Dark Days of Georgian Britain

Dark Days of
Georgian Britain

Rethinking the Regency

By
James Hobson

PEN & SWORD HISTORY

First published in Great Britain in 2017 by
Pen & Sword History
An imprint of
Pen & Sword Books Ltd
47 Church Street
Barnsley
South Yorkshire
S70 2AS

ISBN 978 1 52670 254 8

A CIP catalogue record for this book is
available from the British Library.

Printed and bound in England
By TJ International, Padstow, Cornwall, PL28 8RW

Pen & Sword Books Ltd incorporates the Imprints of Pen & Sword Books Archaeology,
Atlas, Aviation, Battleground, Discovery, Family History, History, Maritime, Military,
Naval, Politics, Railways, Select, Transport, True Crime, Fiction, Frontline Books, Leo
Cooper, Praetorian Press, Seaforth Publishing, Wharncliffe and White Owl.

For a complete list of Pen & Sword titles please contact
PEN & SWORD BOOKS LIMITED
47 Church Street, Barnsley, South Yorkshire, S70 2AS, England
E-mail: enquiries@pen-and-sword.co.uk
Website: www.pen-and-sword.co.uk

For Christine, my wife.

Contents

Introduction

Emma Woodhouse, handsome, clever, and rich, with a comfortable home and ... had lived nearly twenty-one years in the world with very little to distress or vex her.

Jane Austen *Emma* (1815)

This book is not the 'Anti-Austen'. I am not using Emma Woodhouse as a stick to attack Jane Austen; Emma is a fictional character and it is the author who admits that she is insulated from the worst effects of these terrible years. Austen was also more than capable of making judgements about the rich and powerful and wrote about aristocrats and clerics who were neither moral, nor glamorous. This is also the basis of my argument, but my material is different – war, corruption, poverty, class selfishness and political repression.

Dark Days of Georgian Britain is more of an attempt to agree with Jane, probably a wise move on my part. I accept Karl Marx's view that the history of all hitherto existing societies is the history of class struggle, and I think Jane might have at least considered the notion. Her genius would not have been enhanced with a passing reference to bread prices or trade unionism. She manages to be a moralist about society without any of this. However, some grim background might be useful, especially when the Regency is often portrayed through the TV and cinema screen as looking even lovelier than it does in prose.

The point still stands that, if you were not lucky enough to be Emma Woodhouse or one of her ilk, then this era of history was appalling in nearly every way that a period could be. This is no comment on Austen however; portraying this misery was not what she was trying to achieve, so she cannot be condemned for not achieving it. It bears repeating though: the late Regency was terrible, truly appalling, and people at the time knew it.

Indeed, when historians debate the 'worst year in history', the only recent year that is considered is 1816, and its earlier competitors are usually times of vicious epidemic disease or fratricidal civil war. I contend that 1800 to 1819 were the most dismal years in the last three centuries in Britain, with

1815 to 1819 being the worst. They had the full range of calamities – climate crisis, war, austerity, social unrest, a rotten and corrupt system of law, welfare and government, and a ruling class too scared and arrogant to do much about it. Unlike disease and civil war, it was only the lower orders that were affected by the Regency crisis.

The rich and privileged are present in this book, but only in their role as tormentors of the ordinary people or as thoroughly bad examples. They are not presented as cardboard-cut-out villains, but I will admit to having no sympathy for them. The poor are my main interest, although they are not always presented as heroes. There was little scope for heroics when conditions were so bad.

Luckily, this is one of the first eras in history in which the voice of the poor can be heard, albeit faintly and often through the filter of people who had no regard for them. The eighteenth century was a time of rising literacy and for the first time the lower orders could sometimes speak without the squire or the vicar looking over their shoulder. We also have, faintly but with growing confidence, the voice of women. I have tried to find original stories of real people that shine a light on their life.

The book falls into four parts: the appalling experiences of the poor in the years 1811-1820; the failure of the rich to help and their tendency to make things worse; the ramshackle and the corrupt nature of the British state; and finally, some aspects of social history which show how very different we are from our Regency ancestors.

Chapter 1

The Darkness Years

This year has been a very uncommon one. The spring was exceeding cold and backward or rather there was no spring, the summer was cold and wet, or rather we had no summer. The Crop was very bad and unproductive. The Harvest was very late, the crop was not well got in. A Scarcity has taken place. The Quartern loaf is 1/6, other articles in proportion.[1]

There never was so many beggars as thee is at present in our streets. Taxes are high and are levied with Severity. Petitions for a reform have been presented to the Prince Regent from London and other Cities, and have not been well received. Neither trade nor commerce are revived. Tradesmen and labourers are out of employ and are in a state of Starvation. The Regent and his ministers do not seem to care for the grievances under which the Nation groans under, and seem to be deaf to a reform of flagrant abuses that universally exist in the expenditure of the Public money.

Diary of Edward Lucas of Stirling, 31 December 1816.[2]

The title of this book is more than a metaphor. The period 1810 to 1820 was one of the darkest and coldest in the last 200 years. The causes are well known now; in April 1815 there was a colossal eruption of Mount Tambora, in present-day Indonesia. It was the biggest explosion on our planet for 80,000 years, pushing ash and pumice into the air, but more importantly, pushing sulphur above the atmospheric level of the weather. The sulphur became sulphuric acid. The earth cooled, harvests were decimated and trade and transport were hugely affected. Between 1809 and 1820 there had only been one really good harvest in Britain, that was in 1815, just before the eruption. 1816 was the worst; it was 'The Year Without A Summer'; forty days of rain in spring in most of the country; frosts in June and July; orange and brown snow in winter; and bright yellow and reddish-brown sunsets, as clearly shown on Turner's painting from this period.

The cause was not known at the time, although it was suspected by some that the weather was outside of normal variations. The *Leicester Journal* commented in July 1816, 'such inclement weather is scarcely remembered by the oldest person living'.[3]

The temporary cooling was made worse by a cyclical increase in sunspots called the 'Dalton minimum', which also reduced global temperatures. On some days in July 1816 the sunspots could be seen quite easily with the naked eye and some people panicked, thinking the end of the world was approaching.[4] The poor harvests, and the lack of availability of food from the foreign markets which were experiencing the same freak weather effects, increased the price of food, causing riots, misery and repressive measures from the government. The consequences of Tambora can be clearly seen in the early chapters of this book.[5]

These are also the darkness years because of the consequences of Britain's first 'total war'. Britain has experienced two of these in the last century and nobody today is in any doubt about how serious they were. The Napoleonic War is outside our folk memory, but it was a war to the death; a struggle which threatened every aspect of the British state. Britain went to war against a revolutionary enemy, and for most of the time, especially when sympathy with France waned, it was a war of national survival.

The suffering was immense, especially amongst the poor, and the state was nearly bankrupted in an attempt to repel Napoleon and defend the balance of power in Europe. However, the darkness years really started when the war was won; the suffering did not stop when the war ceased.

For almost a generation the war with France had been a national focal point in the same way the Second World War was. Following both world wars of the twentieth century, people expected change and improvement, but after the war with Napoleon, these things did not happen. Indeed the opposite happened. The end of the First World War brought the commemoration of the sacrifices of the many, and a promise of a 'land fit for heroes'; a consequence of the Second World War was a welfare state for all. You will look in vain for cenotaphs and commemorations about the Napoleonic War however. Victory was celebrated but the victors were not. There was no improvement in life after Waterloo. Those lower orders who thought peace would end their problems were whipped up into a fury which disrupted life for a very turbulent five year period.

These were the darkness years because life in Britain was changing and people did not know how to respond. The population had doubled between 1751 and 1821 causing panic and deep pessimism about the future; there was a genuine belief that starvation was on the way – not the near starvation that kept the poor in check, but actual national calamity. Thomas Malthus was the prime source of this fear and uncertainty. His *Essay on the Principle of Population* was in print every year from 1798 to 1817. It suggested two possible futures: either the population increase would lead to mass starvation as agriculture failed to feed the new mouths, or disease, famine and war would hold back population growth. The government was so worried that it took some action – there was a nationwide head count organised in 1801 and another in the midst of a desperate war in 1811.

Malthus's pessimism encouraged many of the ruling classes to change their attitude towards the poor. Malthus regarded unemployment as just another word for overpopulation, and he believed that the vast increase in the number of poor families with poor children was caused by early marriage and encouraged by generous welfare policies. Like many aspects of life in the Regency, the old ways were not working and nothing new was appearing to take its place. William Cobbett, a radical reformer who used his newspaper the *Political Register* to attack the government and its actions, and a man to whom hate came easily, told Malthus that he loathed him more than anything in the world.[6]

The population rise led to new urban areas which ushered in new ways of living, disrupting the traditional ways of doing things. Prior to this, people had mostly lived in small units, where problems were locally based and could be solved face to face, and where the rich felt a responsibility for the poor. It was a hierarchical society, but one based on consensus and some shared values. There were laws forbidding new machinery and other laws guaranteeing hours of work, rates of pay, and protecting apprenticeships. These were swept away in the Regency period, and the social mobility and prosperity needed to mitigate the problems caused did not arrive until later. Although people at the time would not recognise the term – as then you were either a child or an adult with nothing in between – the Regency was the 'awkward adolescence' of modern British industrial society.

To our eyes, the political figures of the Regency were unappealing, and this was magnified by the fact that they lived in a time when critical public opinion had some effective outlets. The Prince Regent was one of the most unpopular members of the royal family in British history. This is partly due to his long list of personal failings, of which we could cite greed, arrogance, and insensitivity as the main three jostling for first place. The major members of the government, Lord Liverpool the prime minister, Lord Sidmouth the home secretary and Viscount Castlereagh the foreign secretary are also unappealing from the modern perspective. They were certainly reactionary – they looked backwards – and they severely curtailed the political freedoms for the population in the darkness years.

The police, justice, finance and welfare systems were no longer fit for purpose, but they were applied with increasing severity during the Regency period by politicians such as Liverpool, Sidmouth and Castlereagh. There was a crime wave caused by poverty and resentment, and a welfare system that was out of control. Reform was about to happen; there were parliamentary inquiries into prisons, poverty, and child labour, and this was the age of William Wilberforce and Elizabeth Fry. There were debates about voting, trade unions and the death penalty. One of the reasons why we consider this an age of darkness is that a new dawn of reform and improvement was approaching – just not yet.

The years after 1820 were slightly better. Austerity slackened a little. Food prices fell and diets improved, slowly. The justice system was reformed. Rights to free speech and agitation were restored. The first reform of parliament happened in the 1830s and the Poor Law was improved administratively, if not humanely. Even the grave robbers were put out of business. Some people continued to be desperate for food, but agricultural improvement saved Britain from the Malthusian trap of mass starvation.

The darkness years of the Regency bears striking resemblance to Britain in the second decade of the twenty-first century. Climate change threatens; childhood seems to be in crisis; relations with Europe and within the nations of the UK are uncertain; the existence of an unpopular ruling elite and the widening gap between the rich and poor are causing tensions; technological change and the destruction of employment is a challenge; an expensive and creaking welfare system may need reform; an unrepresentative electoral system that does not seem to reflect the will of the majority.

We seem to be facing the same challenges in Britain now as 200 years ago. The following chapters explore some of those challenges.

Chapter 2

The Poor Weavers

There is no better example of misery in the Regency period than the handloom weaver. In 1815 they were struggling; by 1840 they were starving. Weavers had initially prospered after spinning was mechanised, when the Jenny produced ample thread for weavers and demand was high. There was plenty of work in the weaving villages of Lancashire, Yorkshire and Scotland from 1790 to about 1805. William Radcliffe, a textiles entrepreneur noted how well the handloom weaver was doing during this period:

> *Their dwellings and small gardens clean and neat, – all the family well clad, – the men with each a watch in his pocket, and the women dressed to their own fancy, – the church crowded to excess every Sunday, – every house well furnished with a clock in elegant mahogany or fancy case, – handsome tea services in Staffordshire ware, with silver or plated sugar-tongs and spoons, – Birmingham, Potteries, and Sheffield wares for necessary use and ornament, wherever a corner cupboard or shelf could be placed to shew them off.*[1]

The most skilled Bolton muslin weavers at the beginning of the nineteenth century were said to parade the streets with a £5 note in their hats, showing off their week's wages, wearing expensive shirts and leather boots, and excluding less wealthy weavers from their favourite public houses.[2]

By 1810 this prosperity had ended and wages began to fall. Decent workable power looms, first invented in 1785 were slowly being gathered in factories. Wages were pushed down not so much by the power looms themselves, as there were no more than a few thousand in the whole country in the 1810s, but the fact that the owners could turn to machines if workers' pay rose too much.

When the war disrupted trade in the 1800s, individual manufacturers reduced the pay for weavers' labour and goods, forcing other manufacturers to follow suit. Many weavers were unable to switch to better paying bosses because they owed money to their present employer, or did not have the money to re-tool when offered better paid work.

There was also an increasing supply of people who could do their job. Irish textile workers moving to Lancashire and Scotland found it easy to transfer their linen producing skills to cotton. Agricultural workers pushed out of the countryside by the enclosure of farming land used by the poor added to the supply of people who could weave. Manufacturers could enforce lower and lower wages at the same time as food prices were rising. It was a vicious pincer movement on their standard of living.

Weavers used a variety of techniques to improve their quality of life. They petitioned the House of Commons and the Prince Regent. When that failed they demonstrated and marched. When these protests were broken up, they formed trade unions, organised strikes and threatened, or used, violence. The famous machine breaking done by weavers, knitters and croppers in the period 1811-12 were the actions of desperate people. These violent acts of poor workers in Nottinghamshire, Yorkshire and Lancashire – 'Luddism' – was the last resort of people who had tried everything else.

The law was the first resort. The weavers of Lancashire and Scotland were initially under the illusion that the House of Commons would enforce minimum wage regulations that already existed in theory. In the eighteenth century it was common for the state to protect workers' conditions. The Spitalfields silk weavers had had the price of their labour regulated by the Justices of the Peace in 1773, admittedly after some vicious rioting and machine breaking – but attitudes were changing and the new general belief was that it was impossible to regulate the value of people's labour. The Weavers Minimum Wage Bill was introduced in the House of Commons but not put to a vote, as there was not a single voice to speak in favour of it. The best advice MPs could offer was to counsel patience and submission to their privations.

Some manufacturers actively supported the workers' demand for predictable wages, and often signed their petitions. Regular wage rates prevented conflict and protected the better employers from the unscrupulous ones, who undercut the rest with poor quality goods and low wages. Many bosses also wanted to stop the ludicrous arrangement where the pay offered by some manufacturers resulted in poverty, which had to be alleviated by poor rates paid by all employers, the good and the bad alike.

Workers also had no geographical mobility due to the Poor Law preventing them from getting support outside their home parish. This 1817 petition to the Prince Regent made these points:

In populous towns of Bolton Stockport ... the owners of houses ... pay
10s in the for poor rates the wages of the weavers are frequently as low

as 6s to 8s a week and he who receives them thinks himself perfectly justified in complaining to his master of his wages and who shall say he is not when he cannot live where he is and is prevented by law of settlements from seeking a better [place] for his labour. But he receives as much from the Parish which comes ... out of the pockets of the same persons manufacturers who employ him.

It was a new society; one where it was every person for themselves and previous mutual obligations between the rich and poor were dissolving. These weavers were totally dependent on variable wages. The only relationship they had with their betters was an uncertain one based on the selling of their labour in unpredictable national and international markets. There was no longer a fixed price for anything; manufacturers could not guarantee a price when they could not be sure of their markets. Tudor rules for protecting the poor were abandoned; they neither worked nor were very convenient. The Elizabethan Statute of Artificers, which protected conditions and apprenticeships, was declared a dead letter in 1808 at the same time as minimum wages were rejected. This encouraged even more of the desperate poor to learn weaving and further depress wages for all.

Thomas Holden was a typical victim of this new society; the economic and political system was stacked against him. Born in 1792, Thomas was a Bolton weaver and would have seen his family's fortunes decline inexorably as he grew up. The Poor Law prevented him from moving to an area where his labour could be more valuable – unlike the owner's capital, which could migrate to wherever was profitable. The Combination Laws of 1799 made forming a trade union illegal; it was also against the law to swear a secret oath – known as being 'twisted in'. Both were banned by the government because of the implications of conspiracy, violence and treason.

Holden did not have the vote because he was poor, and stayed poor because he did not have the vote. The rejection of the Weavers' Minimum Wage Bill was hardly a surprise. The workers were not represented in parliament; their bosses were mostly unrepresented too. In 1811, a weaver activist reported back on another failed attempt to influence parliament: 'Weavers – had you possessed 70,000 votes for election to sit in the House, would your application have been treated with such inattention?'

In response to parliament's lack of concern, between 15,000 and 40,000 weavers, including many from Thomas Holden's Bolton, held a protest march (or riot, depending on the source) at St George's Field, Manchester in May 1808. They presented their grievances to the magistrates; they were working a fourteen-hour day for eight or nine shillings a week and still did not have enough to live on. They were eventually dispersed by the military with one protestor killed.

The establishment press were unsympathetic. In a portent of Peterloo eleven years later, it was reported that the weavers were being supported by the local poor rate so therefore did not need to riot; and it was also reported that many of the poor weavers were Irish, had no poor law settlement and therefore received no poor law support. However, the same conclusion was reached – the weavers were wrong to riot. In the same year that the House of Commons refused to support the weavers, it gave Edmund Cartwright, the man who invented the power loom, a grant of £10,000 in acknowledgement of an invention that reduced the need for weavers' labour.

After the failure of these tactics, the weavers turned to strike action. This was difficult to organise because weavers were spread around many locations. Most of the time, it was not factories full of power looms that they attacked – it was individuals who would not join the strike or went back to work prematurely. Often the lists of rioters and strikers contained recurring surnames and involved illegal action to maintain the effectiveness of the strike. The newspapers reported this:

> *Thomas Eckersley, James Crouchly, Thomas Gregson, Henry Gregson and Thomas Cooper, having assembled in an unlawful manner ... for the purposes of raising wages, and for entered several houses in the townships of Lauton and Golborne, and forcibly taking away a great number of weavers' shuttles.* [3]

It should be noted that these Wigan strikers were not destroying machines, merely putting them out of use. The strikers wanted to stop production, not damage the property of people they would have known personally. When machine breaking started in earnest in 1811, the weavers were desperate enough to destroy the means of production permanently, and the response of the government was correspondingly more severe.

In Bolton, as in Wigan and many other places, industrial action was organised locally. Strikers were often families and co-workers. In the case of Thomas Holden, he was part of a weaving family in Hag End, Bolton, which included his parents John and Ellen. Three other Holdens were involved in the attempt to form trade unions and destroy a weaving mill in Westhoughton near Bolton in April 1812, including a William Holden, who shared the same name as one of Thomas's brothers and seems likely to be the same person.

What was life like in Bolton and other weaving districts to make families like the Holdens desperate? No protest seemed to work. The same pattern occurred more than once between 1808 and 1812. There would be a prolonged and painful strike and then the bosses would raise wages by a large amount – twenty per cent in 1808. Within a few months the pay rise would disappear as unfavourable market forces took their predictable and inexorable toll. Conditions became intolerable. In a parliamentary report in 1812, sympathetic MPs took evidence from Lancashire residents about the life of the local people. John Wood of Bolton-le-Moor, Salford was a former overlooker in a weaving mill, and shop owner, who knew the local weavers well. He reported that in 1800 the spinners and weavers had a large amount of badly paid but skilled work. Now the situation had changed – the pay was still bad, but the work was irregular and the price of food, fuel and rent had increased. The weavers were living on oatmeal porridge and low quality bread, with almost no animal protein at all. [4]

Other witnesses from Stockport and Saddleworth reported the same situation; weavers were sending their children to bed hungry with gruel and water instead of milk; rents were unpaid and evictions were soaring. The only dissenting voice was a Mr Robert McKerrell of Scotland, who thought the root cause of the weavers' problem was that they had enjoyed such a high standard of living in the past that they had been corrupted by it. They were therefore not able to cope with the present misery, and that agitators and seditious people (such as the Holdens, presumably) were exploiting the situation for nefarious purposes. He painted a picture of the Paisley and Glasgow muslin weavers, corrupted by wealth at the beginning of the century and similar to the Bolton muslin workers:

> *The rate of wages prior to 1806 was so extravagant that I should suppose upon a Sunday, going to Church, you would see two or three thousand girls in silk stockings, and as many rouged. The very best teas of the East India Company were not good enough for them. Their whole way of life was built on the same system.*

So, it seemed that while there was no need for a minimum wage, there was a real danger in a high wage. The poor would forget their place; women would become shameless. There is an irony in the fact that McKerrell did not notice that richer people bought more of the labour of other workers and high wages stimulated the demand and reduced poverty. He liked a bit of poverty – for other people.

There were lots of explosions of anger in 1812 and Thomas Holden was involved in them. Four people, James Smith, Thomas Kerfoot, John Fletcher and Abraham Charlson were found guilty of an attack on Westhoughton Mill near Bolton. This mill had 200 power looms and had been operating since 1808. The recent Frame Breaking Act made the damaging of powered looms punishable by death. This did not stop a mob of about thirty attacking the mill near Bolton on 24 April 1812. Unlike other Luddite attacks in the North of England, there was no attempt to be selective about which machines to destroy and which manufacturers to target. The mill and its contents were burned down indiscriminately and afterwards there were riots. The mill had been guarded by the Scots Greys but they had left earlier on the Friday because they believed the threat of attack was a hoax.

Abraham Charlson, one of the people later found guilty, was seen armed with a scythe, helping to break the windows of the mill and one of the first to get inside due to his size, being passed through a window by others. Two young women were seen actively helping – they were Lydia and Mary Molyneux aged 15 and 19, arrested later but acquitted. The doors to the mill were broken open, and then straw from a barn nearby was used as kindling to start a fire, to which was added cloth from the looms. The Scots Greys eventually returned but the destruction was complete. Afterwards, the owners quit the town for good. There were no power looms in the area again until the 1830s.

On Monday, 1 June 1812, the Westhoughton prisoners were tried at the Lancaster special commission. Thomas Holden was one of three men accused of receiving an unlawful oath at Bolton on 14 April 1812. Taking an unlawful oath does not seem to be a terrible crime; however, the authorities were worried about what they were trying to do. Thomas's defence that he went to the meeting merely out of curiosity was rejected; there had been a password on the door and the judge suggested that nobody would be in any doubt that this was an illegal enterprise. They were accused at the trial of planning the attack on Westhoughton mill; according to the government spies who gave evidence, they had talked about the best way to enter the mill and warehouse.

The other Holdens – Arthur (33), James (20), and William (17) were fortunate when the defence pointed out there was a flaw in the indictment (it didn't state that they were assembled for an unlawful purpose), so the prosecution was given up, and the men were acquitted. Thomas Holden was given seven years transportation.

On 13 June 1812, Smith, Kerfoot and Fletcher were executed alongside Abraham Charlson, who was no more than 16 at the time and cried out for his mother as he was hanged. Some sources hostile to the authorities suggested that he was younger than that. Even under the harsh regime of this period, hanging a 16-year-old was uncommon. A clear political point was being made.

On 15 June Thomas wrote to his wife that he was about to be moved from the Lancaster Special Assize. Knowing the criminal system, he asked his wife for money as he would need it to survive in prison, and specifically asked that no new clothes be sent to him because he knew they would be stolen. He was moved on 19 June, and wrote that he still had no money. Thomas was not contrite; organising with his co-workers was not a crime in his view and he said so in a letter to his family:

> To part with my dear Wife and Child, Parents and Friends, to be no more, cut off in the Bloom of my Youth without doing the least wrong to any person on earth. Oh my hard fate, may God have mercy on me... Your affec. Husband until Death.

Nine days after leaving Lancaster, Thomas arrived at the prison ship *Portland* at Langstone Harbour, near Portsmouth, on 28 June 1812. Most prisoners preferred both transportation and life in a penal colony to living on these hulks, and it was mostly pure chance how long was spent there. Holden reported that he had lost his possessions on the ship – they were probably stolen. His journey to the hulk was described to Molly as 'whett and uncomfortable' and for the first eight days on the boat he wore the same clothes.

Thomas spent five months on board the *Portland*, longer than average for a criminal awaiting transportation. He was well enough to do the manual labour expected and complained to his wife that there were many from Bolton on the hulk, but they did not help him at all. Throughout his correspondence, Thomas never mentions any political actions he took, or references any political ideas; he knew that his mail would be opened by the authorities. His disappointment that the people from Bolton showed no solidarity suggests that he was expecting something from their common bond of struggle. The appalling conditions on the hulks and the transportation ships were well known for breaking down the strongest friendships and connections.

Another person who did nothing to help was the Prince Regent. Holden's wife Molly was among many Bolton wives who made an appeal to the acting monarch, who told them that he was unable to help – although Molly makes it clear that it was a political petition initiated solely by women, showing their involvement in radical protest.

Holden's journey to Australia was eventful. He contracted jaundice and spent two weeks in bed, not eating for days at a time, and reliant on the goodwill of other prisoners. Unlike many other criminals, who could use their talents in Botany Bay to make a new life in a way that was not possible in Britain, he did not thrive in Australia. He still wrote to his wife complaining about prices and the behaviour of Aboriginal people. He still hoped to get home: 'I Shall Returne to Ingland and then I hope we Shall Spend the Remainder of our Days in this world in love and happyness togater' [sic].

At least he was willing and able to keep in touch with his family, except his brother William, who refused to write to him – he may have been the man of the same name acquitted of rioting. In her letters, Molly asks Thomas about two other Bolton men, who had also been transported and from whom their families had heard nothing. Thomas's letters are a remarkable, raw piece of evidence direct from the mouth of a poor man, albeit one who knew that the censor was looking over his shoulder. Thomas's story does not have a happy ending. He was given a pardon in February 1817, but never returned to England. He never saw his wife, Molly, or his daughter, Ann, again.[5]

Back in Britain, weavers continued to use methods that had already failed to maintain their standard of living. The Coventry ribbon weavers had an agreement with the masters to pay a fixed price for goods produced. By August 1819, market forces had destroyed the agreement and the workers retaliated by forcing two factory owners to ride through the town on donkeys. One was accused of lowering prices and another was using apprentices on half pay to replace the work of the fully qualified. The weavers' plan was to parade through the streets with asses and find more victims to sit upon them, until the magistrates intervened. Locals would have recognised this kind of protest – it was a 'skimmington' or ritual humiliation of local people who had not behaved according to local standards of morality. The novel aspect was the use of it for owners of capital rather than a nagging wife or an unfaithful husband.

Another, newer, tactic was to target one major employer at a time and refuse to work for them. In 1818, weavers in Preston started to draw the names of employers out of a green bag and the *Lancaster Gazette* reported that it was ridiculous to pick on Horrocks and Company who had done nothing particularly wrong. The weavers were operating from a position of profound weakness, made more obvious and poignant by the fact that the workers also held a procession from Preston to Gallows Hill, burying some weaving equipment in a mock funeral for their trade. The newspaper mocked the weavers' efforts, but still hoped that trade would improve – it was clearly permissible to hope, but not legal to do anything about it.

Weavers made up one of the biggest occupation groups who were killed and injured at St Peter's Field in Manchester in August 1819. This was a demonstration for parliamentary reform and better working conditions. More than 60,000 peaceful men, women and children were attacked by armed cavalry resulting in fifteen deaths and over 600 injuries. In a sarcastic reference to Wellington's triumph in 1815, it was dubbed the 'Peterloo' massacre.

When the *Morning Post* satirised the groups that were at Peterloo, their first target was the handloom weaver:

> *Diggory Dunderhead, a very honest and hard-working stocking weaver, went to the Meeting of the 16th August, to look for his master at Peterloo, with the view of receiving eighteen pence for a whole week's work, on which he had to maintain a wife and thirteen small children (all under three years of age) for seven days. It will be shown that he was one of the many thousands who were mutilated on that day. Mr Dunderhead meeting his master, who was one of the Yeomanry Cavalry, applied (most respectfully taking o' his hat) for his wages. 'Wages!' replied the brute (his master). 'I'll pay thee in a crack;' and with that he lifted up his sword (which had been sharpened for the purpose), and seemed about to strike, when Diggory pathetically exclaimed – 'Squire Jollychops, thee wo' no hurt me, I know;' and, while he was speaking, the same blow took o' his left-hand, and both his ears. The hat fell to the ground, and has not since been recovered, nor has the eighteen pence been paid.*[6]

From his surname, Diggory is deliberately presented as stupid; he has an impossible number of children, with the implication that Poor Law support has produced them. His wages are stated by him as much lower than any poor weaver – he is a liar; his master is presented as a cardboard-cut-out villain, and the terrible deaths and injuries of the day are mocked. Although this was an extreme characterisation, there was not a lot of sympathy in the Regency for the poor handloom weaver. What they did not know, but might have suspected, was that far worse was to come.

Chapter 3

Making Life Worse

The Corn Law, the Budget, the Game Laws and the Lottery

T he British soldiers at Waterloo, with their Prussian allies, defeated
Napoleon in June 1815. The sacrifices had been made by the soldiers and workers, but the government handed the victory to the
landlords and the richest taxpayers. The aristocracy had invested heavily
in their land since the 1790s, putting fields under the plough that had not
been used since medieval times and fencing in land that had previously been
open to the rural labouring poor. In 1815, the price of a quarter (512lbs) of
wheat had fallen to sixty-five shillings; this spelt economic disaster for the
aristocracy and was a great problem for their tenants, as rents would become
unaffordable. Food prices needed to go back to the same levels as during the
Napoleonic War for the ruling class to prosper.

It was in the spirit of protecting the already privileged that Prime Minister,
Lord Liverpool, introduced the Corn Bill in March 1815. Landowners
argued that the wartime investment in agriculture meant Britain was now
self sufficient in food, but the price needed to be maintained to allow landowners to recoup their earlier investment. European and American farmers
would always be able to produce food more cheaply because they were free
from the burdens of tithes and taxes that were levied in Britain. The impor-
tation of cheap food would bankrupt landowners and their tenants and put
Britain at the mercy of foreign food supplies, which would be withdrawn at
times of conflict.

Meetings were held all over the country rehearsing these arguments,
including one in Warminster, Wiltshire in January 1815 organised by local
landowner, John Benett. The Benett family had had a good war. On the proceeds of high wheat prices, Benett had rebuilt his home, Pythouse, adding a
Palladian frontage with pillars, portico and steps. Other buildings included a
huge walled vegetable garden, a dovecote, a stable block, an orangery and an
icehouse. Like many of the British aristocracy, they had spent considerable
amounts on agriculture during the war and had made immense profits from
a closed market. Unlike many others, who were merely grasping, he had a

reputation for being an innovative farmer who also added some value to his estates.

This meeting in Wiltshire was different to the hundreds held around the county in one crucial way. John Benett was not the only substantial land-owner at the meeting. Another, who made Benett's landholding look puny, was Henry Hunt. He was a gentlemen farmer with 3,000 acres in Wiltshire and Somerset. Despite an economic interest in the proposed Corn Law, Hunt was scathing about landlords like Benett and the arguments they employed to justify their profits. Hunt declared the meeting improper; he knew for a fact that the local tradesmen and artisans had been told there was nothing to interest them in this meeting and that they should not attend. He invited Benett to hold an open meeting and then tell the people that he was planning a petition to parliament to raise the price of bread. He then issued a further dare: tell the poor people that he was doing it in their economic interest!

Hunt then explained how the Napoleonic War had created inequality. In the central Wiltshire village of Enford in the previous thirty years, for example, agricultural wages had risen from 6s to 8s; in that period the quartern loaf had doubled in price to 10d. The rents from local estates, for example from the Benett's own Pythouse estate, had quadrupled from £400 pounds to £1,600 a year. Hunt concluded that it was clear to him who gained from high prices. The *Leicester Chronicle* of 14 January 1815 reported:

> *This proves that bread has rised* [sic] *more than three times more than labour, and land more than twice as much as bread, and six times more than labour. At the present price of land, corn, bread and labour, the landlord is benefitted three times more than the farmer, and six times and much as the labourer.*

Some newspapers reported the meeting but completely omitted Hunt's speech. It was not what their readers wanted to hear. [1]

Thousands of petitions from all parts of the country were sent to parliament by the aristocracy and richer farmers asking for protection from the type of competition that ordinary working people encountered every day. Meetings were large and formal, headed by the local aristocracy and gentry and packed with tenants who were so dependent on the landowners for their living that they were politically neutered. The *Bury and Norfolk Post* reported that the 4,000 strong meeting in Stowmarket, Suffolk was interrupted briefly just as the decision to petition parliament was about to be made:

When the assent of the meeting was called for, there was a clamorous cry of No Corn Bill! No Corn Bill!, but on the Sheriff's requiring that those who dissented from the measure should put up their hands, not a single arm was observed to be uplifted.

The powerful were making the rules.

There was no doubt that parliament, who represented the same people as appeared at the county meetings, would legislate to ban foreign importations until home produce reached 80s a quarter. This price was so high that it was a *de facto* ban on foreign imports.

As the bill was about to become a law, petitions against the Corn Bill were produced in both rural and urban areas. The Birmingham petition was signed by 50,000 people. The poet Samuel Taylor Coleridge crafted an anti-Bill petition for the poor people of Calne in Wiltshire. It was quite important to get the wording right; if the obsequiousness was not complete and the wording accurately phrased, the petition would not even be read and if it were read, it would be ignored.

Resentment bubbled up. The London mob appeared in the Palace Yard at Westminster, trying to make their voice felt in the traditional way. On Monday 6 March, big crowds of 'disaffected persons' appeared around the Palace of Westminster, hooting and hissing members of the Lords and Commons and inquiring robustly about how they intended to vote. Later, the crowds stopped coaches reaching their destination, and members had to walk through the crowds, supported by the local militia. The militia pushed the mob into the surrounding streets and, in a clear indication that the mob had been following the debates closely, they destroyed houses of those who initiated and supported the Bill.

It was the biggest London riot since the anti-Catholic disturbances of 1780. Rioting continued into Tuesday when the Corn Law was passed, with parliament protected from the Londoners' wrath by soldiers with fixed bayonets. By Thursday, the panicking government offered outlandish rewards for information about the ringleaders. It was by this mixture of law, violence, and bribery that the state operated against the anger of the lower orders.

The rich were not the only victims of the four days of rioting. Two innocent bystanders were shot in the head outside the house of Frederick John Robinson MP in Old Burlington Street. From early evening on a Tuesday, his house was surrounded by a mob of about sixty throwing stones and brickbats. Robinson was paying the price of introducing the Corn Bill to parliament. However, his price was less than that of 19-year-old midshipman

Edward Vyse, who was walking past the house and was hit with a shot from the pistol that was designed to scare the mob of boys outside. He died immediately at the scene.

There was another fatality that night, a young woman called Jane Watson (in some newspapers she is Mary, and the coverage was considerably less than that of Edward Vyse) who was in her mid-twenties and already a naval widow. In the formulaic words of the time, she 'lingered' in hospital for a few days before dying. When Frederick Robinson went to the Commons to explain the events in his house, he cried, and the sympathetic property and landowners gave him the nickname 'The Blubberer'.

In order to make life even more intolerable for the lower orders, the Property Tax was abolished in 1816, and the money lost was replaced by taxing consumption, which hit the poorest hard. It was the people who supported the Corn Law who also wanted the poor to pay more in indirect taxes when the Property Tax was abolished.

Unlike the Corn Laws, the members of parliament themselves must take the blame for this. The prime minister, Lord Liverpool, and the foreign minister Lord Castlereagh knew how desperate the financial situation was and wanted to keep some form of the tax. The Chancellor of the Exchequer, Nicholas Vansittart, came to the House of Commons with a confident proposition. He would halve the rate of tax to five per cent and he would protect small farmers. He regretted not being able to expire it – 'expire' rather than 'abolish' it – making it clear that it was a time limited expedient. He promised cuts in expenditure from £30 million to £20 million per year and the end of the Property Tax in two years.

Vansittart argued in vain that more indirect taxation on expenditure would hit the poor hard. For many MPs, the fact that there would be government commissioners enquiring about their income and lifestyle was the last straw and they called the tax 'Unnecessary, Unconstitutional and Inquisitorial'.

Such was the outcry about taxing property that even religious organisations with a deserved reputation for humanitarianism were opposed to it. Lord Lansdowne told the Lords that he had a petition from 'some of the persons called Quakers' who opposed the continuance of the Property Tax. Their reasons for this view will never be known for sure; the Lords rejected the petition without reading it, because it had been addressed simply to 'The Upper House' and not the 'Lords Temporal and Spiritual'. The Quakers had refused to use the word 'Lord' as they believed that this should be reserved for the Supreme Being; the forty-four Lords refused to countenance such disrespect and voted thirty-five to nine not to even read it. One reason for the Quakers' opposition to such a tax might have been their objection to the use of government money to finance wars. The Quakers had a long history, especially in the USA, of refusing to take part in transactions that were used to finance war.[2]

Sir William Curtis MP wanted the tax abolished, albeit for different motives. Sir William was a maverick. His fellow MPs used to openly mock him; it was a parliamentary age that was much less polite than now. He had outraged his colleagues by opposing the Corn Law, saying that landlords were already well protected. Perhaps his modest background – the family wealth came from the manufacture of sea biscuits for sailors – made him less worried about the aristocracy. The Regency cartoonists and satirists called him 'Billy Biscuit', and his colleagues, a little more respectfully, 'Sir W. Biscuit'.

Billy was not a great speaker, and not particularly well educated. He had gained his knighthood in 1802 for his record of constantly voting as the government wished, but revolted on the subject of the continuance of the Property Tax. The tax had been a war tax…where was the war now? He was, strictly speaking, correct, as the tax had been introduced in 1799 as a temporary measure to pay for the war with France. Despite selling food to the wartime navy, Billy demanded the demobilisation of 90,000 sailors to prevent the rich being taxed so heavily that they could not continue to help the poor with charity.

On 18 March, the government lost the vote. The debate was ended by William Wilberforce, the man who led the campaign for the abolition of the Slave Trade. Wilberforce suggested that the government simply cut its budget faster and more savagely.

Unlike the Corn Laws, it did not need a ring of soldiers around parliament to abolish the tax and there were no riots. However, it certainly added to the misery of the lower orders. The government now had a yearly deficit and an accumulated debt of £834 million and it was clear that the elders and betters of the establishment were going to allow the poor to pay the price of austerity. The only remaining way of raising the money was by increasing taxes on spending. This indirect taxation pushed up the price of tea, tobacco, sugar and beer. Much of the money raised from the poor would be used to pay interest on the loans given mostly by the wealthy, who had just opted out of making their contribution by allowing the Property Tax to expire.

Britain was already heavily taxed. Tithes were payable to the Church of England clergy. All the adequate roads had fees payable at tollgates. Now, lots of basic items were to be taxed and the burden fell on the poor, who used up more of their income on necessities. A crowd of 35,000, mostly workmen, attended a political meeting in Glasgow in November 1816 where the taxes were listed:

We are grievously harassed and borne down with the salt tax and the leather Tax, the soap tax and candle Tax, the sugar tax, the tea Tax, the spirit tax, the Licenses, the window light and house duty tax, the stamp tax, the Manservant tax, the Cart tax, the Horse tax, the dog tax....

The people of Glasgow did not mention the Coal Tax; it bore a much bigger burden on the poor of London. The Regency government found it very hard to collect indirect taxes, and many of what we call taxes were actually duties – coal was a difficult commodity to tax and some coal attracted no tax. A petition in the *Windsor and Eton Express* in April 1819 showed the vagaries of the system. Coal that entered the Port of London paid a duty, largely because the government was in a position to control its movement. Other ports had a lower rate of taxation, and those people who lived near the source of coal paid no duty at all. So it was the poor of London, with the least access to any kind of fuel, who paid the most. This shows the difference between taxation 200 years ago and today – there was no attempt to create fairness; taxes and duties were only designed to raise revenue. The fact that Regency winters were some of the coldest on record made the situation even worse.

In a decade when food and basic goods were heavily taxed, the government made it even more difficult to take food from the land owned by the aristocracy. The Game Laws were a piece of class-based legislation forbidding the rural poor from taking pheasant, partridge, hares, and rabbits from the lands of the aristocracy. As ever, poverty had a moral aspect, but not the immorality of the poor suffering. The *Morning Post* (July 1816) reported on the thoughts of some members of parliament. The aristocracy had become richer since the original game laws. Game was still given away by the long-standing aristocracy as part of their responsibilities to the poor; it was noted that the newer owners of land were less interested in either giving away game, or even owning it.

This put the poor in moral danger; they could take from the land of the aristocracy with impunity and make a living from the property of others. The strong belief seemed to be that the poor only worked if they had to; possible starvation was motivation. Those who plundered the aristocratic estates would not want to work again; they would end up being transported and depriving the country of their labour, or worse still, hanged. If they were in prison, their relatives would have to be supported by charity or the poor rates. A poached hare was transformed into national ruin in a few illogical steps.

The poor could not eat the game, but the game could eat the poor. Pheasants and partridges would eat their grain; rabbits would consume their grass, and hares would attack parsnips, and nothing could be done about it. The *New Monthly* magazine reported that some landowners would not even allow small boys to chase off rooks, in case there was a precious game bird among them. A farmer whose land was worth more than 40s (£2) in rent per year could vote for a member of parliament, while he had to have £100 a year to even consider killing a partridge.

The law was passed in July 1816 with the same robust punishments that were used to protect other property. Few people were actually transported for the maximum of seven years, but the code was bloody enough even without an enforced visit to Botany Bay.

William Peachy of Saffron Walden was given six months hard labour and imprisonment; he had been spotted on the land of Lord Bristol between the hours of 8.00 pm and 7.00 am. Although nobody saw any poaching, the fact that he was on the land with a gun was enough to convict him. The person watching him also felt the need to show great discretion. He was the only witness and could not be sure that the two men would not kill him to avoid the new punishment. That was always a danger when the punishment for murder and poaching was similar in severity. The 'bloody code' was designed to protect property but it almost encouraged extreme violence.

His partner in property crime – John Rayner – was also found guilty. He had previously spent a week in prison for owning a lurcher – an unlicenced hunting dog. Moses Johnson of Flint was given the same punishment. Ownership of a dog in a location where you were not known was suspicion enough for some gamekeepers, and such a suspicion was enough for magistrates.

Punishments varied, but you could expect a £5 to £20 fine for being caught with nets and snares but no game, or hiding game at home, and three months minimum in prison if found in the act of killing. Many poachers ended up in prison for not being able to pay the fine. The chances of being transported increased if you were thought to be in an organised gang, or were caught with a gun at night trespassing on private property. Both would be enough to send you to Australia.

An early capitalist market in game was developing, and the authorities seemed determined to stop it. On one occasion, baskets full of dead rabbits were traced back to the person who had put them on the stagecoach and the miscreant fined £5 per corpse. There was a demand for game but little supply, so it seems that much of the stealing that took place was done by poachers and corrupt gamekeepers who would send these to market.

It was similar to the modern drugs trade. Opponents of the Game Law pointed out that the main cause of poaching was the demand of people for the food, especially the 'new rich' who held no land but wanted to consume game, and that the London poulterers were the biggest connivers in breaking the law. Often, it was the aristocrats themselves who bought game while in London, knowing it to be stolen goods. However, the 1816 Game Laws were silent about those who stimulated demand by buying it, because these people were the wealthy, not the poor.

The fact that the authorities were aware of this, and the judiciary was more than ready to make an example of those people moving the contraband, shows that they were aware of the developing market. Some magistrates argued that the Game Laws increased the price of game, which in turn encouraged more poaching; the law was the fatal combination of ineffectual and counterproductive.

It seems that some people were arguing for a free, capitalist market in products, with licences issued to allow individuals to hunt on private land. Most people, especially those in power, thought that draconian punishment was the answer. In an era when the free market was painfully being formed, and fewer and fewer people had access to the countryside, this was another backward-looking law.

In the same budget that abolished the Property Tax, the Chancellor announced that the National Lottery in 1815 had made a £200,000 contribution to government funds. The aim of the lottery was solely to raise money for the Treasury. The money raised was used to repay the interest on the bonds held by the rich – it was not used for good causes – although the owners of government debt probably believed that they fell into this category.

Lottery tickets were traded as a government stock with a quoted and variable price depending on demand. Those such as Wilberforce and Cobbett, who opposed the lottery, were invited by the government to suggest other ways of raising the money to pay off the £834 million national debt. They could suggest nothing.[3]

Despite being called the 'state lottery', it was actually privatised. Contractors would bid for the right to run the lottery at a profit. Companies with names such as 'Bish', 'Richardson Goodluck', and 'Hazard' would offer tickets in advertisements in the paper. They would dominate the front pages; they boasted about the number of winning tickets they had sold and that their offices were 'fortunate'. The Richardson Company had paid £50 to a Mrs Goodluck for the right to use her name. Hazard would regularly advertise in the press, advising customers to apply early if they wanted their lucky number.

These companies were based in London but to achieve nationwide distribution they would appoint agents all over the country. Booksellers were preferred, as it was thought that this added lustre to their brand, but high-class grocers, goldsmiths, and watchmakers were also acceptable. These were selected as places where the poor would not go, but they still did, and the lottery did nothing to make their lives better.

The lottery was another device that redistributed money from the poor to the rich. On most occasions there were 20,000 tickets and £200,000 in prize money. The two main prizes were of £25,000 each and 4,600 prizes of £10, with others in between. Basic mathematics showed that they were poor value for money. Each ticket had an intrinsic value of £10 (£200,000 in prizes divided by 20,000 tickets). However, a whole ticket, which the lottery contractors purchased from the state for around £14, was sold for £24. This was well beyond the means of all but the richest individuals. A sixteenth of a ticket could be purchased for just over a pound and that was the way the poor participated. This was still a significant amount for the poor to pay for a gamble on the lottery. Lottery clubs were organised illegally by the poor, where they would gamble on the results without buying an official ticket, usually by taking side bets whether a certain number would come out of the giant wheel used to pick winners but, like everything else in Regency Britain, the lottery was rigged against the poor.

Lord Byron had a trenchant view on the subject

To Wellington

... and I shall be delighted to learn who.

Save you and yours, have gained from Waterloo? [4]

Chapter 4

Why People Rioted

R ioting was a common feature of late Georgian Britain and the motivations were easy to see. It was a period of high bread prices, and other basic commodities were heavily taxed. It was a time when jobs and lifestyles were being destroyed by new technologies and machines. This was exacerbated by laws that seemed designed to make the situation worse.

It was an age of transition, and this showed in the attitudes of the powerful towards the suffering of the poor. Two sets of conflicting ideas existed. Britain was still a community-minded society where the rich felt the need to help the poor under certain conditions. However, it was also one where market forces and laissez-faire economics were all the rage, and were used to condone the suffering of the poor. A more fatalistic view of suffering was developing as Britain industrialised.

Conflicting ideologies were evident in the speech 'On Rioting' by the Recorder of the Guildford Quarter Sessions, Sergeant Best. In October 1816, whilst summing up after the Guildford Riot, he favoured the jury with his thoughts on the current rioting problem. He started by accepting that the massive rise in the price of bread was the main cause. 'Whether the recent increase in the price of bread in this town was justifiable, I am not prepared to say.' Best's audience would know that he was trying to blame the bread retailers, who were traditionally held culpable when prices rose. Criticism of millers and bakers were always popular with the public and these complaints became physical attacks when times were bad.

Sergeant Best then condemned anybody who had increased the price of bread through what he vaguely called 'false reports'. He praised the assize of bread, which still monitored and sanctioned price increases. He praised the medieval institution for trying to help the poor. Then he became a little more modern and stated that ultimately, only the 'exciting of competition can keep down the price of necessities'. Therefore he supported both free markets and traditional community control at the same time, neither of which were being any help to the poor.

Best's ambiguity shows a society where the establishment could not make its mind up. One thing that had not changed was that there was absolutely no excuse for rioting. If you suffered in silence, you would be entitled to the pity and protection of your betters. This would bring all the people together, getting through the high prices caused by poor harvest that was God's Providence, which must be endured but not questioned. Best came very close to the position of the evangelical, and lecturer of the poor, Hannah More, who believed that starvation was God's way of reminding the poor how much they needed the rich.

Nothing could be done to reduce the price of bread, as only the law of supply and demand could decide. However it was possible to manipulate markets by a ban on imports until domestic grain reached the very high figure of 80s. Best did not mention the Corn Laws of 1815, which increased the danger of starvation dramatically; perhaps because it had led to four days of rioting in London, the ransacking of his own residence, and could not be explained by God's providence.

April 1816 saw a traditional riot, but not of the 'bread and blood' variety that would dominate the rest of 1816. The tanners of Bermondsey organised a street fracas, their main complaint being the behaviour of William Timbrell. Timbrell owned a tanner's yard in Bermondsey. He asked his workers to forego their two days traditional Easter holiday and to do paid work instead. This was, according to the papers, welcomed by the workers, and is not surprising as work was in short supply.

A group of 300 journeyman tanners turned up with fife and drums and tanners' aprons on poles and asked the working tanners to 'play out' rather than work on a holiday. When the workers refused, the journeyman rushed Mr Timbrell senior and Mr Timbrell junior fired a gun over their heads. The protesters then spilled out of the street, assaulting Timbrell's workers, dousing people with water, assaulting a pregnant woman thought to be the wife of a working tanner, and then marched to demolish Timbrell's house in George Street.

This was a riot in an earlier tradition. The mob were attacking other workers for ignoring a historic holiday. The capitalists were not the targets, and in the spirit of forgiveness rather than class war, Mr Timbrell later asked for mercy for the six accused and it was given, reluctantly, by the magistrate. The Timbrells only asked for peace in return. They did not get it; by September the father was bankrupt, and by 1824 the son was in the King's Bench debtors' prison.

In May 1816, the Riot Act of 1714 was read to the manufacturing poor of Bridport who had assembled to complain peaceably about the price of bread and lack of employment, but then went on to rampage through the streets, breaking windows of bakers' shops, and stealing three hogshead of beer from Gundry's Brewery. The Riot Act, when read word for word by a Justice of the Peace, allowed punitive action if a group of twelve or more people refused to disperse after sixty minutes. Any local militia cavalry unit who maimed or killed after a failure to disperse would be immune from prosecution. There was, however, no such military force available in the area. Instead a group of local worthies entered into debate with the rioters, smashed their hogshead of beer and persuaded 2,000 to go home peacefully. The ringleaders were dispatched to prison and then the government sent a troop of the Light Dragoons to Radipole, which is nearer Weymouth than Bridport and probably an indication of how stretched the state's machinery of coercion were.

At the Dorchester Assizes in August, eight men received prison sentences of between nine and twelve months; 16-year-old William Fry, who had stolen the beer, was one of them. Hannah Powell, Susan Saunders and Elizabeth Phillips were imprisoned, alongside three men who tried to prevent John Edwards from persuading the mob to go home. Mr Justice Holroyd dealt with this in one day and was still able to order his tea for 4 o'clock.

Nationwide rioting continued into May. On the same day as the Bridport disturbances, local press began to report with some unease that ricks and barns and other places that the rich stored food were being burned down at night. This kind of anonymous arson was typical of rioters who thought that there was no point in face-to-face negotiations, as the application of law and justice gave the landowners such great advantages. Rioting continued in Kent, Essex and all over East Anglia, particularly in Brandon, near Bury, and Norwich.

The Downham Riot of May 1816 acts almost as a 'check list' for Regency rioting. Desperate farmers converged on a local centre of population, armed with modified agricultural implements; their numbers increasing as each village was passed, in this case growing to over a thousand. Then an attack on a flour producer, in this case William Baldwin's, followed by intimidation of retailers to make them lower their prices. Butchers' shops were also looted and free beer was demanded from publicans. There were cries of 'bread or blood' and loaves were paraded on the end of pointed sticks. As their courage and drunkenness increased, there would be an attack on a particularly cruel magistrate, the reading of the Riot Act, a show of strength by the yeomanry cavalry using the safer, flat side of their swords, and then the sacrifice of a ringleader. It was almost choreographed – in an age which forbad workers forming unions to defend them; it was 'collective bargaining by riot'.[1]

Two selected ringleaders were executed in Norwich Castle in September. It was theft that brought them to the scaffold, not rioting. Thoday and Harwood, both labourers in their twenties, had their execution delayed until 1.30 pm as there was a rumour of a pardon. When this rumour turned out to be untrue, Thoday had a shrieking panic attack and had to be restrained by six men before being hanged. Harwood used his time to say goodbye to his pregnant fiancée.

As prices rose, the poor were being urged to eat potatoes instead of bread. However, potatoes themselves had a value and were being exported. On Friday 17 May, a large group of men, women, and children armed with crude weapons appeared at Bideford docks to prevent their only remaining sustenance being placed on ships. An intermediary by the name of Watts had purchased most of the potatoes from local farms and intended to send them to London to achieve a higher price. The distribution of goods was far less efficient than today, and prices for basic goods could vary greatly across the country. Some secondary accounts of events say that the food was going abroad, but as far as the starving lower orders of Dorset were concerned, it might well have been.

Rioting against the movement of food was not new in British history – what was novel was the fact that the poor had been told by the rich that they should be eating potatoes, and now the rich would be eating these too. To many it was as if a bond had been broken – how were the rich helping the poor by exporting something once deemed only good enough for the Irish labourer? The potato scarcity was created by man, not God, and patient resignation to the divine will was not the appropriate response.

Four women were identified as the ringleaders. Using simple weapons and the support of about 150 others, they prevented the potatoes from being loaded. In the Regency period many of the small-scale 'just price' riots were initiated by women, who would obstruct the movement of goods and force supplies to be sold at the traditional price. In this case, they were detained in the local lock-up gaol by the forces of law and order without much difficulty. A local magistrate appeared at the quay with just enough special constables to quell the riot.

Traditionally, this is where the historic small town riot ended. Ringleaders would be punished and then the conditions that caused the riot would be ameliorated by the concerned principal citizens, usually in the form of a temporary reduction in prices and a public subscription for the non-rioting poor.

On this occasion, however, the lower orders of Bideford continued to resist. A group of 200 carpenters and apprentices, on hearing of the committal of the four women to prison, sailed into the harbour, met up with the 150 original protesters, and marched on the prison, intent on a Bastille-like liberation of the women.

It was 29-year-old Thomas Trace, a local shipwright and former soldier, who seemed to be co-ordinating the attack. It was he who demanded the release of the prisoners, ignored the reading of the Riot Act and arranged for a dozen men to smash down the doors of the prison with two 14ft pieces of timber. Trace also seemed to be behind the fight with the constables, the stoning of the guards and the eventual rescue of the four women. Trace was rewarded at the Exeter Assizes with the longest of all the sentences – two years in gaol which, due to the appalling conditions, was often a death penalty in another form.

Thomas Croscombe appeared to be Trace's right-hand man and was later awarded a commensurate sentence of eighteen months. He seemed to have been involved in the provocative procession through the town, with the four women being held shoulder high by the mob. The town quietened at night, with the North Devon yeomanry cavalry patrolling the streets. These part-timers were stood down the next morning when the Inniskilling Dragoons arrived. Using their skills as naval shipwrights, the male ringleaders of the riot had escaped by sea.

Lord Sidmouth, the Home Secretary and Devon peer, was so outraged by the audacity of the lower orders that he sent his best detective, John Stafford of Bow Street, to hunt down the escapees. Stafford was the state's main spymaster and would later help to track down major revolutionaries and quash the attempt to assassinate members of the government in 1820. By August, the men had been found and were tried at the Exeter Assizes.

Presiding at Exeter was the same Lord Justice Holroyd that punished the Bridport rioters at Dorchester, but this time he was not able to stop for tea at 4 o' clock. In a thirteen-hour session, Croscombe and Trace were convicted. William Mayrick and James Stapledon, who had fought with constables, were given a custodial sentence and George Veal received six months for the bad luck of being known by all the special constables who gave evidence. Hundreds went unpunished. The fate of these five men was designed by the government as a salutary lesson to all; although in Georgian Britain the death penalty was not used for riot unless other crimes had been committed. Even in the much more serious riots in Ely and Littleport in May, when Fenland farmers armed themselves to fight local troops and militias, the five ringleaders who were eventually hanged were convicted of robbery rather than riot.

Thomas Trace survived the British penal system, and was still living aged 64 in the Bideford Old Town in 1851 with his wife Elizabeth. He was marked in the records as a 'former shipwright', but this may be due to his retirement from his skilled job or a lifetime of being blacklisted. A reference to a Thomas Trace with the same named wife appeared on the 1841 census, but with the word 'pauper' where the occupation should be suggests that there was no happy ending in this case.

Part of the traditional Georgian riot was an attack on the machinery creating the unemployment that was making bread unaffordable. In May,1816 newspapers reported that in Essex '(the rioters) visited Rob Smith's farm and destroyed a plough of a new construction that displeased them'.[2] However, as industries grew and new industrial communities were created, the nature of rioting began to change.

Merthyr Tydfil was one of the most urban and industrial parts of the United Kingdom, with one of the biggest ironworks in the world during the Regency period. In 1802 Nelson himself had visited to see cannon for HMS *Victory* produced, but the end of the war had reduced the demand and their product was no longer wanted, but profit was still required. In October 1816, owners of the ironworks tried to reduce wages to a level that maintained their profit margins.

At least 1,500 people were involved in mining coal and the production of iron in the Merthyr area. Many were relatively unskilled but there were a smaller number of iron puddlers, who stirred the molten iron in the furnace and used their skill and experience to know when the iron was exactly ready.

The disturbance started on Friday 18 October, with workers from Nantyglo, Blaenavon and surrounding villages converging on Merthyr and successfully disabling the furnaces by removing the blast from them as they marched. Armed with skilfully made iron weapons, they overpowered the small number of special constables sent to stop them. At this point, some protesters seemed to have been killed while trying to take control of a blast furnace and the next-door house, although many papers afterwards claimed that there had been no fatalities.

On the first evening of the disturbance, the Riot Act was read to the protestors by the magistrate and they were warned that they would be fired upon, but they stood firm. Annoyed by the language of the mob, the magistrates ordered the Cardiff yeomanry to charge, using their bayonets and the flat side of their swords. The workmen, armed with only a few sticks and clubs, were no match for the soldiers, and after around thirty of them had been seized, the rest dispersed quietly. By evening the town of Merthyr Tydfil was peaceful, the climax of the disturbances had passed without bloodshed. On Sunday three of the ringleaders, Rawlins Haddock, a 22-year-old labourer, and Thomas Jones and Steven Jarrett, aged 44 and 36 respectively, were escorted to the county gaol by the Cardiff cavalry. An anonymous letter from a member of the Light Dragoons was published in *Bell's Weekly Messenger*. He reports that he had arrived in Merthyr after a forced march over the mountains and was welcomed by the local people, 'There is nothing to fear from the rioters; they have no plan, no arms, and flee at the sight of a soldier.' However, most of the crowd control had already been done by the local volunteer militia.

Monday was quiet in Merthyr. The Light Dragoons were battle-hardened Waterloo veterans who had 'the cruel gleam that is only won only where blood flows like water'.[3] The soldiers also impressed the locals with their full moustaches and beards, a rare sight in South Wales.

At this point the riot changed into a strike. It proved difficult to maintain any solidarity between the different groups of workers however, and difficult to recruit other workers, such as the local colliers. Some of the more skilled men seemed to have gone back to work first – mostly the iron puddlers, who worked four to a blast furnace and were essential for the ironworks to operate. There was sufficient stock of materials to allow the owners to wait until the labourers ran out of money so, effectively, the strike became a lock out. The *Hampshire Chronicle* could not help sounding pleased. 'The higher class of mechanic employed in the ironworks continue in their occupation; but the other classes do not seem ready to return.'

In the pragmatic tradition of British criminal law, one ringleader bore the brunt of the retribution for the thousands of others whom the state did not have the resources to capture and punish. Rawlins Haddock received a one-year prison sentence for rioting, breaking into the Cyfartha Ironworks and sabotaging the blast furnace. He defiantly pleaded not guilty.

The owners of the ironworks put out a public statement about the dispute – one that was helpfully republished word-for-word as far away as York. They rejected the assertion in the newspapers that labourers were to have their pay reduced to one shilling a day and then went on to publicise the new pay rates; nobody would be on less than ten shillings a week; the best paid would still earn a guinea. They claimed that, even after the wage cuts, many rural workers would have envied these pay rates. It was an attempt to divide and rule. The owners also wondered, in print, why the workers had failed to return even though the riot had finished and the mob had been dispersed. They concluded that they were aware that their workers could not feed their families on the new wages, but they could do nothing about it. What they meant in reality was that the workers could do nothing about it. It was a terrible indictment of life in 1816.

There were similar riots all over the country, bearing strong similarities to the ones described. In Bury, Lancashire and Calton in Scotland, machines were destroyed that took employment away from spinners. In October, there was a riot in Sunderland that was very similar to that in Bideford, with women leading the fight against price rises by intimidating retailers. In Preston there were riots against wage reductions similar to Merthyr, and the Newcastle miners struck against wage reductions in May. In Great Halstead in Essex there were 'freedom riots' to release from prison four men who had been breaking machines. In December 1816 there was violence in Dundee over the price of bread, with the plundering of one hundred food shops.

Bread did not reach the 1815 price of 65 shillings per quarter until 1820 and traditional riots continued. Despite the ferocity of the 1816 rioting, it was the final flourish of 'bread and blood' riots that had been common in Georgian England. William Cobbett understood the 1816 riots, pointing out that the poor man would risk his life because he gained so little enjoyment from the living of it, but he did not support them. He told his readers that their suffering was caused by corruption and lack of political representation. In 1818, Cobbett took the credit for the lack of further riots. His advice was to organise rather than riot. Many people listened and the nature of protest started to change into something novel and even more worrying to the government.

Chapter 5

Bread and Potatoes

The price of bread mattered to everybody in the nineteenth century, not just those who were obliged to eat it in large quantities to survive. High bread prices allowed rich landowners to charge high rents. These rents enabled their consumption of luxury goods and fine new houses. Luxury goods and construction provided employment for urban tradesmen, allowing them to eat the overpriced bread that the rich were profiting from. Apart from bread, the diet of the Regency poor consisted of potatoes, oatmeal, cheese, meat, and seasonal domestic fruit, usually in that order. Meat meant scraps of ham, bacon, and offal such as pigs' ears, cow heel, sheep's trotters, and fruit meant apples and pears.

A nineteenth century agricultural labourer who required 4,000 calories a day would need at least one quartern loaf of slightly more than 4lbs pounds; a family loaf today is less than 2lbs, so a lot of bread, whether from wheat in the south of England or oats or barley elsewhere, was eaten during the Regency. In 2016 the *Grocer* magazine reported that bread consumption had sunk to a new low with less than half of the British population eating it daily and average consumption measured in slices per day.

Britain was running out of bread by 1800. High grain prices caused by Napoleon's attempted blockade had not yet been mitigated by increased domestic production. The government response to the crisis was the Stale Bread Act of 1800. This was not an attempt to protect the consumer against old bread. On the contrary, it made it go further by ensuring that all bread sold was stale when it was eaten. Parliament believed that half of all bread bought in London was bought fresh and eaten immediately. This was no longer a luxury that the lower classes should be allowed to indulge in. Under the new law, bakers had to leave bread for twenty-four hours to dry after being produced, or face a fine of 5s per loaf. Stale bread was believed to add twenty per cent to the stomach filling capacity of the loaf; overall bread consumption would also fall due to the final product being less appetising. The difficulty in applying this law effectively was hinted at when a reward of 2s 6d was offered to anybody who informed on the bakers.

The Act lasted less than a year. The government understood that nothing undermined their authority more than a law than cannot be enforced. It was expected instead that the poor would keep their bread for three days to increase its ability to fill the stomach. This was as unreasonable as the original law, and by the Regency period there were shops selling cheap, stale bread products to meet the demand for cheap food.

At first glance, it seems that well-established medieval customs protected the consumer from high prices. Bread sizes and weights were controlled. Bread was made in three main sizes: the peck, the half peck and the quartern loaf, with a half peck being exactly twice the weight of a quartern loaf. In most jurisdictions, no other sizes were permitted and hawking bread on the street was illegal. The price was also fixed by the Assize of Bread, first established in 1315, which regulated prices but brought little relief to the poor.

The weekly assize was led by the magistrate or the mayor. Its job was to determine the cost of bread based on the market price of wheat, and add an allowance for the profits of the miller and baker. It was assumed that about ninety per cent of the price of a loaf was made up by the ingredients. The assize of bread was a *de facto* control mechanism on millers and bakers and put a local limit on their profits. It did not stop the price rising; it merely suggested the highest possible price and this was still based on the market-determined price of the ingredients and the cost of labour. The protection offered to the poor was a mirage.

Bakers were watched by government and public because they had more power than they do today. The alternative – baking your own bread – was less viable than it might seem. The scarcity of fuel, especially in the south, made it economically unjustifiable to produce bread at home, or indeed any other foodstuffs that needed heat to prepare. Even the Sunday lunch, which may have involved the roasting of meat, was often done in the local baker's oven. In the early nineteenth century, as flour prices rose, the poor also found it more difficult and expensive to buy small amounts, as it was now more profitable for producers to sell larger quantities to middlemen.

Suspicion continued despite regulation. In Cheltenham in 1811, the local principal citizens advertised their crusade against bakers in the newspaper. They resolved to print a handbill listing the punishments available to those who sold underweight or overpriced goods. They asked the clerk to the market to do 'no notice' raids, to inspect the bakers' weights and measures. In Derby the same year, the Assize ordered bakers to bake their initials into their product so they could be tracked down if necessary.

Most people who believed that market forces increased prices made an exception when it came to bakers, who were simply blamed for their greed. William Cobbett, the radical observer of Regency life in his newspaper *The Political Register* knew the truth about the new market system. He pointed out that bakers who raised their price out of greed would soon lose custom to those who sold at a fair price, and that the rise in prices was caused by taxes and scarcity. This did not impress people; most of them had a notion of a 'fair price', both for their labour and their necessities, and were increasingly perturbed that these rules did not seem to apply any more.

The end of the war brought no relief to the suffering of the poor. The 1815 Corn Law banned the import of wheat until the very high price of 80s per quarter was reached. Bakers and millers still suffered, despite the blame that people placed on the government and landlords for this selfish law. There were accusations of both profiteering and adulteration in the newspapers. Conspiracy theorists commented that bakers had been receiving secret deliveries of potatoes to add to their bread. Bakers were often one of the first victims of rioters after the introduction of the Corn Law. The Spa Fields protesters of November 1816 smashed shops and paraded the streets with loaves on the end of a stick. The Downham rioters of 1816 attacked the bakers first and the butchers second.

Bakers were forbidden by law to adulterate their product to make it go further or taste better. Alum was the major illegal ingredient used. It was usually only discovered when officials or informers found it on the premises. It had no legal use in the baking process, and even possessing it was an indication of guilt. The *Rex v Dixon* 'bad bread case' of 1814 gave some examples of the extent and technique of adulteration. John Dixon, master baker, had been accused of selling 257 loaves of alum-laced bread to the Royal Military Asylum in Chelsea. This was an orphanage for children of soldiers who had died whilst fighting the French. In 1814, it contained a depressing 1,200 children:

> *It appeared from the evidence of the Quarter-Master of the Institution, of the Commandant, and seven of the children, that the bread delivered by the defendant on the day in question was served out to the children. They found it so rough and dry, that the majority of them rejected their breakfast, and complained of the badness of the bread, chewing lumps of alum of the size of a horse-bean, which they found sticking therein. The Commandant caused half a dozen spare of the loaves to be cut, and found them taste very sour. The Commandant took the piece of bread, with a*

*lump of alum in it (which was produced in Court), to the Lord Mayor,
for whom the defendant said he did not care. His Lordship attended in
Court to identify it. Mr Mac Gregor, surgeon to the Asylum, testified as
to the unwholesomeness of alum in bread, particularly to children, some
of whom were of the age of only five years. Its tendency was to produce
nausea on the stomach, and constipation in the bowels.*[1]

The defendant was the baker's foreman and was in no personal jeopardy –
his master was on trial. He was therefore able to give revealingly honest evidence. He had been putting alum in bread for eleven years. It was general
usage. Half a pound of alum in a sack of flour would not be noticed by the
consumer. It sped up the process, saved fuel, and made the loaves look more
attractive. He knew it was not allowed, so he bought the alum himself and
smuggled it in under his coat. This would seem to be a straightforward case.
As the master was responsible for the actions of his servant, the foreman
went free but the master baker, John Dixon, was found guilty.

Dixon appealed. He did not know about the alum. He had received no
bill for it. Alum was not harmful in small quantities. The judges pointed
out that this was a contradictory position. If alum was no problem, why
did they not advertise the fact that they used it? If they were to do that,
the judges suggested, the defendant would soon have no large complex
business to oversee, which was Dixon's next excuse. The judgement and
the punishment stood – a fine of £100 and six weeks in the King's Bench
prison.

Adulteration was illegal, but eking out bread with legal substances and
new ideas was encouraged. The quality of flour fell after 1815, and flour
that would have been formerly thrown away was now consumed. The Royal
Navy, as part of its post-war disposals, offered defective flour for sale after
1815, clearly advertised as such. Recipes suggested that the poor could turn
the worst quality wheat into nutritious ships' biscuits instead; one correspondent suggested that adding carbonate of potassium to poor quality
flour would render it 'less black, damp and tenacious'. Mr John Saines of
Masham seemed to have written to newspapers all over the country in 1816
with his plan to make bread out of unsound corn.[2]

Some commentators suggested adding rice to eke out the bread. For the
rich of Regency Britain, rice went into a dessert. One expert suggested that
boiling rice for ten minutes would make the bread go further. He had probably never seen the highly inefficient fireplace of the average poor person, and
did not take into account the price of the fuel needed. However, he did have

time for sarcasm; you could save 2d per loaf, while still 'paying the baker amply for his trouble'.

Others suggested the poor should eat less expensive grains. The plan was to feed oats of the cheaper variety to the king's horses, and leave the better ones for purchase by the poor. The drawbacks were obvious. The cavalry would need the same amount of oatmeal, and therefore the price of the cheapest oatmeal would rise, as the king's subjects went into direct competition with the king's horses for food.

Cheap salmon and oysters were another suggestion. A religiously inspired letter in the newspaper justified the use of more fish in the labourers' diet, with the biblical reference: 'Man cannot live by bread alone.'[3] It was true that in certain places and times of the year, fish were a cheap supplement to the diet of the poor, the best example being the salted Cornish pilchard. However, they tended to be a cheap luxury with some bread and butter, not the basis of a diet. Only in public houses were salted fish and a slice from a quartern loaf offered as a snack – this is because the fish could be cooked in large, economically viable quantities in a large establishment.

The newspaper editorials suggested that the populace should eat more 'household' bread that contained more bran; and if the people would not eat it (especially those in cities who had a loathing of the coarse brown bread), then at least it could be used to feed those in the workhouse. King George III himself ate a slice of brown bran bread every day with his lunch, which earned him accusations of tokenism and the new, unflattering nickname of 'Brown George'.

Petitions were made to parliament to stop the distillation of grain to produce spirits. The rich sent letters to the papers asking people not to waste bread – as if this was the main reason for the problem. The concerned citizens of Cambridge organised subsidised household bread for the poor, with a stern warning for those who tried to buy better quality bread with their charity ticket.

Poor people were spending all their available income on feeding themselves and their families. Here are some 1816 prices for the quartern wheaten loaf, which would be the same weight as two family-sized loaves today. All figures are for Leicester:

February:	9 ½ d
April:	10d
November:	14 ½ d
December:	17d

These increases meant less demand for manufactured goods and raw materials, which fell in price after 1815, causing more unemployment and thereby making it even more difficult to buy basic foodstuffs. It is not an accident that food prices were on the front page of Regency newspapers; these were vitally important, and they changed regularly – usually upwards.

By August 1816 the price of domestic wheat had risen to 80s a quarter, the price at which imports were allowed. However, even with the increase in imports in the latter part of the year, prices did not fall. Foreign imports had stopped by December because the catastrophically poor weather had led to shortages in Europe as well. There were no available surpluses in the USA either. The domestic harvest for other foodstuffs had also been mediocre and this exacerbated the situation. In Oxford, the quartern loaf was 8d in January 1816; by December it had increased to 14d and wheat reached 94s. Conditions were much worse in France and the rest of the continent, as the British papers gleefully reported: 'In many parts of France bread is absolutely twice dearer than in England'.[4]

It was clear that this was a food crisis all over Europe, perhaps the last one in Western Europe where people starved in significant numbers all over the continent.

Potatoes were suggested as an alternative to bread but they were regarded as low status food, especially in the south of England. The poor, the friends of the poor, and the apologists for the suffering of the poor, all took a moral position against the lowly tuber. To the poor, potatoes were a food fit only for hogs, possibly poisonous, the content of charity soups, and the staple diet of the Irish.

Cobbett, a vocal critic of the system and the sufferings caused by it, concurred, calling it 'Ireland's lazy root', believing that the potato diet would be a race to the bottom for the English poor, who would not ever see bread, beef, and beer again. In his book, *Cottage Economy* he continued his prejudices by stating the potato 'reduced the English labourer down to the state of the Irish', whose diet is 'but one remove away from a pig, and an ill fed pig too'.

Malthus, who fretted about the rapid rise in population, believed that the crop was the cause of early marriage, rapid population growth, and by implication, too many Catholic Irish of doubtful loyalty. Adam Smith, the economist, took a rational, evidence-based view; he had seen many Irish, mostly porters and prostitutes, and they were much better physical specimens than those brought up on wheaten bread in England.

The lower orders were blamed for their ignorance about food preparation. On 28 December 1816, a letter in the *Northampton Mercury* suggested that the poor were not cooking their potatoes well enough – it was only 'done well in Ireland and Lancashire' – a reference to the poor Irish peasant and the Irish diaspora in Liverpool and Manchester. Critics pointed out that too much of the potato was peeled away before cooking, that people could not spot a good quality potato from a poor one, and they were ignorant of the fact that it needed to be dry when stored.

The crop was also unpredictable. This situation was made worse by the damp rainy summers in the years after 1816 and the potato failed in Ireland in 1817 and at regular intervals after that. Even years of surplus were not very valuable, because the crop could not be stored for any length of time. Attempts to store potatoes in underground pits were unsuccessful. The difficulty of storing was made worse by the fact that they did not crop throughout the year. There would be a few months of scarcity, but this only mattered to those who did not have other options.

In a good year, the Irish peasant would have milk with their potatoes; the Reverend David Davies, who studied the poor of his own parish in 1797 noted:

> *Wheaten Bread may be eaten alone with pleasure; but potatoes need either milk or meat to make them go down; you cannot make hearty meals of them with salt and water only. Poor people indeed give them to their children in the greasy water they have boiled their greens and their morsel of bacon.*

The newspapers had mixed feelings about the potato. 'We use the potato, we abuse it and despise those who eat it.' The paper went on to do some despising – with the price of potatoes being so cheap:

> [Potatoes are sent to] *Spitalfields, to sell at 3s and 4s per cwt., or 5 or 6lbs. of good food for 2d? Who need to starve? Another serious consideration arises, – who need to work, when the chief sustenance of a family can be procured so cheaply?*
>
> *In 1815, in Hampshire, this was felt: 14lbs. of potatoes for 4d. made the labourer too careless. Have you got the potatoes? was the only question of the morning, for the provision of the wife and four or five children of the cottage*

The bountiful nature of the potato brought a moral problem. It would stop the lower classes working. This opinion would have been particularly galling for those who had been rioting for food for the past two years. Cobbett would have been outraged by the establishment newspapers' invitation to the lower orders to subsist miserably on potatoes while feeling guilty at the same time. The report continued to reference a beggar woman who regularly earned 8s a day, made herself fat on cheap potatoes but stayed poor, 'as it was gin and brandy that impoverish' – once again, cheap food was a problem because it led to vice, idleness and drunkenness.[5]

Despite everything, there was a shift towards the potato during the Regency for the practical reason that it filled the belly of people who could not afford bread. In places such as Manchester and Liverpool the diet of the urban poor was potatoes, oatmeal and bacon by 1815. If Cobbett had travelled to any of these places he would have realised the potato ('the root of extreme unction') was linked more with exploitation than religion. The Irish handloom weavers in Manchester in 1820 were living on salt and potatoes because of their occupation, not their religion.[6]

An advantage of the potato was that it could be grown in a poor person's garden. Despite Cobbett's doubtful assertions about the nutritional value of the tuber, common sense and experience suggested that it could feed the most family members with the least amount of land, as the poor Irish survived in this way. According to one newspaper correspondent it produced other advantages:[7]

> *Mr Cobbett has forgot to state, that in the country a great majority of the working classes have a small garden in which they cultivate Potatoes with their own hands in over hours, literally, without expense. No money goes out. It is all amusement and clear gain. By this their homesteads are endeared to them, and they are kept from the alehouse.*

Growing your own food was a source of satisfaction for the lower orders, he continued. The correspondent also challenged Cobbett's arguments that the potato needed 500 fires a year and therefore wasted fuel and time. The paper's correspondent pointed out that the urban poor would usually have a non-working member of the family at home and that a fire was lit for other purposes such as cooking other foods and keeping warm in winter. If fuel was short, men would make a sandwich of dry bread and cheese for their lunch before leaving for work in the morning to save the wood or coal for their family in the evening. It was also pointed out that the worst cuts of meat end up with the poor, that no additional fuel was needed to boil or roast potatoes, and they were an ideal complement to a stew or a cheap joint and then 'add a herring and the meal is sumptuous'.

In 1819 there was a flurry of charitable societies who tried to create allotments and cottage gardens for the poor. The growing of potatoes, including cultivation of early crops and better preservation of surpluses became a hobby for the rich, even if they did not eat the produce themselves. Some people asked the landowning aristocracy to give up land to create small farms. Mr Phillips, a regular correspondent to newspapers, had written an essay on 'Relieving the Distresses of the Labouring Poor' and now wanted to do more: [8]

> *At present he is pursuing a plan in which we most heartily wish he may succeed: he is confident the liberality of the Nobility and Gentry will raise a fund sufficient for the hire of large quantities of land in different parts of England, for the purpose of re-letting, in small farms, plots of land to the cottagers, and pasturage for cows, sheep, etc. When we reflect how many thousand families may be replaced, from a state of pauperism and misery, to profitable pursuits and employment, we cannot too often or too loudly call the attention of the Public to the question.*

Some cynical observers commented that the nobility and gentry were merely giving back, as an act of charity, land that had been cultivated by the rural poor as a matter of custom and right a mere thirty years earlier. In April 1819 the Poor Law authorities in Titchfield, Hampshire tried to use enclosed land to allow paupers to grow potatoes – in other words, to allow it to return to its historic and customary use. However, the plan was successfully challenged by the new owners; new property rights trumped the need to help the poor.

When the potato crop failed in the United Kingdom in 1844, it was first spotted in the Isle of Wight, not Ireland. Prime Minister Sir Robert Peel's first concern was the diet of the English working class, who were eating potatoes every day by this time. Peter Gaskell, in his *Condition of the Manufacturing Population* (1836) suggested that the 'staple diet of the town-mill artisans is potatoes and wheaten bread, washed down by tea or coffee'.

Apart from coffee and a little more tea, it was still mostly bread and potatoes for the lower orders thirty years after the Regency.

Chapter 6

The Poor Law

Although it was called the Poor Law, it was a law about the poor, not a law against poverty. There was no concern in Regency Britain about people being poor; it was considered a natural state, and it allowed others to live in luxury, which was another natural state. Poverty encouraged social order – it was believed that people could escape the worst of their condition by sobriety, obedience and constant hard work every day of the week except Sunday. People could be as poor as they could bear, and they were obliged by God to bear it. It only became a problem when the people became indigent – unable to survive without help.

Britain's system of looking after the poor was falling apart by the late Regency period. Over the centuries, a local system had developed whereby money was collected by a 'poor rate' and distributed according to need. It worked well when there was shortage of labour, because it made economic sense to retain a skilled workforce even if they went through a temporary bad patch. It was an inexpensive system when bread was cheap and work was regular. It was popular when it was clear that local people rather than strangers were being helped. All these conditions reversed by 1790, the cost of helping the poor increased far faster than anybody's income. The apparent generosity of the system was ended by a new, harsher Poor Law in 1834, which introduced the workhouse as a deliberately cruel punishment and abolished other payments to the poor.

Lots of experiments were tried before this harshness was implemented in 1834. A minimum wage for all citizens may seem a modern idea, but it has been tried before. It started in the Pelican public house in Speenhamland, Berkshire on 9 May 1795. Officials had used locally raised taxes to help the poor of their parishes for centuries, and this was an attempt to regularise the system. The meeting started with a request from concerned magistrates to employers to pay their labourers better wages 'to enable them to provide for themselves and their families...in proportion to the present unavoidable price of bread'. Wages were falling in the countryside as land was enclosed and rural employment fell. High bread prices meant that the locals were starving, while those who owned the land were thriving.

Despite the exhortation to the rich to pay more, the magistrates then did something that stopped employers increasing wages and arguably led to rural poverty wages for the next forty years. They offered to subsidise labourers' wages based on the price of bread. Each man would receive 3s, and his wife and children 1s 6d when the price of two quartern loaves (often called a gallon or half peck loaf) reached 1s. This money would only be available to the poor who were industrious and who 'endeavoured as far as they can to support and maintain their own family' – but it was still an indexed-linked minimum wage over 200 years before it was officially introduced in the United Kingdom. The money would be raised by a Poor Law rate, paid by the wealthier members of the local community. However burdensome the Poor Law rates were, this was still cheaper for the employer than raising wages or offering regular employment.

It was unintentionally ironic that the Pelican Inn was the site of this important decision. The pelican, in Christian mythology, injured its own breast and drew its own blood to feed its offspring. In a sense, this is what the authorities had decided to do. It could never solve the problem of poverty, only mitigate the consequences, and they arguably made things worse by providing taxpayer-funded subsidies to employers.

The Speenhamland system was the main example of outdoor relief – payments to the poor in money or goods. It was cash payments to the able-bodied that caused most resentment. The fact that the Poor Law officials tried to stop such payments, and they continued nevertheless, shows the scale of the emergency of this period. It was still a cheaper option than admitting people into the workhouse.

When the economy collapsed in 1815, the cost of the poor law spiralled out of control. It was not only expensive, but in the eyes of the rich, dangerously demoralising for the poor themselves. The Speenhamland system paid allowances for children and therefore encouraged the poor to marry earlier and produce too many children.

It was widely believed that the system was exploited by malingerers. This item syndicated in lots of newspapers:

An itinerant dealer in toys died last week at Lincoln at the age of 70. By perpetually pleading poverty, he had obtained for some time parochial assistance for his own support, and his wife and family were occasionally admitted into the work-house. On his death he bequeathed property to the amount of £1000 to a person no way related to him.

'Name and shame' became popular. At its root was the belief that much poverty was voluntary. In 1817, 200 rate payers in Great Yarmouth petitioned the local magistrates to allow the names of all of those claiming outdoor relief (cash and offers of work) to be published: 'The list…was printed as expeditiously as possible, and the outdoor relief has since been reduced from about £120 per week to little more than £60, and the rate [has fallen] to six shillings in the pound.'

This small article was published in newspapers in Stamford, Carlisle, Cambridge, Northampton, Bristol, and almost every major area in the country. In 1818 the Portsea Workhouse near Portsmouth printed a list of 900 families in receipt of outdoor relief with the stated aim of flushing out those who were cheating the system. It also announced that there were 900 people in the Workhouse, being a total of 8,000 people being supported by the poor rate. Shame became a form of rationing, and more stigma was attached to being poor, and much of it stuck.

Workhouses would often give money to the poor to get them back to work. In January 1819, the workhouse of St Saviour in Southwark gave money to George Adams to redeem his glazier's diamond – a glass cutting implement that would have been indispensible. He had clearly pawned it to feed his family. Clothes were sometimes provided – Theodosia Brown received shoes from St George the Martyr workhouse nearly every August between the years 1815-1820. Sometimes she received money as well, yet she was always back in the workhouse in October. She had been given the grant to go hop picking in Kent, presumably wearing out her shoes. Theodosia was a good example of an 'In and Out', who left and entered the workhouse according to need; it was this ability which made the workhouse slightly different from prison. She died aged 80 on 14 January 1824 at the same workhouse; she did not need to go hopping any more.

Shoes, breeches, gowns, stockings, petticoats, shirts, waistcoats, smocks, greatcoats and bed gowns were distributed. They were hardwearing and plain, so that the poor did not come to expect finery, and would be connected with the needs of employment and respectability – John Agar was a workhouse apprentice who was given a shirt, stockings and pair of shoes to start his apprenticeship with Mr Deane in Southwark in 1816. Critics complained about the able-bodied poor receiving clothes; they believed the paupers should join a clothing club – saving from their wages in the same way as they did for their funerals.

Help was limited in another important way. Paupers could only be helped in one place in the country – their place of settlement, which could be gained by birth, marriage or work in a particular parish. This law of settlement worked well in a rural economy, but was not working in the more industrialised 1800s. It now distorted the labour market, reduced workers' rights and created an inefficient economy. The poor were stopped from moving to a place where they had the best chance of good wages, and wages were being controlled at the same time that it was agreed that bread prices could not be regulated. Farmers and manufacturers could send their goods away for the higher price while workers were constrained by the place of their birth like medieval peasants; it was capitalism for the rich and feudalism for the poor.

One example can stand for thousands; at the Michaelmas hiring fair at Kimbolton, Huntingdonshire in September 1815, Thomas Lewin hired Sarah Swales as a domestic servant. She was a pauper from the neighbouring parish of Great Staughton. The overseers of the poor in Great Staughton would have been very pleased with this arrangement. Overseers were responsible for payments to the local poor and the administration of the workhouse, and Sarah would be off their books for a year. A year would be long enough for Sarah to gain settlement rights in Swineshead, her new place of residence, meaning she would no longer be a burden on Staughton.

For the sake of propriety, Mrs Lewin supervised the 16-year-old and she was paid £3 per year in arrears plus her food and lodgings. However, with eight days of her year to go, she was dismissed by the Lewins for oversleeping. Mr Lewin, giving evidence at the local Quarter Sessions, which dealt with disputes between Poor Law parishes, said that he had to make his own breakfast at times and had warned Sarah a dozen times:

> *Mr Lewin said he was a farmer who paid rates; he had told the girl many times of her fault, and it had got worse and worse; and was a bad one and saucy; they had borne with her as long as they could ; he had no thoughts of her settlement.*[1]

Mr Lewin must have been very angry with Sarah. He seems to have forgotten that he paid a property tax to support the poor, and if he did not sack Sarah soon, there would be another resident of his parish that he was responsible for. Sarah herself admitted occasional oversleeping, but also said that her master had told her that sacking her in this way was always his plan. She was sent back to Great Staughton with £3 minus a shilling for the eight days she had not worked. She was not particularly concerned. When Mr Lewin told her not to expect a full year's salary, she said that the idea never entered her head. This was not a court case about the rights of servants or a judgement on her work habits, and her relaxed attitude proved that she was aware of that.

This action was taken by Great Staughton to prove to the ratepayers of neighbouring parishes that they were not a 'soft touch'. They won their case. Mr Lewin was not believed – partly because he went on to incriminate himself by saying that many employers in the area used the same methods. The parish of Swineshead was stuck with the now jobless Sarah. The cost of looking after her had not changed. Only the lawyers had benefitted.

Overseers were also prepared to use more strong-arm tactics and to send people much further away. Heaven help you if you became an orphan while living away from your parish of settlement. In 1810, the *Suffolk Chronicle* reported the fate of an 8-year-old Halifax child whose father had died. Rather than bearing the cost of feeding the orphan, or paying the premium for him to become an apprentice to a tradesman, he was sent back to Rutland, accompanied by the overseer at Halifax.

The overseer at Rutland took the boy in, paid the expenses of his removal, and then beat up the lad in front of the Halifax official. Later the Rutland overseer gave him some bread and cheese and a shilling and told him to make his own way back to Halifax, a distance of 150 miles. He was lucky enough to meet some soldiers with fifty miles to go; it was clear that he had been walking up to that point. The newspaper does not report the fate of the boy or the Halifax overseer; it was just another example of a system that created wastefulness and unnecessary cruelty.

Being born in a parish gave you settlement rights, and the overseers of the poor became worried by pregnant women. It sometimes reached the level of paranoia. According to the *Cambridge Chronicle* (1819):

> ...*a woman by the name of Jane Bulman was seen in the Parish of Wicken. When the overseers of the Poor noticed that she was pregnant, they panicked and asked the magistrate for a removal order. However, she was neither a pauper, nor a recipient of relief and had no intention of staying in the area. The magistrate quashed the order and fined the overseers £2.*

Sometimes pregnant women would be dumped in another Poor Law area prior to birth, or forced to marry somebody from another parish. Families who had lived and worked in a parish for years would be moved away if their circumstances changed and there was a fear that they would become a burden. There was particular discrimination against women, as they were more likely to be a burden on the parish if the main breadwinner had died. Many recently widowed young women had their worries added to by being forcibly removed by the overseers.

This story from Cumberland appeared in *Kentish Gazette* in June 1816. A poor Irish women, unnamed, was becoming a burden on the parish. She had been ill and was about to give birth or, in the delicate language of the time, she was at her *accouchement*. As the overseer was away, his wife took it upon herself to get rid of the woman, putting her on a cart and dumping her in the road in the neighbouring parish. Like many overseers of the poor in this period, this one hoped that money would make the problem go away:

The overseer having made pecuniary compensation...and pleaded guilty, and expected to have been discharged; but the Bench, determined to punish that which is in the highest degree reprehensible...and had been of late much practiced, fined the parties £5 or to remain in prison until such fine be paid.

The treatment of people in workhouses varied tremendously from place to place, depending on the desire to save money and the political situation. At the most extreme end, paupers were at the mercy of the bad temper of the aristocracy. There was a particularly shocking case in Somerset. Sir William Manners owned most of the houses in Ilchester and therefore felt entitled to control both the members that it sent to parliament. However, when voters proved hostile, he took the roofs off their houses and evicted them, thus taking their vote away; he built a workhouse to accommodate them instead. In 1818 his selected candidates for election, one of whom was his son, were not elected, and he closed the workhouse down in a fit of pique.

In January 1819, all of the staff and 163 inhabitants were evicted from the house and ended up sleeping on the streets, or using cattle cribs in the fields and barns. In one case of obtaining possession of a house, reported the *Morning Chronicle*, 'a wagon load of soil from the common sewers was thrown in the room over them' – 'soil' was very much a euphemism. The inflexible settlement system made moving away even more difficult than remaining. As ever, in the midst of starvation and homelessness, the moral dimension was never far away:

About 20 old men and women, pregnant women, young men and boys promiscuously huddled together in one common bed on the stone floor of the Town Hall, where the numbers have been reduced by the deaths of

Ann Pope and Nelly Lye; and where one women daily expects the pangs of child-birth, without anything to divide or screen her from the view of people of different ages and sexes!

Many of these victims were not even paupers a few years earlier. The newly created paupers were given an allowance to find themselves shelter, but there was none to be had. When they strayed into neighbouring parishes they were forbidden relief and threatened with the county gaol.

The Rector, churchwardens, and principal citizens petitioned parliament in April 1819 for an investigation. Honourable members, while accepting the cruelty of the situation, felt that the Commons could not intervene on a matter which rested on the actions of an individual; actions that were not, in themselves, illegal. These houses and tenancies were property, so the Manners family had a perfect right to take the roofs off their houses and dispose of their other property in the town as they wished. The petition was withdrawn. The fact that the Manners had done nothing illegal was a reminder about the type of people who were making the laws. When MPs tried to console the poor with the idea that the law was open to all, the *Westmoreland Gazette* repeated the words of the reformer Horne Tooke on the subject – that the public house was also open to all, but was not a place of joy for those with no money.

It is not easy to see inside the workhouse or House of Industry in the Regency period, and less easy to make a judgement because of the massive differences between them. The Swansea workhouse advertised its own virtues in a long notice in July 1817 and it gave some insights into attitudes and living conditions.

They reported that that they had acquired a new, convenient building, quite cheaply. It had a kitchen, an oven, and a system of ropes and pulleys around the oven, which allowed them to boil 110lbs of potatoes at any one time. This potato-cooking contraption cost £20 but could cost-effectively feed 120 people at a time with potatoes and broth. In a further attempt to be cheap, the inmates were living on hard biscuit rather than wheaten bread. The organisers vowed to replace this with proper wheaten bread when the price fell. The weekly diet was typical of many workhouses:

Diet – Breakfast, water gruel, with three ounces of bread. Dinners, Sunday, Tuesday and Thursday, half a pound of fresh meat (butchers weight), boiled, and one pound of potatoes. Monday, Wednesday and Friday, the broth made from the meat, with a little oatmeal and potatoes...At present we have varied it by cutting cabbages previously steamed, into a broth, and substituting occasionally four ounces of bread for the potatoes. Saturday, fish and potatoes, with any of the remaining scraps. Supper, the same as breakfast.

The dietary highlight of the week was cabbage soup. The cost was clearly calculated at 2s 4d per person. The workhouse also had a kitchen garden, which it hoped would soon contribute cheap food and redeeming work for the poor.

The workhouse was not there to provide financially profitable work. It was not possible, as soon became obvious. 'Experience has proved that no manufacturing or general business can be carried out at a trading profit in a house of industry', admitted the Swansea report. If a workhouse could provide profitable work, then the poor-but-guiltless would be employed outside the workhouse doing it, where the highlight of the week would be something more interesting than cabbage. The job of the Swansea house of industry was twofold: to reduce the price of pauperism, and to inculcate good habits into the poor in the future.

The workhouse report goes on to admit that most of their inmates have no handicraft skills at all. So the inmates have to be occupied doing work that was unskilled and not required on the outside. Their economically meaningless but morally important work of choice was picking oakum – unravelling thick ropes for the fibres – which defrayed half the cost of feeding the paupers. Beds were made of wrought iron, which prevented vermin and were cheap, as the economic depression had caused a collapse in raw material prices. Mattresses were thin linen cloth stuffed with straw. The price of straw was being watched keenly by the overseers and they fretted that it was more expensive in Swansea than elsewhere. There were few treats in the workhouse, though tobacco was available for the most industrious men.

The report announced with a level of grim satisfaction that half of their inmates were children because they had stopped paying Speenhamland-style outdoor relief and instead had started taking in the children of the poor and leaving their parents outside:

Whenever the latter [parents] are incapable of maintaining their children, we have taken a proportion of them into the house, by which the man himself is saved of the disgrace of being a pauper; being independent of his employer he can make a better bargain with him, and his children are brought up in the habits of cleanliness, industry and morality.

The overseers at Swansea were genuinely angry that the local employers were providing starvation wages, but their response was to take away 'surplus children' to allow workers to make 'a better bargain' with their employers. They were not suggesting a trade union style negotiation (throughout the Regency, unions were illegal), merely that with fewer children to feed, wages would go further. Wage rates were already depressed because employers had to pay a property tax to support the children in the House of Industry – who were there because wages were depressed. It was the most vicious of circles.

These captured children were educated from age 5 to 9 – reading but not usually writing – and then taught mostly low-skilled trades, which would mean flooding the market with even more hat makers, tailors, cobblers and basket makers that would eventually increase poverty. It was a system with no future; there was no radical reform in our period; there would be improvements in the future, but of the ungenerous kind.

One newspaper, from a correspondent who called himself 'PHILANTHROPY', shows how the desire for a tougher Poor Law was building up. He starts with attitudes that we would recognise today. Poverty was terrible and individual charity didn't help because it was unpredictable and could not cope with long-term, deep-rooted problems. He criticised the Poor Law system; the support was different in different areas, people were tied to their parish, there needed to be a national system. At this point, it seems that PHILANTHROPY is a visionary with views similar to ours. However, he turns out merely to be a visionary who predicted the New Poor Law of the 1830s.[2]

He then suggested:

> an establishment of district workhouses for the purpose of giving some kind of employment to all who are able and separate houses for the abandoned and vile, with a remedy for the corruption of morals, which has ended to increase pauperism; and also for a proposition for regulating wages, for want of which the poor laws have increased

His vision was to come true. In 1834, larger workhouses were set up with a new, crueller regime, and outdoor relief was (in theory) abolished. Outdoor relief went the same way as independent domestic work, rights to use common land and the protection of apprenticeships. The treatment of the poor continued to be a problem after the Regency period, for just like today, we try to solve the problems of poverty by dealing with the consequences rather than the causes of it.

Chapter 7

Cold Charity

The Regency period is full of examples of the rich being helped by the poor. The poor did the fighting against Napoleon, and then the sailors and soldiers were demobilised into poverty. The poor paid taxes on bread to keep aristocratic rents high; they paid tax on everything else in order to abolish the Property Tax, and they were evicted from the smallholding by enclosure, losing land and entitlements held in their families for generations. There was a rapid and brutal descent into poverty for the lower orders in the relatively short period of thirty years.

It was not a one-way street, however. The rich also helped the poor, but the rules were different. It was conditional help, and one major assumption ran through it. It was the simple, brutal, universally held belief that the lower orders in their natural state were idle, would not work at all if they could get away with it, and would do something far worse if they had the spare time. William Hutton, a dissenting bookseller from Birmingham and no particular enemy of the poor, put this comment in his diary (1795):

> *If a man can support his family with 3 days of labour, he will not work six ... If the body is unemployed, it becomes a nursery of disease. If the mind is unemployed, a languor commences, and a man becomes a burthen to himself.*

All attempts to alleviate the poor had this idea in the forefront. Idleness was far more dangerous than poverty.

The second popular principle was that it was a mistake to give money to the poor. You had no control over how it was spent, and the poor, in their demoralised state, would waste it. An article in the *Leeds Intelligencer*, reprinted nationally, put forward the idea that the poor should be given provisions instead of money – 'by this method the possibility of the money being spent improperly will be done away with':

> *A Correspondent suggests, that, to give provision instead of money, to the distressed poor, would be the most proper mode of really relieving*

wants. Suppose a family of 5, the husband out of employ, the wife unable and the children too young to work, should be relieved at 7 shillings per week; instead of money, supply them with provisions, viz

One Stone of Flour	*2s 4 d*
Half a stone of oatmeal	*10d*
Meat	*2s 10d*
1 ounce tea	*5d*
Half a pound of sugar	*4d*
One peck potatoes	*7d*
Six soup tickets	*6d*
Total	*7 shilling.*[1]

This gives a lot of insights into the attitudes of the time. Children were clearly designed for work and needed to reduce family poverty. Work was their natural state – it explains how parents in mill towns were able to send their children into factories relatively easily, without the reservations people would have today.

With an allowance of flour they were clearly meant to produce their own bread. This shows no understanding of the domestic arrangements of the poor, who mostly bought bread from shops. In the same newspaper, 200lb of flour of the worst quality cost £2 8s. If the poor could buy this, they would survive; but this was four weeks wages for a weaver, and the poor could not buy in such bulk. The two shillings or so allocated to flour by the rich commentator worked mathematically but not in the real world of the poor.

There was a lot of oatmeal gruel in the suggested diet. Meat at these allowances would produce no more than bacon and offal. A peck of potatoes is about 9 kilos, which would be about fifty medium size potatoes per week. That would be seven potatoes per week per person if distributed evenly. The inclusion of tea and sugar showed how entrenched these non-nutritional foods had become into the diet of the poor. It seems that the only vegetables to be found would be in the charity soups. Rent is not mentioned at all. The author also admits that there is no provision for coal, and says that he feels that there was probably a way that the money for this could be earned – thus destroying the whole basis of his argument that the poor can survive without money. Neither would this family buy a newspaper, a toy for their children, or a subscription to a burial club. It looked a little like Caribbean slavery, and for humanitarian reasons the trade in slaves was abolished in 1807. There was no such sympathetic feeling for the British lower orders.

The most formalised way of helping people in distress was the sub-scription society. Many of these societies were designed to help formerly well-established people who had hit hard times rather than the truly poor. The 'National Benevolent Society for the Relief of Distressed People in the Middle Ranks of Life' was formed in Gloucester in 1812 with the belief that not enough was being done for this respectable (but now neglected) class. Considering the immense suffering of the rest of the country in 1812, there was a sense of entitlement here. The Institute's 1815 report records that they had raised £1,835 and provided fifteen persons including the daughter of a clergymen, aged 71, who had found herself in the workhouse 'with persons of low reputation and suffering terrible privations'; the widow of an officer who had been shot during the war with France; the wife of a chief justice, and the widow of a soldier who had been forced to sell his commission in the army. Not only were these people not 'the deserving poor', they were often not poor at all, just members of the establishment who had had some bad luck.

There was a flurry of attempts to use charity to help the widows and families of those who had died at Waterloo in 1815. The ordinary seamen had been discharged from their warships and there was not enough trade to absorb these men into the merchant navy. The fate of the poor British sol-diers and sailors would have been obvious to the public. Unlike today, mili-tary men appeared in public in their uniform and they were a very common sight during the Napoleonic Wars, especially in the southern coastal towns. By 1818 sailors were regularly spotted in the streets, shoeless, near naked, and with empty bellies, to the extent that the newspapers worried that pro-fessional 'sturdy beggars' were impersonating them.

A fund set up by William Wilberforce raised £7,000 in 1817–18. It could do little to help the 65,000 sailors – two out of three of the whole Royal Navy – demobilised since 1815. The debate in parliament was concluded by William Wilberforce himself, who suggested that the government simply cut its naval budget faster and more savagely. People at the time would not have seen this as a contradiction; charity was voluntary, targeted and conditional. Income tax, another way of redistributing wealth, was fixed, compulsory, and a wartime tax only.

Unlike the help for the middle ranks, the money from Wilberforce's 'Society for the Aid of Destitute Seamen' was spread out amongst considerably more people. Each applicant was examined by a Royal Navy officer. The 250 men – many more had to be sent away – were given temporary low-grade lodg-ings and given a wholesome breakfast of porridge every morning. The papers reported that they were particularly grateful when the accumulated filth of the streets was washed off their bodies and they were given second-hand clothes. The society also applied to other missionary societies for bibles for the distressed sailors – the need for moral reformation was seen as a crucial part of the rehabilitation process. Bibles were also ordered in foreign languages – the British army and navy that defeated Napoleon was multi-racial.

Each city and town organised a subscription society to alleviate the distress of the poor. The society meeting in Norwich in January 1817 will serve as an example. It was a meeting of the most respectable members of the local society. In this case, the chair was William Hankes and the first speaker was Alderman Harvey. They were desperate to distance themselves from radicals and revolutionaries; there would be a loyal toast somewhere in the proceeding, even to the Prince Regent, whose unpopularity united all classes except the ruling one.

These meetings normally started with an explanation of the local distress. In the case of Norwich, the cotton manufactory had lost 900 of its 1,000 workers, exports from small workshops had collapsed due to lack of demand in Europe, and the second year of poor weather had produced high prices for all foodstuffs. Factories in Manchester were undercutting local workshops. The workhouse was now full with 700 inmates, and there were 3,000 people applying for 'outdoor relief' – supplements to their wages. Alderman Harvey stressed that the 3,000 were 'honest, laborious men'; another element of these distress societies was the determination to only help the deserving poor. Alderman Harvey also pointed out that the poor of Norwich were some of the most grateful paupers in the country. In the eyes of the 'Respectability' present at the meeting, it was absolutely vital that the poor were humble and grateful. This gratitude acknowledged the contribution of the rich and avoided the poor being spoilt and demoralised by too much help.

That was certainly the case in Norwich. Mr Gurney, the next speaker, gave some examples:

Mr Gurney then related several cases of extreme distress that had come under his notice, where from the want of work, industrious men with large families have been obliged to part with their clothes, and even sell their dishes for their dinner, before they would apply for relief; and one weaver, who had a wife and three children, and earned 7 shilling a week, and in better times had saved up a little money, burst into tears on being obliged to part with his furniture and resort to the Court of Guardians for relief. Such deserving persons were peculiar objects of attention.

Mr Alderson spoke next and modified the philanthropic atmosphere. He pointed out that people had migrated to Norwich from as far away as Berwick-upon-Tweed; that distress was no worse than last year apart from the increased price of bread, and that was due to a bad harvest caused by God's providence, 'and it was the duty of the poor and the rich to submit to it'. He had clearly forgotten about the Corn Laws.

Mr Alderson was a Poor Law overseer and administered the workhouse and outdoor relief. He welcomed further subscriptions from the concerned citizens as this would keep the Poor Law rates under control. He had perhaps also forgotten that those in the room would be the people paying the most on poor rates. He worried a little that the working man, while needing relief, also needed his independent spirit maintaining for the future. He wanted non-Norwich people removed, in case they became a burden. They would be forcibly removed from Norwich to their place of settlement if they became unemployed or ill. His view about who qualified as deserving poor was trenchant and specific – you had be guilty about receiving help, grateful and hard working. And from Norwich.

Mr Gurney took the stage again. He, too, asserted that more money was needed. Some of the independent-minded poor had not even asked for relief; they needed to be sought out, but their self-reliance was laudable, if a little misplaced. Many of this praiseworthy, independent sort had sold all their possessions at the pawnbroker, but now even the pawnbrokers were running short of capital as their shops were overflowing with pledged items.

The gentlemen ended their meeting with some resolutions. There would be soup kitchens; a door-to-door collection; a subscription, and a distribution to the deserving poor. The initial idea – to employ the poor in repaving the town – was not followed up. It would have cost too much to buy the raw materials – it would also have created real jobs.

The concerned citizens of Norwich seem to have forgotten the events of their town in the previous year, 1816, when relations between the classes were a little less rosy. There had been vandalism in the city in May as part of the rural food riots all over East Anglia. When windows were broken, the Poor Law officials announced that, yes, they would repair all the damage, but the cost would be subtracted from the funds available to the poor.

Other poor people had showed similar ingratitude. The weavers of Calton, Glasgow were under pressure from Irish immigration and new technology which allowed the unskilled to do their weaving jobs and an increase in bread prices. It was 11d per quartern loaf in Glasgow market in July 1816, with a 1d discount if you had a ticket from the Calton Bread Society and bought it from them directly. The organisation was set up in 1810, employed its own staff and set itself up in competition against the local bakers. It urged the workers to spend any money saved from buying cheaper bread on material and moral improvements. The real problem however, was that the quartern loaf was 2d in 1810, and in Glasgow in July 1816 it was 11d, and such a small discount made no difference at all.

On Thursday 1 August, in response to the worsening distress in Calton, a soup kitchen was set up. At first glance this seemed to be a generous gesture; there was no attempt to vet the recipients in order to rule out those whose poverty was the result of moral failings. There was no ostentatious display of names and amounts pledged in the newspapers that was an almost inevitable part of the distress societies. This one seemed to be a 'no strings attached' charity.

The attitude of the local people was novel. First they threw stones at the soup kitchen and then went on to break the windows of those who generously set them up. By 4pm the military had selected the ringleaders and imprisoned them. Then a larger crowd attacked the soldiers, and they fired back and injured people. The riot continued into the next day until sufficient military force of dragoons could be mustered. One youngster had died in an accident; he was discovered with a chisel in his head (some reports say it was a shard of glass in the eye) and this was removed in an unsuccessful and uniquely painful trepanation of the skull.

The *Oxford Chronicle* reported that on the first day of the riot, the mob began 'in the usual way of throwing stones at the soup kitchen, breaking the windows'. The tone had a world-weariness about it, as it seemed to have been a popular method of protest for the poor in 1816. The newspaper speculated somewhat sarcastically that it was the quality of the broth that was the root cause, but then settled on the belief that it was a handful of mischievous people exploiting the economic distress for their own political ends.

The Calton rioters were not forelock-tugging agricultural labourers. They were a tight-knit community of skilled workers who had no time for broth as the answer to their problems. They had been suffering for more than twenty years and had rioted previously in 1797 and 1800. They knew that soup kitchens were a consequence of their problems and not the cure. A truer cause of the anger can probably be seen in the fact that the rioters tried to burn down a factory that manufactured the type of power looms that was creating unemployment and depressing wages.

The local Justices of the Peace announced at the end of the disturbances that they would still be providing relief for the poor weavers of Calton, despite their goodwill being mightily tested. The local subscription society put a notice in the papers after the riots, complaining about ingratitude. Why would benevolent gentlemen volunteer to help with a reaction like this?

Individuals did contribute to charity for the poor. The Prince Regent was always ready to have more of any luxury item that was not selling well. In December 1816, in response to starvation in East London, the prince generously spent more of his taxpayer subsidy on Spitalfields silk. He purchased 2,000 yards of silk for the Princess Charlotte and her new husband, the Prince of Coburg. His influence meant that people who appeared at court followed his example. As people were starving, it was suggested that courtiers should wear plain velvets, which were quick to manufacture and able to produce wages before even more people perished. This was not the end of the prince's generosity with the money of others. On Christmas Eve of the same year, 1816, the 'Prince Regent's Bounty' distributed 9,500lbs of beef and 10,000 loaves of bread to 6,000 poor people.

Each town and city would have local worthies ready to make donations to the poor, aping the example of the monarch and aristocracy. It was thought particularly important that the poor should eat at Christmas. One example that will stand for thousands is that of John Fenton Cawthorne, who donated 1,300lbs of beef (two fat bullocks) and potatoes to feed 400 poor families of his native Lancaster from 1810 to at least 1823. In 1815 he donated 10 guineas to the Lancaster Waterloo fund for soldiers and their families; he also gave £100 and some land to build a school for girls. He was a generous man, but it was generosity with a self-interested purpose.

Cawthorne, a lifelong opponent of Catholics and supporter of the slave trade, had arrived in Lancaster in disgrace after being found guilty of embezzlement of the funds of the Westminster Militia. After a socially embarrassing court martial he wished to reinstate himself as a member of parliament. 'His personal interest there had been established through largesse and was strong enough to secure his unopposed return in 1806, and again in 1812.'[2]

Despite his annual generosity to the poor, he was a harsh landlord and factory owner. In most of the primary references to Cawthorne he is at the local race track; and it is perhaps not a coincidence that when he died in 1831 he left less than £100, and his fine house, Wyreside Hall, had to be sold. Politics and gambling were the most expensive hobbies a member of the local 'Respectability' could have. Although Cawthorne was perhaps a little more villainous than most benevolent gentlemen, it does rather suggest that the motivation of the rich was sometimes suspect.

Charity was a social hobby. It was thought to be a particularly good occupation for the ladies. Many charities would specifically invite ladies to meetings and give publicity to their donations. It would be part of the social round for the young too, as this 1818 poem/joke from the *Northamptonshire Mercury* suggests:

CHARITY BEGINS AT HOME

As a belle of high fashion was boasting one day
Of the clothing and food that she had just given away
To the poor, A satirical elf,
Her Uncle, exclaimed 'you the hungry may feed
But as to you clothing the naked – indeed
You had better begin with yourself!

The young woman is boasting about her charity; her uncle, like elder relations throughout the ages, disapproves of what she wears, and clothing the naked may have been the reality rather than an expression.

Evening balls and afternoon lunches were a common vehicle for the rich to enjoy themselves and help the local poor. The superbly named Grateful Society of Bristol, who still do charitable work today, met on 13 November 1818 to raise money by a divine service, sermon, and lunch ('dinner will be on the table at precisely 3pm'). Ladies were particularly welcome to contribute money at the church doors after the service and their recommendations for charity were actively solicited, possibly because of the number of poor women the charity helped. Since 1758, the society had helped 7,376 women who were about to give birth and had provided apprenticeships for 214 Bristol boys.

Other charitable events on November 1818 included an acting performance in Dublin in support of the local Society for the Suppression of Street Begging. Despite its name, it did have charitable intentions, as it was designed to protect children from being used, endangering their physical and moral welfare. The Mendacity Society report of 1818 believed that vulnerable looking children – the blind were particularly sought after – were hired out for the purpose of begging, and that parents used their begging money to drink spirits and ruin children's lives.

The Exeter Sunday Schools also announced in November 1818 that it had provided reading and religious instruction for 372 of the poor through voluntary subscription. The Bishop of Chester promised a charity sermon (an idea that shows how very far we are today from the ideas of two centuries ago) in favour of the local Blue Coat Charity hospital. Since 1815, these institutions had provided a basic education to poor children – it rarely included writing, as this would encourage ideas above their station. Some charitable schools did more. Thomas Finigan, master of the Irish Free School, not only organised the education of the Irish poor of St Giles, but also provided food and clothes for children. He also stopped asking for parental contributions to the schooling, as the parents could no longer afford them. As usual, there was a catch; the school was trying to wean the youngsters off their native religion by offering what they called a 'non sectarian' religious education.

Charity was usually provided via education or a copy of the New Testament. No money was provided by voluntary organisations without the most careful scrutiny of individual circumstances. The only cash payments were made by the Poor Law officials, and they would examine the recipients carefully before handing over any money. Some charities would hand over goods, such as clothes for the poor, but surveillance and instruction were never far below the surface. A letter to the *Carlisle Patriot* in November 1818 welcomed the new charity for clothing the poor; it would make sure that they had no excuse to miss Sunday school, and asked whether it could be arranged that only children who worked during the week could receive these clothes, as their only chance for an education was on Sunday. The implication was that even regular work could not guarantee regular clothing.

Not everybody was grateful. Leigh Hunt's *The Examiner* suggested that somebody who gave £50 to help a local organisation was going through the process of almsgiving, not charity. If that person enforced high rents for his tenants or drove down the wages of his workers, they were in no way charitable.

William Cobbett was scathing of charities; they came with too many strings attached. He would have objected to the November 1818 meeting of the organisation to 'Relieve the Poor Widows and Orphans of the Clergy of Ely' – not because these people did not deserve support, but because the rich clergy were not paying the bill. It was coming directly from the rich of Cambridgeshire and therefore indirectly from the poor who paid their taxes and rents and ate expensive bread.

Chapter 8

Old Corruption: The General Election, 1818

P arliamentary reform – that is, the fair geographical distribution of seats, the widening of the franchise so that more people could vote, and the end of corruption that gave power to those with money – was not a new subject in the Regency. Prime Minister William Pitt was in favour of reform in the 1780s:

> *Without a parliamentary reform the nation will be plunged into new wars; without a parliamentary reform you cannot be safe against bad ministers nor can good ministers be of use to you*

This was one of the many necessary changes put on hold by the war with France and the fear of revolutionary ideas.

Instead of reform, the British lower orders were constantly encouraged to love their constitution. They certainly enjoyed more liberty than was available on the continent and they were constantly reminded of this too, but the country was not democratic; indeed the word was an insult to the ears of almost everybody, creating images of anarchy, chaos and the worst excesses of the French Revolution. Reform was therefore halted and a rigid system, pickled in precedent from medieval times, was in place, but also under attack during the Regency.

Parliament consisted of an unelected House of Lords (which remains the same in the twenty-first century) and a House of Commons of 658 members, a very similar number to today. One hundred Irish MPs were added in 1801 with the union of the two countries. There were fifty-three from Scotland, twenty-seven from Wales and 484 from England.

It was property, not people, that was represented in the House of Commons; or to be more precise, property when it belonged to the right kind of people. The same principle applied to the qualification for being an MP. There were no women, Catholics, or practising Jews as members of parliament. Except in Scotland, MPs had to be members of the established Anglican Church; so people who rejected the role of bishops in Church governance were acceptable MPs in Scotland but not in England.

There were two types of MP. Some represented the shires – such as Yorkshire or Middlesex. There were two MPs for each shire in England, and one in the other countries of the United Kingdom. In order to vote, people had to own (not rent) land, on which they paid at least £2 a year in land tax. This qualification was first set in the middle of the fifteenth century, and inflation had increased the number of people who qualified. As it was not people who were being represented, it was not considered a problem that some shire seats had four times as many voters as others.

Most MPs represented boroughs – mostly towns that had been granted a royal charter in medieval times. Voting rights varied massively between different boroughs. The householder boroughs had the largest electorate. All men who did not receive poor relief had the vote. There were only twelve of these constituencies, but they could still be controlled by families, or the electors could be bribed. The electorate was still not very big – Northampton, one of the largest, was just over 1,000. There were another six where nearly all adult males had the vote, but these were small towns, so the number of actual voters was still small.

About one hundred seats were controlled by the freemen of the borough. Some of these did allow a proper election but most were under the control of the corporation – a form of unelected local council.

There were thirty-seven boroughs in which the franchise was restricted to those paying 'scot and lot', a form of local taxation. Some, like Westminster, the biggest constituency in the country, had 12,000 voters but most had far fewer. Gatton in Surrey had two, and most others numbered their voters in the hundreds.

There were twenty-seven boroughs where the unelected members of the local corporation had the only votes. There were few contested elections here, as seats would be distributed by agreement of the borough's most influential families.

In burgage boroughs, only those who owned a particular property or plot of land could vote. These were the most open to corruption as one person could buy up enough of the property to buy the election. Most were therefore uncontested, and instead of elections, the aristocratic class nominated their family, friends and supporters to be the members of parliament.

The General Election of 1818 produced a victory with a reduced majority for Lord Liverpool's government. The election took a month, although the hustings, where people voted, were not open every day during that period. There were 113,000 eligible voters in the whole country. Because most of the constituencies were already under the control of rich families, 260 of the 380 seats were uncontested, so even most of the qualified voters did not vote. However, this was, by historic terms, a very active election; it was the largest number of seats contested since 1734, which shows how little voting usually took place.

There was little election fever in Old Sarum, a deserted hill in Wiltshire, and a burgage borough in which only the ownership of property mattered – a good thing really, as the resident population was zero. It had been purchased in 1802 by the Earl of Caledon for £60,000, and he then used it to advance his own political interests. On earlier occasions he had given the seat to a government nominee in the hope of favourable treatment. In 1818 both of the successful candidates were his relatives and political allies. At the same time, Leeds, Sheffield, Manchester, and Birmingham had no MPs of their own.

How could this be justified? In March 1818, the Reverend Robert Fellows gave it a go. The duty of government was the public good, he argued; a vital part of the public good was the protection of property and prosperity. Giving the vote to the poor 'dependent population' would mean that those without property would decide what happened to wealth. As they were poor, they could not be wise or impartial. So it wasn't a problem that six people chose two MPs in Old Sarum in 1818. What would happen if there was universal suffrage, the vote for all men? Fellowes was gloomy about the prospect, and used the three infamous 'rotten borough' as examples:

> *The boroughs of Old Sarum, St Mawe's and Higham Ferrers would be transferred from their ancient possessors or from persons of high family and generous sentiments to be revived in forms of aggravated corruption and depravity in the district of some overgrown capitalist or occupier who had some hundreds of the dependent population at his beck.*
>
> *Six or seven voters at Old Sarum may be thought too little to send two members to parliament but what is the difference as to the result whether the representative be nominated by two or three voters or by two or three thousand more than nine hundred out of each thousand of whom have no will of their own but are mere puppets.*

Wisdom was not to be found in numbers. The ideal voter was the independently rich, as they could not be bought for money. It would be 200 years before MPs were paid a salary, and in the Regency period MPs had to have a substantial property qualification in order to stand.

The establishment view was that the ancient and randomly organised system provided virtual representation through the collective intelligence of the elite. Thomas Oldfield, who wrote a book, *A key to the House of Commons*, describing in detail the corruption of the 1818 election in each constituency, wondered why those who believed fervently in virtual representation were not content with virtual taxation as well; a properly representative parliament would not need the protection of a ring of soldiers when passing the Corn Law; and would not have done such a partisan thing in any case.[1]

There was a slightly more exciting election in Brecon, a Welsh borough returning one MP. It was not the result that made it exciting, but the fact that it was the first contested election since 1740. The Morgan family of Tredegar controlled the fifteen members of the corporation, who in turn elected seven voting freeman in a seat that contained 4,000 adults. In 1818 Walter Wilkins stood against the nominated George Gould Morgan and, predictably, lost seven to zero.[2]

In the growing industrial city of Manchester, some people could vote in the 1818 election, albeit not in the city itself. Manchester had been a much smaller place a few centuries earlier when the borough seats were created, so they had no direct representation in parliament – Manchester was represented by the Lancashire county constituency. Any voters, therefore, needed to meet the 40 shilling freeholder qualification – they needed to be a landowner; there were many traders and business people who did not meet this target and who would certainly have had a vote if Manchester had been a borough. Instead, affluent and entrepreneurial Mancunians had to travel to the county town of Lancaster to cast their vote.

Many voters around the country had to travel long distances on poor quality roads – indeed one of the perks of being an elector was toll-free travel on the turnpikes in order to cast a vote and return home. However, it would have been prudent for voters in Manchester to read the newspaper before starting the journey. They would have discovered that the Lancashire seat had already been divided up between the aristocratic Stanley family, the Earls of Derby, and major landowner Jack Blackburne. There was no contest. In reality, nobody in Manchester had a vote in the 1818 election.

In places where there was a contested election, it was commonplace to provide food and drink to first entertain and then persuade those whose vote was free from the control of a landlord. A wine merchant in Reading had published this advertisement in the local paper:

> *As there will be a general election shortly, you might perhaps think it is right to provide wines for the occasion; we therefore beg to mention that we can supply you with every kind of white wine.*

It was a logical investment. Receiving hospitality was not illegal. All votes were declared openly. A vote was a form of property, and it made perfect sense to sweat your asset at election time. It could work out to be very expensive and it is clear why some people actually bought control of a rotten borough like Old Sarum or Brecon rather than buying the voters. It made economic sense.

Those who wished for parliamentary reform stood in the 1818 election, mostly for borough seats with enough independent voters to give them a chance. On 30 June, the *Manchester Mercury* bemoaned the character of the reformers who were standing for election, some of whom, said the newspaper, you would not trust with sixpence, never mind the nation. Henry Hunt was standing for Westminster and the paper reported that 'it was Gin and Beer all round for his supporters' and that 'they meddle little with wines, which they consider rather aristocratic'. It was a common quip of the age that general elections brought in more money for the tax collectors due to candidates buying alcohol to consolidate their support. It is to be hoped that Hunt did not spend as much money as the hostile newspapers reported, as he secured a mere eighty-four votes against his fellow reformer and sworn enemy Sir Francis Burdett who topped the poll with 5,238.

Hunt and Burdett were both meant to be on the same side. However, they disagreed with each other – something that both egotistical men found easy. Burdett wanted a uniform property qualification with a redistribution of seats. Hunt wanted universal suffrage – the vote for all men. Thirteen years later, when parliament was voting on a reform similar to the wishes of Burdett, Hunt was initially opposed to it, as the extension of the voting qualification was so modest.

The mostly biased press reported the 1818 Westminster election in great detail. It had a large electorate of skilled tradesmen, shopkeepers, craftsmen, and artisans who were willing to listen to radical ideas. It also had a large number of disenfranchised rowdy poor who were willing to riot.

It was almost a national campaign, with both sides sending out propaganda to newspapers to try to influence public opinion. Burdett was claimed (by hostile media) to be spending £3,000 a day. Burdett denied it. Money was certainly spent on a 'rent-a-mob' by both sides. These supporters were not necessarily voters themselves, but were paid to promote their candidates interests. Their role was to provide a visible presence in the streets, with a music band, banners, and libellous placards about their opponents. The voting took place in public and the mob would try to intimidate any opposition voters, who would cast their vote in public and therefore be vulnerable. Burdett's supporters did all these things despite him being the most vocal proponent of parliamentary reform. Although apparently playing no part in the proceeding, Burdett seemed to travel every morning from his home in rural Wimbledon to St James to do nothing all day. The hostile press saw him as the mastermind behind the scenes.

There was a lot of mudslinging at the election and not all of it was metaphorical. When Burdett's opponent, Murray Maxwell, decked out a mock boat full of supporters dressed as patriotic sailors, exploiting Maxwell's heroic naval career, the boat was ambushed and pelted with mud and worse. Burdett supporters gained possession of the boat, untied the horses that were moving it, and dragged the boat in triumph to the hustings. When it arrived at the hustings they were misidentified as Maxwell supporters and pelted with cabbages. After that misunderstanding the mob broke up the boat into handy weapon-like staves and attacked Maxwell's headquarters, using the wheels of the carriage as a battering ram. A riot started and the magistrates called out the dragoons. The Riot Act was read and ignored, and the soldiers were pelted with vegetable looted from Covent Garden carts. Disorder lasted all evening, and this was neither the first nor last time that there was violence in this constituency.

So, larger constituencies did not guarantee either more transparency or honesty – often the opposite was true. Some of the enemies of universal suffrage suggested that the so-called 'democratic' seats had some of the lowest and most reprehensible people and behaviour, and this was just a hint of the horrors that a more democratic constitution would provide. In the eyes of some, every election would be like Westminster if Hunt had his way, and he would get more than eighty-four votes.

A secret ballot would have ended much of the intimidation at elections. It would also have stopped landlords ordering their tenants to vote for a certain candidate. In contested elections, it would stop people selling their vote for beer and beef. The political establishment opposed the secret ballot – not only was it not English to hide your opinion, but a secret ballot would take away the legitimate influence of the aristocracy. It would also double the amount of corruption because it would enable people to take bribes from both sides. Another argument used was that if a ruffian or a villain was elected, it would be easy to track down those whose judgement was poor enough to vote for him by checking the poll books which listed who each elector voted for.

The results were often contested afterwards. There were election laws and they were regularly broken. No less than 40 of the 120 contested elections were the subject of a petition to the House of Commons after the 1818 election. Thirty-eight of them were declared to have some merit, and some MPs lost their seats.

Manasseh Lopes was one of the victims of the rules in 1818. He was, in the words of his radical opponents, a 'boroughmonger'. Lopes was involved in manipulating the result in various boroughs, including Westbury, New Romney and Evesham. He had been ejected from Evesham in 1807 for bribery and in 1816 he attempted to buy the borough of Grampound in Cornwall, which became quite significant in the mid-sixteenth century when it was awarded two members of parliament. There were ten boroughs in Cornwall even smaller than Grampound, but none where the voters aggressively sold their votes to the highest bidder.

Lopes had, through an agent, tried to bribe forty-five of the voters and thought that this would be enough with an electorate of sixty. This was not a property transaction – these men had a vote by virtue of their status as freemen of the borough. His agent could not rustle up forty-five, so settled for about forty, whom he met in a hotel in Grampound, where the freemen asked for £50 and settled for £35 a vote. These were loans, claimed the defendant at the later trial, but it became clear that only men with votes were given money.

Lopes was not as discreet as other people who bought and sold seats, and the subterfuge came to the knowledge of an equally ambitious character, John Teed. Armed with a list of bribed electors, Teed attempted not to get justice, but to convince Lopes to share the two Grampound seats in exchange for his silence. Lopes refused. Teed and his supporters then waited until the 1818 election, when they caused a disturbance at the hustings. They used their list of bribed electors to challenge the voter William Allen and demand that he took the bribery oath, which he was not keen on doing because he had been bought for £35. Lopes's two nominees were elected, and the defeated candidates petitioned the House of Commons on the basis of bribery.

Lopes's defence tells us a lot about the state of the system. It went like this: if it was bribery, it happened two years before the election and a prosecution after such a lapse of time was unknown. In any case, there was no bribery, as none of the paperwork proved this. Teed himself was by no means an 'unspotted champion of parliamentary purity'. Teed had been the MP for Grampound in 1808; he had tried to do a deal with Lopes, not tell the authorities. Lopes pointed out that if there was bribery (which of course there hadn't been) it made the freemen of Grampound look dishonourable. He failed to mention that he had offered Teed £7,800 to make the problem go away after the election.

The jury took less than sixty seconds to find him guilty of bribery. He was later sentenced to a £10,000 fine and a two-year stretch in Exeter gaol. The thirty-five bribed electors were punished with three months in the much less salubrious Bodmin gaol. As Lopes started his sentence in November 1819, the government ordered that the £10,000 fine be paid immediately so that interest could accrue and bring the figure up to £11,000.

In a bad month for Lopes, a House of Commons report concluded that there was sufficient evidence that he had also bribed the freemen electors of Barnstaple, where he stood in 1818. Using the same *modus operandi* as in Grampound, he gave £3,000 to voters in exchange for their support using a local agent. When he was put on trial later in 1819, Lopes was found not guilty through lack of evidence.

He also had active control of the borough of Westbury, but had done this legally by buying property from their rightful owners, whereas in Grampound and Barnstaple he just seemed to bribe people, which was illegal. In March 1819, more petitions were presented to the Commons. In Penryn – another borough that Lopes had dabbled in – there was clear evidence of voters being given money. Sir Frances Burdett, a keen reformer, argued: 'corruption was so generally to be found in all boroughs, that he thought it would be a great injustice to think about disenfranchising Penryn...bribery is as notorious as the sun at noonday'.

The determination to prosecute Lopes while ignoring other people seemed to have a hint of anti-Semitism about it. His Jewish background and the very recent accumulation of his wealth through trade was well known. His conversion to Christianity and his election as MP for New Romsey a few months later were cynically commented on. In 1806 an attorney by the name of Dance received twelve months in Newgate for libelling Lopes with the phrase 'Jew Baronet'– it clearly seemed to some that there was no such thing as effective Jewish assimilation. In 1819, when discussing Grampound, the radical Leigh Hunt suggested that Lopes's background might have encouraged his prosecution.

Lopes's sentence was respited in September 1820 after less than a year, and in November he was elected, legally, to be the MP for Westbury.

Lopes, the ultimate borough monger, may have done more for parliamentary reform than he intended. Grampound lost its two MPs and they were given to the county of Yorkshire although Lord John Russell, the Whig leader, wanted to give the seats to Manchester. In any case, the spell was broken and the constitution was clearly changeable. Eleven years later, in 1831, with the middle classes swelling and cities becoming even more important, Russell became Prime Minister. Once again, the curse of the Regency was maintained. Improvement was coming – just not yet.

Chapter 9

All About The Money

In our age when money seems to rule everything, it may come as a surprise to know that the Regency was far worse. Money, rather than merit, mattered. Everything came at a price, and without that price, nothing would happen. Military ranks were bought and sold; parliamentary seats and influence could be purchased for money; names of bankrupts were printed prominently in newspapers as a warning not to trade with them; cash was routinely given to informers as rewards; ecclesiastical livings in the established church were bought and sold. Vicars neglected the people of poor parishes if they held a more lucrative living elsewhere. The government took money from the poor in taxes and gave it to the rich in the form of sinecures – jobs that carried a salary but no work.

None of this was corruption and fraud, although that existed too. Bakers adulterated their bread, politicians paid voters to support them and mobs to intimidate their enemies; bribes were paid to witnesses to lie in court, and police officials used trumped-up charges to create felonies that would lead to rewards.

One form of property was the right to nominate the next occupant of a parish. In 1818 this right – 'the advowson' – was offered for the Rectory of Fiddington in Somerset. The advertisement laid more stress on the agricultural than pastoral. It was a healthy spot, convenient for the turnpike, and:

> *the Glebe contains about forty acres, near the parsonage house, and the parish consists of 770 acres of very fertile land and large proportion of this is annually tilled.*
> *The present incumbent is 81 years of age.*

With the present rector not far from death, and with a house and medium size farm to go with it, this was an exciting potential purchase.

The parish eventually changed hands in 1821, when the Reverend H.W. Rawlins succeeded the 84-year-old former incumbent. Since 1810, Rawlins, a theology graduate of Balliol College, Oxford, had also been Rector of Staplegrove, and after 1821 he continued in both jobs as each provided an income. He did not reside at Fiddington, leaving St Martin's Church to be served either by a curate or nobody. This probably did not worry the parishioners of Fiddington, as there had been an absent rector for most of the eighteenth century. To modern eyes this seems to be the sign of a lazy and selfish character. However, Rawlins seemed to have been at least a passable cleric. In 1810 he donated two guineas to the widow and eight children of Lambert Kiddle. Rawlins was secretary of the Taunton Adult School Society and raised money for the Ladies' Bible Association. What he did was normal for the time. A clerical posting was a piece of property and the incumbents had to find any way possible to earn a living. Jane Austen's father, the Reverend George Austen, had a boys' schools in his parish at Steventon in Hampshire. He also farmed, or more accurately, allowed others to farm for him.[1]

Money could also buy a commission in the armed forces, but there were limits. It never applied to the navy, and only really applied to infantry and cavalry regiments, who were regarded as socially superior to the Royal Artillery or Royal Engineers, where qualifications and seniority were the requirements. There was absolutely no stigma attached to purchase of rank, and it was regarded as another form of property – you bought your rank from somebody who was relinquishing it, either through his promotion or 'selling out'. Even the Duke of Wellington once considered selling his rank in the army to pay off gambling debts.

This notice appeared in the newspapers. It was one of many:

Military Promotions

War Office, May 22nd 1818

2nd Regiment of Life Guards – Lieutenant William Elliot to be Captain of a troop, by purchase, vice Irby – Commission dated April 14 1818

The newly promoted Captain Elliot has chosen well – the Life Guards, with their link to the monarch and light duties around London, were a most desirable regiment. He would have paid the difference between the price of a captaincy and that of the lower rank. Money would not have been enough; he would have been vetted for social acceptability. Although a fixed set of fees existed, more money may have been necessary to secure the deal if there were other strong applicants. He replaced the Honourable Henry Edward Irby, son of Frederick Irby, Lord Boston, so William was already moving in elite social circles.

You did not always need to pay to be promoted. Captain Elliot knew this already. This from the *London Gazette* of December 1812, which listed all changes in armed forces personnel:

> *War Office Dec 15; 2d regiment of life guards; cornet and sub lieu-*
> *tenant William Elliot to be lieutenant without purchase*

How had William achieved this without money? There are three possible ways. This was 1812, and people bought fewer commissions during war-time, when the 2nd Regiment of Guards would be fighting in Spain with Wellington rather than spending summer evenings at fashionable social occasions in their attractive uniforms. Another possibility was that William was replacing somebody who had been killed in battle, or he may have sim-ply been promoted on merit and bravery. The system worked tolerably well with this mixture of paths to promotion, but it was money that was needed to scramble up the ladder, especially in peacetime. He would have paid for his first rank as a cornet, as well as needing to know the right people; both were important.

Money could not just be used to get you on in the military. It could be used to get you out. This is one of seven advertisements in the *Morning Post* on one day in August 1810:

> *MILITIA – A gentlemen who has been drawn in the militia and is in*
> *want of a substitute, to serve for five years or during the war, and to*
> *who a very liberal bounty will be given, by an application to Mr Jones,*
> *Charles Street…any young man who may have received a decent edu-*
> *cation and is presently out of employ, will find this a most desirable*
> *opportunity.*

Mr Jones had been drawn at random to join a local militia. This was a home based force that was a serious commitment, and vital in times of war. However, if you did not want to do your duty you could pay to evade it. He would probably pay between £30 and £50 for his substitute. This made sense; he would have had to pay fines of a similar amount if he refused to serve in person, and would still be liable to be entered in future ballots. He was also being canny by directing his advertisement at the unemployed. His substitute would receive help for himself and his family if they fell on hard times, and medical help if they were injured. It was a reasonable bargain on both sides.

Whole businesses were set up to evade the militia; you could insure your-self against being picked out of the ballot; agencies recruited substitutes in advance – men between 18 and 45 over 5ft 4in – and acted as intermedi-aries for gentlemen with more money than patriotism. Mr Charonneau of the High Holborn Military Insurance Office offered not only bounties but rewards for 'bringers', people who procured substitutes. Although the whole system may seem dishonest to people today, that was not the view of the time. The substitutes were often more welcome by militia than reluctant recruits; it provided work and a transfer of money from the rich to the ambi-tious poor.[2]

Money was also vital to political promotion. Today, prime ministers get to the top mostly in their late fifties. This is partly because it takes a long time to secure a seat in parliament; during the Regency the belief was differ-ent. If a person was born to rule, then it was thought best if they got on with it, and start by purchasing a seat in parliament or rely on a political patron to lend them one. William Pitt's ability to be Britain's youngest prime min-ister at the age of 24 was helped considerably by being elected as MP for the rotten borough of Appleby, in the pocket of the Lowther family. The prime minister for most of the darkness years was Robert Jenkinson, later Lord Liverpool, who became MP for Rye in 1790, one year too early to take up his seat legally, so he was made to wait. Rye had six voters and was controlled by the Lamb family, who offered a seat to the young Jenkinson as his father was a member of Pitt's government and Lamb expected this generosity to be recognised. Lord Liverpool became prime minister at 42 and died at 58, when the career of a modern politician would just be reaching its peak.

One area of controversy in the Regency period was the distribution of sinecures to members of the establishment. A sinecure was a job that either involved little work, or was vastly overpaid for the work required, or could be done by employing substitutes. Often receiving the annual tranche of taxpayers' money was the only responsibility. They were well known to the public; Cobbett railed against them, and when the Chorley weavers peti-tioned Parliament in 1812, they had specific people in mind. They were concerned that while they worked and starved:

> *vast sums of the public money are bestowed upon individuals, as the salaries of sinecure places…selecting a few instances out of a great vari-ety of the same nature, they beg leave to remind the House, that the right honourable George Rose holds the sinecure office of clerk of the parliament, with a salary of £3,278 per annum; that the right hon.*

George Lord Arden holds the sinecure offices of register of the high court of admiralty and of register of the high court of appeal for prizes, for which he receives, clear of deductions, 12,554l. per annum; and that the earl Camden, and the marquis of Buckingham, hold the sinecure offices of tellers of the exchequer, for which offices they receive, the latter 23,093l. the former 23,117l. per annum.

The petition went on to complain about the numbers of smaller grants to thousands of people, including foreigners (mostly in war subsidies). George Arden probably received more money than anybody for doing little; probably three times as much as the weavers' estimate. In 1816, the hostile newspaper *The Examiner* stated that Arden received £38,566 per year.

The number of sinecures was one of the problems that was postponed for the duration of the war. There was growing political opposition to them. Pressure mounted from both sides of political opinion, from the radicals and from the new business class. To both of them it seemed reprehensible that these payments should be made to the elite in times of austerity and national debt.

When asked by a Parliamentary Commission in 1810 whether any inconvenience would arise if his sinecures were abolished, George Arden refused to even consider the question as appropriate, or talk about his sinecure – Register of the High Court of Admiralty – apart from the amount of money earned. It was a hereditary sinecure, as he gained it from his dead brother. Arden regarded the post as a piece of property and felt a discussion of the value of the sinecure would jeopardise it. Second and third on the list were the Marquis of Buckingham and the Marquis of Camden who both acquired £23,000. They were in receipt of this cash in 1807, when radical MP Thomas Cochrane pointed out that this was slightly more that the total paid out annually to wounded officers and widows of the whole Royal Navy.

Although the majority of the Church of England clerics were doomed to continue to be without a parish, and instead doing the work of those who had the money and connections, it was very lucrative at the top. In 1820 the Archbishop of Canterbury received £19,000. He headed an organisation that made no official payments to the widows and orphans of the clergy but relied on others to provide charity.

In 1820, journalist John Wade calculated that 2,344 persons received £2.5 million annually.[3] These included members of the government, armed forces and the established Church. Some were salaries for actual posts. Lord Liverpool received £13,500 for being prime minister (The First Lord of the

Treasury) and that was probably value for money. Lord Eldon, Speaker of the House of Lords, earned £18,000 from work and another £24,000 from sinecures.

Sinecures led to power, which allowed nepotism. Lord Eldon's brother took £6,000 for doing nothing, and after retirement took a £4,000 a year pension to get over the exertion. Stratford Canning, the cousin of Foreign Secretary George Canning was given a sinecure in the Foreign Office in 1807 and by 1815 was working on the peace with France from a base in Switzerland on nearly £500 per year. John Wade also pointed out that large numbers of non-existent jobs were given to the younger members of the aristocracy:

> *Many Noble Lords and their sons, Rt. Hon. and Hon. Gentlemen, fill the offices of Clerks, Tide-Waiters, Harbour-Masters, Searchers, Guagers* [Collectors of excise], *Packers, Craners, Wharfingers, Prothonotaries* [law clerks], *and other degrading situations.*

They were not degrading because they attracted no work. In the spirit of equality, women were included too:

> *There is one fine lady, a baroness, who is Sweeper of the Mall in the Park, for £340 a year; Lady Arabella Heneage is Chief Usher in the Court of Exchequer; and the Honourable Louisa Browning and Lady B. Martyn are* Custos Brevium *in the Court of Common Pleas.*

Arabella Heneage was the wife of John Walker Heneage and the sinecure reverted to her when her husband died in 1806. He had, in turn, inherited it from his father. Heneage was an MP for Cricklade for four years in the 1790s and never spoke in the Commons.[4]

It was almost a social security system for the aristocracy and establishment. John Wade and many other radicals such as Cobbett, Burdett and Hone opposed the system; they called the sinecurists 'state paupers'. Wade became less radical in later life, and his ranting against sinecures ended when Prime Minister Palmerston organised a weekly pension for him in his old age.

At the other end of the spectrum, the low cost of the legal system was an illusion. Its creaking apparatus was oiled by dubious payments. In order to catch criminals, rewards known as 'blood money' were offered to the informant on conviction. Despite the name, it wasn't a compensation for a victim's family, nor did it necessarily involve blood, but it did pervert the course of justice. Witnesses could be bought; honest witnesses could be suspected of being bought. Some reforms started in 1818, but it remained a process that was open to abuse.

Local groups were set up all over the country to plug the gaps of the justice system by offering their own informal reward system. Property owners would form a subscription society. There were hundreds all over the country; as usual one must stand for them all, they were more or less the same. The 'Audlem and Wrenbury Association for the Discovery, Apprehension and Prosecution of Felons' did exactly what it said. Forty or so local property owners offered rewards for help in apprehending criminals. The crimes had to be local and had to be to the detriment of one of the subscribers. Ten guineas was offered for horse stealing, housebreaking, and highway robbery; five guineas for large farmyard animals; two for small animals and fowl; and a guinea for the apprehension of people stealing crops or destroying farm property. Like the whole judicial system, it was unashamedly designed for the protection of property.

George Vaughan was a Bow Street officer who knew that justice was all about the reward money. He was paid a basic weekly retainer of £1. It was not much for a high profile police officer, but he had other sources of money. Small amounts were available for court appearances and night work, but most of his money came in the form of blood money.

There was no official reward for the detection of minor crimes, only for solving felonies. This meant that petty criminals and juveniles were ignored, even encouraged, until they 'weighed £40' – that is, committed a felony that was worth a reward.

At 12.30 am one day in 1814, Vaughan went to the Falcon public house in Gray's Inn Lane and noticed local thieves John Farthing and John Thomas 'drinking out of the same pot'. The officer now thought they weighed the right amount, so Vaughan followed them when they left the pub in haste. A few streets later, Vaughan apprehended Thomas with a flitch of bacon under his coat. The bacon was worth seven shillings. This made the crime 'grand larceny' – and a reward payable to Vaughan. However there was nobody who came forward to say that they owned the bacon or had seen the robbery. If there had been witnesses, they would have been given a share of the reward, to be decided by the arresting police officer. The scope for corruption was obvious.

Vaughan had enjoyed a distinguished career, and had been publicly thanked by the magistrates at various times. He was a successful witness against bigamists, forgers, highway robbers and burglars.

He visited the house of James Poole late in the evening in December 1815, when it had become too dark for James to cut any more cloth for his tailoring business. Vaughan warned him that his house was about to be robbed and he was here to prevent it. Could Poole imagine the danger to his wife and children? Perhaps they would be murdered in their beds! Poole was frightened. Vaughan asked Poole to mark his cloth so it could be identified later; Poole was unsure how to do this and Vaughan did it for him, surprisingly skilfully. They left the house, leaving the door on a latch on Vaughan's instructions.

Poole was told to continue his business; he went to visit a customer but returned earlier than planned and on the way back saw thieves carrying his rolls of calico. He cried 'stop thief'. 'After I seized him, the officers came up immediately; I don't know where they came from.'

When he met Vaughan, Poole was displeased. Contrary to Vaughan's promises, he had lost three rolls of cloth. Vaughan was also angry: 'he said he knew where to find them, and he knew where to find the other thieves; but I had spiked the job by calling out "stop thief"; for he knew where they had gone.'

He never saw his cloth again. Poole also ruined the later prosecution by admitting that he could recognise their faces without artificial light. The crime was reduced from burglary to the daylight crime of stealing from a dwelling house and the reward disappeared. Vaughan told Poole that he had spoiled it: 'by saying it was so light…you have deprived me of the three rewards of forty pounds, which you would have had part of for taking the one man'.

Vaughan had also been deprived of the reward for John Farthing, the man from the unproven bacon theft, who was also picked up from the street on the night of the robbery and added to the charge list as revenge for escaping last time.

Vaughan was, in fact, a corrupt officer who was setting up crimes to take the reward. He knew the date and time of the crime because he had organised it. He was caught by the evidence of Constable William Barrett. Barrett and Vaughan were drinking with John 'Jack-a-Dandy' Donnelly in the Falcon inn and Vaughan was told of a raid on Poole's house to steal the cloth – the 'broady'. It was agreed that Vaughan would facilitate the burglary by scaring Poole and making it easier to break into the house. Donnelly would escape, and the others would be captured, Donnelly would get a reward and would then leave the country.

Vaughan lost more than his reward. Due to the diligence of fellow officers and John Donnelly's statements at the trial, Vaughan was subsequently found guilty of abetting a theft of more than 40 shillings, having avoided a greater charge on a technicality. Vaughan was already doomed however, as this was not the first time that he had been caught in 1816.

Vaughan was about to receive five years' hard labour for organising a burglary at Mrs Ann McDonald's house in Holborn. This time it was a one-legged criminal called William Drake who had sold information to Vaughan. Young boys were often taken by thieves to make entry into houses, and 13-year-old William Wood claimed in court that Drake had sent him for money from Vaughan to get the four thieves 'lush' (drunk) before the crime; jemmies and skeleton keys were also provided, and Vaughan arranged for Mrs McDonald to be out drinking on the night of the robbery. The first attempt was aborted when one of the robbers failed to turn up; this would have reduced the reward. After the robbery, Vaughan's corrupt comrade, Robert McKay, planted a ring on one of them. McKay put his hand in his pocket and exclaimed 'so you have a phorney (ring)' to which the accused answered, 'I do now, coz you have just put it there.' It turned out that this was a useful precaution, for the amateur thieves were too scared to actually steal anything themselves, having been scared by the rustling of the trees.

It was the Hatton Garden officers Limbrick and Read who secured the conviction. This included chasing Vaughan when he skipped bail, appre-hending him in his uncle's house with two pistols and a notebook listing his conspiratorial activities. There is no evidence of any of Vaughan's earlier cases being reviewed. In 1814, Vaughan's evidence had condemned three children to death for burglary – Moses Solomon, Joseph Burrell and John Morris. The first two boys were 9 years of age and John was 8. They were respited; but Vaughan was quite clearly ready to see them executed for a crime that he may well have organised. It was certainly all about the money.

Chapter 10

The Disgusting Prince Regent?

According to Thomas Scott of the Society for Promoting Christian Knowledge, the Prince of Wales, George Augustus Frederick, was a 'British Prince, in the exercise of his father's venerable authority, assaulted and insulted by a lawless multitude, in defiance of the majesty of the laws and every sense of decency and justice'. Scott then compared the forgiving nature of the prince to that of Christ himself. Reverend Scott thought enough of himself to publish his sermons, and this one was in response to the so-called assassination attempt on the Regent in January 1817.

George, who had been ruling as Regent since his father's illness in 1811, attended the state opening of parliament and gave the customary speech. It was a lacklustre and indistinct effort, but the loyal *Ladies Monthly Magazine* suggested that it was the poor morale of the people that had depressed the prince too much for him to produce anything better. It would have seemed a very generous interpretation to most people in Britain. By 1811, the Prince Regent had been unpopular with the ordinary people for nearly twenty years, and much of the establishment only pretended to like him because it was politically necessary.

The prince finished his mumbling in the House of Lords ('Excellent Speech' – *Morning Post*) and started his journey to Carlton House. As the coach arrived at St James Park, an ominously large crowd blocked its way. It seemed that the people, in their third year of terrible economic conditions, were inflamed by the ostentatious mode of transport used:

> *The state carriage, with the eight beautiful cream coloured horses, ornamented with light blue ribbons; the Master of the Horse's carriage, with six fine black horses, ornamented with red ribbons; and two other Royal carriages, with six bays, ornamented with red ribbons...His Royal Highness wore regimentals, with his splendid Orders of the Ribbons of the Garter.*

Hails of stones appeared, along with insults and attacks on the horse guards and the horses themselves. A bullet-sized hole punctured the window of the prince's coach. There were dents in the protective copper panels, added after a similar attack on his father in 1795. The Prince Regent arrived home in a panic and summoned the Home Secretary, who added insult to injury by not turning up for a very long time.

The newspapers raged the next morning. 'HORRIBLE AND TREASONABLE ATTEMPT TO ASSASSINATE THE PRINCE REGENT!' was one example. Even before an investigation started, the *Morning Post* already knew who was responsible. 'There is no doubt that this is a deep laid plot, the offspring of the doctrines, if not the very conception of our mischievous reformers.' On that very day, the parliamentary reformers Henry Hunt and Lord Thomas Cochrane were presenting a petition to the House, and a few days earlier the revolutionary Spencean Philanthropists were put in prison awaiting trial for high treason. It is not certain which of these groups were the 'mischievous people' the newspaper was worrying about; as Hunt had spoken at the Spa Fields meeting in 1816 which had led to the Spenceans being imprisoned, it is probable that both groups were in the frame.

The main suspect was a Thomas Scott (no relation to the Reverend who had denounced him from the pulpit). This Thomas Scott resided in Goodge Street, but did not fit the archetype that the newspaper needed. The paper was perplexed to report that he was a minor property owner who did not need to work (in the Regency there was a big moral difference between not working and not needing to work). Despite having soft hands that had seen no manual work, Scott was no friend of the establishment. He was not going to take his arrest without protest; the slightly less deferential *Morning Chronicle* reported that Scott pleaded not guilty, but understood that somebody had to be arrested, so it was clearly going to be him. He insinuated that some informer would receive a reward for his indictment.

The evidence against Scott was not very convincing. There had been two bullet shaped holes in the carriage. No bullet was found in the coach. No gun was heard discharging. No smoke was seen. Rather than conclude that the event had not happened, it was decided that the weapon of choice must have been an airgun.

An attempt to make the charge stick came a week later at Bow Street Magistrates. Scott, 'a small robust man, with the look of a stable keeper' was in the groaning, hissing and stone-throwing crowd and the witness heard somebody call the Prince Regent a '----------- -------------', and to 'pull the ---------- out!' The witness saw Scott throwing stones; Scott said he had not. Another witness heard the mob, including Scott, hurl abuse at the

Life Guards: 'Piccadilly Butchers', a name they had gained during earlier riots in 1811. Another witness testified that Scott had attacked no soldiers; Scott himself commented that it would have been foolish to assault a soldier armed with a drawn sabre.

Despite the underwhelming evidence, he was sent to the King's Bench Prison to be examined on the more serious crime of high treason. Scott did not seem at all surprised. Judge Hicks allowed him to see relatives in prison, but no strangers, thus implying that Scott was part of a plot of desperate men who might try to rescue him.

It was standing room only on Saturday 1 February when Scott was examined. Lord James Murray, in the coach with the Prince Regent, used his military credibility to convince people that he recognised bullet holes in glass when he saw them; they had been fired by a stick gun from above, possibly from a tree. Yes, the holes were pea sized, and no, the fact that they were fired downward did not mean that the bullets were in the coach. The glass could not be inspected as it had shattered completely when hit by more stones. No other witness was able to link Scott with any crime and the second examination was concluded.

The case against Scott collapsed in the third examination on 5 February. Some Life Guards disputed whether there were bullets at all; Scott was seen with an umbrella, protecting himself from the horses. He was bailed for £400, which he was able to find, and was indicted instead for aiding and abetting a riot. The judge lamented the fact that, out of a huge mob, only one person had been arrested.

Why was the Prince Regent so unpopular? Why were his Life Guards so unpopular? Why were the horses so hated? The horses were fed with better quality oats than many of the people, now in their second decade of high food prices. The Life Guards were part of the victors of Waterloo, but were now seen as an oppressive force. However, it was the prince who was really unpopular, and had been so for two decades. The government then made itself unpopular by suspending *habeas corpus*, which protected a person's right not to be imprisoned without trial. Sidmouth genuinely believed that the unrest and misery in the country was about to translate into conspiracy and insurrection.

Respectable newspapers of the time were a poor source for criticisms of 'Fat Prinny'. Not only did they fail to criticise; they rarely made the mistake of repeating insults in order to condemn them. The radical press that had grown up since the French Revolution was different – they were both braver and more foolhardy. In response to a particularly obsequious report in the *Morning Post* in March 1812, John and Leigh Hunt in the *Examiner* produced an angry, sarcastic and insulting editorial. 'Why', said the brothers on page one, 'were the papers full of the most trivial information about the prince?' It started with a not so guarded comment about greed and parasitism and a quite graphic image.

> *The Prince Regent is in everybody's mouth*
> *   If a person takes a newspaper, the first thing he does when he reads*
> *it, is to give out the old groan and say - what of the Prince Regent now?*

The *Examiner* continued its parody of a world where the Regent was everything, with a description of a Prinny-dominated evening:

> *At dinner the Prince Regent quite eclipses the goose or the calf's head;*
> *the tea table rings of the Prince Regent. If the company go to the theatre*
> *to see 'The Hypocrite'...they cannot help thinking about the Prince*
> *Regent...People, in their nightcap, will see something to remind them of*
> *the Prince Regent.*

They finished with pure insults rather than mere innuendo:

> *That this Breather of Eloquence could not say a few decent extempore*
> *words – if we are to judge at least from what he said to his regiment on its*
> *embarkation to Portugal! That this Conqueror of Hearts was the disap-*
> *pointer of hopes! That this Exciter of Desire—this Adonis in loveliness,*
> *was a corpulent man of fifty!— In short, this delightful, blissful, wise,*
> *pleasurable, honourable, virtuous, true, and immortal PRINCE, was a*
> *violator of his word, a libertine over head and ears in debt and disgrace,*
> *a despiser of domestic ties, the companion of gamblers and demireps, a*
> *man who had just closed half a century without one single claim on the*
> *gratitude of his country, or the respect of posterity.*

To sum up: Prinny was a stupid, unattractive, cowardly, fat, debt-ridden, mendacious, gambling womaniser, with appalling friends and no redeeming achievements. The government's desire to strike back was understandable.

When their editorial was read back to the brothers Hunt at Bow Street in December 1812 they pleaded not guilty to libel. The prosecution case was that this was a deliberate planned attack of such falsity and ferocity that there could be no defence, especially to the assertion that the prince had done nothing at all for his country. Lord Brougham, for the defence argued that this was an unimportant, hastily written article in an obscure magazine, and that the government and the prince should ignore such 'small shots' as these.

Brougham was unsuccessful. Both brothers received two-year prison sentences. John Hunt was dispatched to Coldbath Fields in London, and Leigh Hunt to the New Jail in Surrey. Both were fined £500, but still had enough money to live in reasonable comfort in a prison system where anything was available for cash. Leigh Hunt was visited by Byron and both men had the vocal support of Shelley and Keats. Despite the libel conviction, and the realisation that they would never be able to write about the prince ever again, many people realised that their comments were substantially true. His unpopularity continued. Prinny could pass 10,000 people in his coach, as he did in 1812, to a dead silence that said more than the traditional groaning and hissing.

Was he the repulsive specimen that the Hunt brothers portrayed? His excessive lifestyle took a toll quite early. Caricatures by Gilray and Cruikshank laying out Prinny's weaknesses were on open sale in the Regency. In 1792, he is represented as a fat spherical object that moves around on a board with wheels. Prinny is a debauched physical specimen in another Gilray print, '*A Voluptuary under the Horrors of Digestion*'. The Prince is slumped in his chair, with unpaid bills and full chamber pots around him, picking his teeth with a fork. Dice and lists of horses at Newmarket races show his addiction to gambling; his coat of arms is a crossed knife and fork and he has medicine for stinking breath and piles next to him. Those looking carefully would see the name of two quack medicines designed to ease the symptoms of venereal disease.

Was he a libertine? He had mistresses throughout his life. This would make him no different to many other aristocratic men, including Wellington, the hero of Waterloo. The use of taxpayer's money was the main difference. His first mistress was Mary Robinson, an actress to whom he gave extravagant gifts of money. Later she used his love letters to blackmail him. Grace Elliott was a scandalous member of the court set, by whom the prince may have had an illegitimate child. Lady Melbourne also had an affair with the Prince of Wales during the period 1780 to 1784. At the same time as Lady Melbourne, Elizabeth Armistead, wife of his friend and political ally Charles James Fox, was the prince's mistress. Later, as king, George gave Elizabeth a pension of £500 per year. Frances, Lady Jersey, was his mistress when he married Princess Caroline of Brunswick for money in 1795.

In the period of his regency, his main paramour was Isabella, Lady Hartford, who lasted until he became king in 1820. His affair with her was common knowledge and satirical cartoons could be bought on the street for pennies. Cartoons show them on a new style bicycle, the velocipede, going on a journey from 'Wales to Hertford'. Another shows the prince handing over the content of the privy purse to his lover at her home at Manchester House. In the eyes of the establishment, the prince's sin was not his behaviour, but his unwillingness to show any discretion.

He treated his wife appallingly and did not hide it. In 1795 he had married Caroline of Brunswick only because his father promised to pay off his debt of £670,000 which had been accumulated over a mere seven years. He graciously allowed the taxpayer to pay £52,000 for a wedding that he did not want, was drunk on the day and extremely drunk on his wedding night. Lady Jersey, his mistress, was appointed the Queen's Lady of the Bedchamber to humiliate Caroline and to spy on her. In 1806 he urged the government to launch the mis-named 'Delicate Investigation' to find out whether Caroline had produced an illegitimate child with her butler. Even when exonerated, her access to Charlotte, their only child, was restricted, and when Charlotte died in 1817 after an agonizing fifty-one hours of childbirth, the prince refused to tell Caroline and failed to attend their daughter's funeral because, the newspapers claimed, he was 'overcome with grief'.

Caroline did not know of her own child's death immediately because she had moved to Italy with her lover, Bartolomeo Pergami, and £35,000 from the taxpayer. Caroline enjoyed a lavish and lascivious lifestyle in Milan but claimed to be living the simple life – promenades, theatre, reading, – with her platonic companion Pergami. These lies were not believed by anybody in Britain. Yet she was still more popular than the Regent.

When Charlotte died, George was determined to remove her mother from the line of succession. He spent £30,000 on spies to collect evidence of the queen's adultery. The quality of the witnesses and their bought evidence was so poor that the findings of the 'Milan Commission' were rejected in 1819, bringing disrepute to the prince and the government. A famous cartoon of Caroline and Pergami in the bath was bought widely on the streets, even if it did contradict the prince's whispering that she never bathed and smelled appallingly.

When he became king in 1820, George continued to persecute his wife. He regurgitated the adultery case against Pergami and tried to use an Act of Parliament to divorce her. When she was banned from George's coronation in 1821 (cost: £243,000) it caused pro-Caroline riots in the streets from the poor, who had no reason to support the spendthrift princess. Throughout the Regency and during his reign, support for Caroline was mostly a proxy for hatred of George. So, on the charge of womaniser, the jury is still out, but he can be called out as a cowardly and callous husband and a roaring hypocrite. Jane Austen disliked the prince – but still found it convenient to dedicate *Emma* (1815) to him. In 1813 she showed her support for Princess Caroline in a letter to a friend: 'Poor woman, I shall support her as long as I can, because she *is* a Woman and because I hate her Husband.'

Was he a gambler? In an aristocratic world where excessive gambling was common, Prinny stood out as one of the most extravagant. While other members of the aristocracy would blow their brains out after suffering massive losses, George just asked for more money, and got it.

Was he a poor soldier? He never actually led soldiers into battle, but his constitutional position precluded that. He was made a Colonel in the 10th Hussars, with his promotion backdated a year to ensure his precedence over others of the same rank. He enjoyed his review of the Hussars every year in August at Belle Vue Fields in Brighton and liked going on manoeuvres in tents, but his tent was especially luxurious. He also enthusiastically reviewed the various county militia at the annual Brighton camp or Wimbledon common. To reward the Life Guards and Blues, who bravely led the cavalry charge at Waterloo, he made himself their Captain General. He also enjoyed redesigning uniforms for the army. In 1811 he simplified some British army uniforms, while exempting his own, perhaps not coincidentally. So perhaps it would be unfair to call him a bad soldier, but he was certainly a dabbler and a fantasist, with the public paying the bill.

The Marine Pavilion at Brighton is claimed as one of the prince's lasting contributions to British life. The design of the building divides opinion today and it was mocked mercilessly from the moment it was built. It was originally a modest cottage on the Steine at Brighton and the prince moved there in 1787 as an economy measure after one of the regular clearings of his debts. Economy was abandoned when a stable block for sixty-four horses was built and there was a seven-year remodelling which started in 1815. Dorothea Lieven, wife of the Russian ambassador, visited Brighton in 1818 and estimated the cost of the Pavilion at £700,000. She was also invited inside, according to her biographer:

Here the Prince held a continuous house Party in his brilliantly illuminated, centrally heated, lavishly decorated Pavilion. Daily, thirty or forty people came here for consistently excellent dinners…at midnight they sipped iced champagne punch or lemonade, and nibbled on sandwiches.

George used the expensive services of John Nash to create the building we see today, but the mixture of styles was the result of the Prince's changing fads and preoccupations and unlimited amount of other peoples' cash. This little ditty was penned in 1817, and was first published in a newspaper in 1828, when people had stopped worrying what the Prince Regent thought:

Master Nash, Master Nash, You merit the lash,
For debauching the taste of our Heir to the throne:
Then cross not the Seas, To rob the Chinese.

Cobbett called it the 'Kremlin'. William Hone, in his satirical poem *The Joss and his Folly*, presented it as the work of an oversized despotic ruler:

The queerest of all the queer sights
I've set sights on;
Is the what d'ye call't thing, here,
The Folly at Brighton

The outside – huge teapots,
All drill'd round with holes,
Relieved by extinguishers,
Sticking on poles;

The inside – all tea-things,
And dragons, and bells,
The show-rooms – all show,
The sleeping rooms – cells.

But the grand Curiosity's
Not to be seen –
The owner himself –
An old fat Mandarin.

The building was an 'opium dream,' according to some observers.[1] A lot of artistic work was done under the influence of opium – Thomas De

Quincey's *Confessions of an English Opium-Eater* was written as the Pavilion was being built. There was no reason to believe that the prince took opium for artistic inspiration, but he did take laudanum to relieve the effects of over indulgence.

Was he a spendthrift? This seems an easy judgement. He always had debts and he spent money easily and the debts were always paid off by others. In 1816, with his new yacht 'Royal George' harboured in Cowes, and chandeliers costing £5,600 recently installed in the Pavilion, he received a rare warning letter from the prime minister to tell him that he was inflaming the lower orders with his excessive spending. There are hundreds of examples of his spending habits; some of them on art, science, and literature, and he could be randomly generous to individuals in distress. However, it was never his money, nor his responsibility. When he died in 1830, £10,000 in cash was found in nearly 500 different pocket books that he had simply forgotten about. To give that figure some perspective, this was exactly the same amount of money that Jane Austen's Mr Darcy had per year, and he was a rich man.

His ten-year reign reflected the utter lack of promise of his Regency. While his people suffered he bought himself a giraffe and paid £200 for a painting of it. He was a near blind recluse by 1830. Carlton House, his main residence was demolished in 1827 while still unfinished. The king had spend £300,000 of public money on the edifice but it was still structurally unsound – an extended metaphor for the state of the monarchy, which he left at a very low ebb. Harriet Arbuthnot chronicled his last days, a mixture of emergency medication and, during brief recoveries, appalling overeating and drinking. 'Last night they gave him some physic…and after that he drank three glasses of port wine and a glass of brandy. No wonder he is likely to die! But they say that he will have all these things and nobody can prevent him.'[2]

Three weeks after his funeral, the *Times* was scathing:

> *What eye wept for him? What heart has heaved one sob of unmercenary sorrow?…If George IV ever had a friend – a devoted friend in any rank of life – we protest that the name of him or her has never reached us.…Selfishness is the true repellent of human sympathy. Selfishness feels no attachment, and invites none*

The *Times* was merely saying what the Hunt brothers had said eighteen years earlier. In that period, these sentiments had gone from being criminal libel to established fact. That was the achievement of the Prince Regent.

Chapter 11

Arthur Thistlewood – The Gentleman Revolutionary

Arthur Thistlewood was one of the few people who openly advocated revolutionary violence during the Regency; he was infamous for a botched and pathetic attempt to assassinate the members of the Cabinet in 1820, but deadly in his seriousness. This became known as the 'Cato Street' conspiracy.

Thistlewood was the illegitimate son of a minor Lincolnshire landowner. Arthur was treated well by his father, so had no pressing reason to rebel against anything. The family were respectable gentry and the son seemed dutiful at first, but underneath there appears to have been a rebellious streak. He rejected his father's ambition for him to become a land surveyor and in the 1790s joined the militia and served in the West Indies. He spent time in the USA and later in France during the era of Robespierre. He became a deist, influenced by Thomas Paine, accepting the Supreme Being but not other aspects of established religion. He fought for the French around 1794–5, accepting the Jacobin view that violence should be used for political ends. He supported a regime that had put his hero Thomas Paine in a damp, rotting prison. It is not recorded how he dealt with this contradiction. Both his friends and enemies accept that he was an excellent swordsman, had an obsession with military matters and a burning desire to protect the vulnerable and poor, especially those in the armed forces.[1]

Although some commentators suggest he was taking part in massacres as part of the French Army in 1799, this seems to be only in the imagination of hostile sources.[2] By 1798 however, he was a gentlemen member of the West Riding militia. His marriage was duly reported in the *Gentlemen's Magazine* in 1804, but his next appearance in the newspapers in May 1805 was for a sad reason. His wife, Jane, had died in childbirth on 29 April, aged 30. The couple lived at Bawtry, West Yorkshire 'in some splendour', according to his unreliable post-mortem biographies. Also in 1805, a man of the same name and location subscribed to a progressive but far from revolutionary book of religious and political discussions called 'Essays on Various Subjects'. Was he a revolutionary Jacobin or a typical member of the Georgian minor gentry? Was he reliable and steady or was he a wild man?

Thistlewood seems to have married Jane Worsley for money, although biographers cannot agree about the figure. This was in a tradition common among Georgian gentlemen, but he seemed to have been particularly intense in his courtship. A hostile biographer stated jocularly that he 'ha[d] laid siege to her at Lincoln', but after her death he found out that the majority of her money would not revert to him. For most of his life, he seemed to be both lucky and careless with money.

Some primary sources suggest that he was financially stranded with a small annuity. However, the house Thistlewood bought in Lincoln around the time of Jane's death in 1805 seems far from ordinary. He sold it a mere two years later, in May 1807 according to this notice in the *Stamford Mercury*:

> *FOR SALE. All that substantial dwelling-house, in complete repair; consisting of commodious kitchen, breakfast, dining and drawing rooms; four lodging rooms on the first floor, and several good attics and rooms for servants; with brewhouse, stabling for three horses, kitchen and pleasure gardens, and a very excellent paddock immediately behind the Dwelling-house, containing upwards of 2a acres, and late in the occupation of Henry Rutter, Esq. But now of Arthur Thistlewood, Esq.*[3]

The house, in the medieval centre of Lincoln near St Mary's Church had previously belonged to the eminent solicitor and substantial Lincoln citizen Henry Rutter so it seems that Thistlewood was living the life of the gentry, despite his Jacobin beliefs.

Later, when he was on the run from a charge of high treason in 1817, the *Cambridge Chronicle* suggested that he had property worth £15,000 from the death of his first wife. This sum may have purchased the Lincoln property; the paper claimed that he later gambled much of the proceeds away. The post-mortem biographies suggest something similar; that by 1805, he had lost money at Lincoln races and failed to pay his creditors. The motives of the biographers will always be suspect but the constant and varying references to gambling at different times in his life makes the charge credible.

There is some evidence for his dissolute lifestyle, the details of which can be seen in a law suit of 1815, referring to an incident that occurred at an unknown earlier date – possibly 1806 or 1807.[4] In this case, Thistlewood's brother John had sent Arthur to London to collect the £800 proceeds of a property deal. Arthur had drunk 'too freely' and found himself 'by accident' in a drinking den in St James with the notorious gambler and ruffian Hill Darley. During the night he lost all of his brother's money at the game of hazard, a dice game, and usually a game of chance unless you are drunk and playing with criminals, in which case you have already lost.

Many later biographies, especially those written at the time of his execution, suggest that Thistlewood had fallen in with a dissolute London crowd and had gambled regularly, but the Hill Darley episode seems to be an example of an innocent man out of his depth. The 1815 lawsuit then explains how Thistlewood sobered up and went to ask for his money back, which would have been naive if he was really part of the 'Hellfire' set. Many primary sources suggest that he was a professional gambler. The *Calcutta Chronicles*, a newspaper for the British in India, produced at the time of his execution, suggested that Thistlewood had lost £2,000 on that night in St James. Was he a professional gambler or merely inept with money? Once again, the sources do not agree. He may have lied in the lawsuit – he was both desperate enough and sufficiently contemptuous of the legal system to do so.

According to the *Calcutta Chronicles*, Thistlewood fled to France after losing the £2,000, where he was imprisoned for having no passport and was involved in violence and atrocities in the army of the enemy. It also claimed that he learnt French moderately well; which was not a compliment on his language skills but a comment on his loyalty to the British constitution. His enemies also place him in Paris in 1814 and 1815, either gambling at the Palais Royal or plotting against the French monarchy.

He may have been a fool with money, but he seemed skilled in the art of marrying it. In May 1808 he married Susannah Wilkinson, the daughter of a wealthy Horncastle butcher, who came with a dowry of £2,000. He then quit his commission in the army and, with the help of his family, bought a farm. The farm was not a success; by 1811, Thistlewood was back in London with his wife and son. In March he was in the local press as the secretary of a committee to defend Peter Finnerty, who was being prosecuted for libelling Lord Castlereagh. In that meeting, Thistlewood was present with the reformer Major John Cartwright and would have known Sir Francis Burdett. The meeting took place at the Crown and Anchor in the Strand, the home of political dissent in London, suggesting that Thistlewood was active in the radical movement at that time but at a relatively humble level.[5]

He first encountered the revolutionary Spencean Philanthropists in 1814. Their views would have chimed with his; opposition to most forms of private property, a rejection of the established Church and conventional

The end of the war did not improve life for John Bull, despite expectations. Cartoon by
Cruikshank, 1814.

Hannah More (1745–1833) suggested humility and patient resignation to the will of God when
prosperity did not return. Many others agreed.

Traditional handloom weaving.
(Wellcome Library, London).

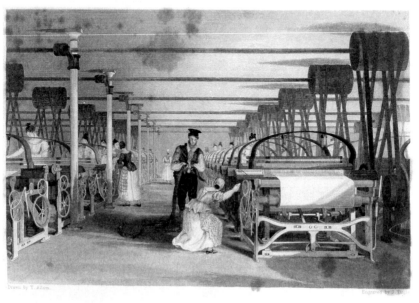

Factory weaving: the new supervision and discipline. Engraving, about 1840.

George IV withdraws from society with gout. The pictures on the wall are him in his youth. (Wellcome Library, London)

Carlton House, Pall Mall, home of the Prince Regent. Demolished while still unfinished, 1827. (Brayley, 1820)

Gambling – the vice of the rich. Satirical print about 1800.

Gin and disorder, the vice of the poor. (Wellcome Library, London)

Unnamed hulk, 1810. Notice the washing.

THE LANDING of the CONVICTS at BOTANY BAY

Arrival at Botany Bay, late eighteenth century.

Above: The danger of hiring a young servant: 'Get out of my house, you hussey, I hired you to do your own business, not mine.' Cartoon, about 1793.

Left: A completely inaccurate grave robbery scene. (Wellcome library London)

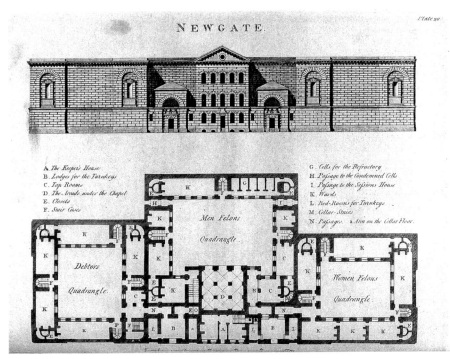

A plan of Newgate, *circa* 1800. (Charles Dance)

Public view of an execution before the Debtor's Door of Newgate, 1809.

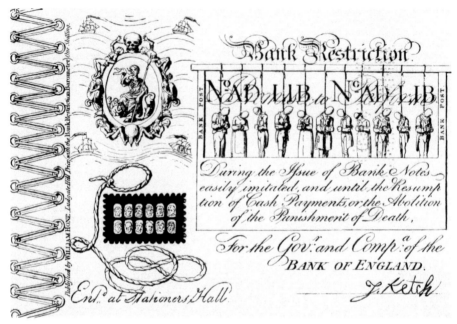

A protest about excessive punishment for counterfeiting, by William Hone. Signed by Jack Ketch, the public hangman.

A young William Cobbett – an opponent of paper money, and many other things. Engraved by Francisco Bartolozzi.

religion, a call for communal ownership of land, and the belief that violent action could, and should, overthrow a rotten government. He must have been increasingly active in the movement, because although he did not become leader after the death of Thomas Spence in 1814, he was certainly in charge a year later.

The Spenceans planned an armed revolt against the government in December 1816. They believed that their thirty activists could start a chain reaction among the lower classes. When it failed dismally, Thistlewood and other leading Spenceans – James Watson, Thomas Preston and John Hooper – were tried for high treason in March 1817. The others were a surgeon (meaning a chemist or apothecary), a cordwainer and a labourer. Thistlewood had no occupation; he was a 'gent' and he seemed to have left most of the heavy revolutionary work to the others. Preston wrote the inflammatory leaflets and posted them around London; Watson visited the public houses of Holborn and Paddington and tried to agitate the navigators building the Regent's canal. These Irishmen would provide muscle, have a grievance against the protestant state and could be found easily in pubs, the favourite place of the Spenceans.

The day of the attempted coup was 2 December 1816. This second Spa Fields protest started by looking very similar to the first – the same field, the same public house, and the same flooding of London with pamphlets and handbills beforehand. However, the tactics of the Spenceans had changed. A petition to the Prince Regent had been presented after the first mass meeting on 15 November. They already knew that the Prince Regent had refused permission to even present it to him and they were determined to incite a riot and then try to turn it into an armed revolution against the Lord Liverpool government.

The other similarity between the two meetings was the planned speech by Henry Hunt at 1pm. However, the Spenceans seemed to have pre-empted Hunt's arrival when they appeared an hour early with a cattle wagon full of flags and banners proclaiming: 'Nature, Truth and Justice', 'Feed the Hungry' and 'Protect the Oppressed'.

There was also gunpowder, guns, and pikes in the wagon and this seems very likely to be the work of Thistlewood, although the 200 metal pikes were provided by one of their new members, John Castle. Thistlewood was there, clearly focussing on the military aspect, but the main speaker, who introduced himself as 'Mr Smith', was actually James Watson junior. He told the crowd that their petition had been rejected. He attacked the monarchy – 'This Brunswick Family' – 'people with a million pounds who give the poor £5,000'.

Henry Hunt was late. He couldn't resist a meeting, even with people with whose views he did not fully agree. In reality, the Spenceans did not rate Henry Hunt very highly, and they knew only his ego had brought him back to address another mass meeting. Hunt was caught between the moderate reform positions of Cobbett and Burdett, and the unconstitutional ambitions of the Spenceans, and trying to be the leader of both.

John Castle, Hunt's driver, was under orders to delay Hunt so that the others could start without him. 'Mr Smith' continued his speech, comparing Hunt to Wat Tyler, the leader of the 1381 Peasants' Revolt, and made it clear that this was a good thing. About 200 of the crowd of protesters never heard Hunt speak, as they had successfully been peeled off by Watson's inflammatory speech. They accepted the Spenceans' offer to arm themselves and defend their English liberty with force. The *Chester Courant* said that the 'trail was soon discernible by fragments of lamps and windows'. They stormed away to the Tower of London and the Royal Exchange by way of all the gun shops. The ease with which they located them suggested that some research had been done.

This serious violence was to continue for many hours. Meanwhile, Hunt arrived at about 1 pm and reported what the crowd already knew – that the Prince Regent had declined to see their petition. The Prince Regent had contributed £5,000 to the Soup Committee, which provided sustenance to distressed mariners, but he had no interest in any political or economic change. Hunt reported back his exchange of exaggeratedly polite correspondence with Lord Sidmouth, the Home Secretary. Despite the formulaic good manners of his letters, Sidmouth was now convinced of a conspiracy to overthrow the government. Hunt continued to better his two hour speech of 15 November, when the hostile press claimed that he had 'talked down the sun', with an even longer exhortation to face the artillery of evil with the more powerful artillery of truth and with condemnations of corrupt sinecurists, unrepresentative parliaments, taxation, and a standing army designed to oppress the people.

Meanwhile, a few miles away, state power was reasserting itself. Despite arming themselves with the proceeds of looted guns shops, the Spenceans were unable to defeat the Life Guards and Dragoons set against them. The Riot Act had already been read at 4 pm. There were failed attacks on the Tower by a very drunk Watson; the members of Lloyds Coffee House were conscripted as special constables. Sir William Curtis MP – also known as 'Billy Biscuit' – organised a spirited defence of the Royal Exchange. Thistlewood was at the Tower of London. Despite banners with slogans such as 'We consider the soldiers our friends', the army remained loyal to the government. The insurrection ended about 9 pm. Two Spenceans, Hooper and Cashman were arrested immediately. There was a least one casualty, a warehouseman called Platt, shot in the groin by a Spencean, probably Watson, and probably still drunk.

Thistlewood was on the run from December 1816 to February 1817. A reward of £500 was offered and this newspaper description makes him sound like the desperate soldier he was:

Arthur Thistlewood is about forty-five years of age, five feet 11 inches high, has a sallow complexion, long visage, dark hair (a little grey) small whiskers, dark hazel eyes, and arched eye-brows, a wide mouth, and a good set of teeth, has a scar under his right jaw, is slender made, walks very upright, and has much the appearance of a military man; was born in Lincolnshire, and apprenticed to an apothecary at Newark, and has been a lieutenant in the army; he usually wore a French-grey coloured coat, buff waistcoat, grey coloured Wellington pantaloons, with Hessian boots under them, and at times a dark-brown greatcoat.

His fine teeth and his financial ability to hide for four months showed his gentry background. His scar and his bearing show the importance of the army to his life. He was never an apothecary's apprentice – that was his brother. During the hunt, the newspapers, prompted by the authorities, put out the rumour that he had returned to France, where the French were bankrolling the treason. As the *Stamford Mercury* said, 'his purse was always open to treat his deluded followers'.

On 20 April, he was apprehended trying to board the *Perseus* from Gravesend with his wife and 10-year-old child under the name 'Wilkinson', which was his wife's maiden name. The newspapers described Thistlewood's wife as 'interesting' and 'amiable' – probably a euphemism for something bad, but from a modern perspective she seems to have been a determined women. The *Newgate Chronicles*, a relatively dispassionate source, said that 'she perfectly coincided with the political views of her husband'. The unnamed child was about 10, possibly born in 1807 and therefore neither the child of his first or second wife. His hostile post-mortem biographers did suggest that Thistlewood had an illegitimate child by the seduction of a servant. He was always the Georgian gentlemen, even when trying to overthrow the government.

John Castle was the main trial witness. The Spenceans were tried separately, with James Watson being first. Castle gave some indications of Thistlewood's activity during his attempt to incriminate Watson. He claimed that Thistlewood had provided him with money to buy pikes, and had treated the Paddington navigators with beer on the promise of 500 men at Spa Fields; he confirmed that Thistlewood went to Tower Hill and failed to convince the soldiers to change sides and had also provided the revolutionary icons. Thistlewood seemed already hanged.

However, the case collapsed when it became clear that Castle himself was a spy and agent provocateur for the Home Department. Watson was found not guilty and no evidence was offered against Thistlewood himself. He left to the sound of cheering. Thomas Preston, one of the other released men, thanked the jury but warned their supporters not to be provoked or trapped by the government.

Thistlewood was not listening to the advice of his comrade. He continued to believe in the value of the mass insurrection even when others rejected it. He seemed to have lost whatever judgement he had at this point. His enemies and friends agreed that he was a fiery, tempestuous man, but with a simple hearted desire to help the poor; it must have occurred to him that his every move was now being watched. The Bow Street authorities successfully re-infiltrated the Spenceans with a spy called Edward Ruthven, who reported that the Spenceans were still active, still meeting in pubs, getting drunk, insulting the Prince Regent and being blasphemous.

John Stafford, who held the innocent sounding title of the Chief Clerk to the Bow Street Runners, was certainly watching him. Some sources put him at the Spa Fields riot in December, being responsible for breaking the revolutionary flags and banners, and preventing the Spenceans from using them to inflame the masses. He ushered the spy Castle up to the witness stand and this was the point that Castle's evidence and credibility began to unravel, as Stafford's real job as spymaster was well known.

Thistlewood was a man of few words and the Spenceans produced few radical publications. In July 1817, in a fundraiser organised by Henry Hunt at the Crown and Anchor Public House (the *Morning Post* sniffily said that there were less than sixty people present), James Watson gave a long, eloquent speech of lies about his involvement at Spa Fields; Thistlewood muttered a few thanks.

In early February 1817, Thistlewood wrote to Lord Sidmouth, the Home Secretary who had instigated the treason trial, asking the noble lord for a satisfaction through a duel: 'I leave the choice of pistol or sword to your

Lordship…as for time, I will admit of no delay.'[6] This does not seem very logical; Thistlewood was asking for the return of the £180 he had spent trying to avoid the law. A reasonable person would have known that he would be committed to prison for this action. What it does sound like is the behaviour of an angry Georgian gentleman; clearly none of the other revolutionaries would have the social background to even consider a duel. Perhaps they would also have had more sense.

He was apprehended on 11 February at his home in Stanhope Street, Clare Market (having helpfully given Lord Sidmouth his address on his letter). He pleaded guilty on the first occasion, but asked permission to change his plea in court two days later. He told the judge, Lord Ellenborough, that he did not know that pleading guilty would lead immediately to sentencing and that he wished to have a say, so he was given permission to change his plea. This does not sound like a man with a firm grip on reality, or even a person who had been through the courts for high treason a year earlier.

He seemed to be in a poor state when he came to trial in May. Looking ill, and mumbling an incoherent set of criticisms about his treatment, he also claimed that he had been forbidden to call witnesses who would have proved his innocence, despite the only evidence being a letter that he had clearly written himself. Therefore, he offered no defence and asked for a retrial. In the true spirit of revolutionaries, he claimed the whole process was illegal. He was denied a retrial; it was put to him that he missed the deadline for calling witnesses because he had deliberately made his application on a day when the court was closed – once again it looks like Thistlewood was not in charge of proceedings at all. He was sentenced to twelve months' imprisonment in Horsham Gaol.

By July 1819, Thistlewood, along with James Watson, was back on the 'monster meeting' trail, with Henry Hunt leading the speeches. Thistlewood was seen by the authorities carrying banners with 'Peace and Goodwill' and 'Universal Suffrage' – slightly less revolutionary than at Spa Fields. This was one of the same series of meetings that led to the tragedy of Peterloo in August. Thistlewood and Watson continued leading mass meetings and organising petitions. Thistlewood was becoming a major figure in the reform movement, rivalling Hunt himself.

By November 1819 they had fallen out; Hunt, ironically as it turned out, warned about spies in the reform movement. By December they were trading insults in public through the newspapers, who gleefully documented their disagreements. Thistlewood wrote to Lord Sidmouth again – 'would the noble Lord please send him the £180 he was owed when he tried to leave the country?' The newspapers were both indignant and amazed. The *Public*

Ledger caught the mood of the establishment: 'Is it Bedlam or Newgate that this man is so anxiously seeking a berth?'

Always conscious of the value of the disgruntled Irish to the revolutionary movement, Thistlewood was in Ireland in January of the year of his execution. The newspapers reported that he was being watched everywhere; Spencean meetings were now reported in the newspapers.

It was at this point that Thistlewood tried to organise a violent coup against the state. His motives and reasoning are hard to fathom. He knew he was being followed and spied on. Although he had fallen out with Hunt after Hunt had called him 'the dupe of spies', he didn't need Hunt to tell him about spies after Spa Fields. It was a new member of the group, by the name of Edwards, who told Thistlewood that the cabinet would meet for dinner on 23 February. Despite barely knowing Edwards, Thistlewood still decided to assassinate the Cabinet. Edwards was another spy.

Thistlewood had tired of Hunt's egotistical speechifying and had lost confidence in mass meetings as a catalyst for change. The unpopular Prince Regent had become king in January and was already planning a coronation costing a quarter of a million pounds. The political mood was ugly and the establishment were worried. Since Peterloo there had been more people drilling and collecting arms in Scotland, Yorkshire and Lancashire. Thistlewood felt encouraged.

The reckless gambler was returning. He seemed to be ignoring facts, however. Never before had a Cabinet dinner been advertised in advance, and the only supporting evidence was a newspaper, the *New Times*, a well known stooge of the government. The spy Edwards had shown Thistlewood the details of the meeting just a day before it happened and Thistlewood scrambled to get a group together to assassinate the whole Cabinet. They checked that Lord Harrowby was actually hosting the dinner by visiting his house, and when a servant told the visitor that the noble Lord was out of town, Thistlewood saw this as part of the conspiracy and refused to believe it. Twenty-seven people agreed to take part, most new and desperate revolutionary friends who had replaced Watson and the others who had taken part in Spa Fields.

The conspirators gathered in a hayloft in Cato Street on the evening of the proposed coup. They had weapons, and bags in which to put the heads of Castlereagh and Sidmouth. They planned to parade them among the labouring poor in the hope of starting a chain reaction across the country. They were intercepted while still preparing their attack by the Bow Street Runners and in the fracas Thistlewood killed a police officer, Richard Smithers.

At the trial for treason, the government showed that it had learned its lessons from the Spa Field's trial. Neither of the two spies – Ruthven and Edwards – were called, and lesser members of the conspiracy were encouraged to turn King's evidence. On 28 April 1820, Thistlewood, alongside William Davidson, James Ings, Richard Tidd, and John Brunt, were found guilty of high treason and sentenced to death.

Thistlewood's speech after judgement helps to explain his anger at the state of Britain. It was long, well argued, and well presented; but it was also angry, personal and emotional. Thistlewood seemed to have no coherent plan for life after a successful insurrection, merely hatred of the present system. They were striking a blow against Castlereagh and Sidmouth who were 'privileged traitors who lord it over the life and property of a sovereign people with a barefaced impunity'. He had been convicted by a handpicked jury that was already prejudiced against him, without the right to call witnesses that would prove the existence of spies. Edwards was a government spy, stated Thistlewood, who never had money to buy a pint of beer in the pub but was always able to procure weapons. When Edwards had tried to provoke them into blowing up the House of Commons, Thistlewood had refused because it would kill the innocent and make him no better than the barbarians at Peterloo who had applauded the massacre, and the Prince Regent who was 'still reeking with the gore of the hapless victims'.

Thistlewood confessed himself disappointed with the reaction to Peterloo. 'If one spark of independence still glimmered in the breasts of Englishmen, they would have risen like a man.' He decided to take vengeance on despotism himself. 'I resolved that the lives of the instigators should be the requiem to the souls of the murdered innocents.'

The Governor of Newgate visited the four men the following day to deliver the death warrant and ask if they wanted a visit from a clergyman. They all refused. When a cleric was foisted on them the next morning, they declared themselves deists and disbelievers in the divinity of Christ. James Ings was the only exception, but he also rejected the established Anglican Church by asking for a Methodist minister. They were in such good spirits that their solidarity was deliberately broken by putting them into separate cells. According to the hostile sources Ings was reconverted to conventional Christianity by an unplanned nocturnal visit by the Reverend Horace Cotton, chaplain of Newgate.[7] It was implied that the Methodist minister, a Mr Rennet (a mere journeyman tailor), was rejected by Ings as being too unlearned to guide him to eternity. The paper also reported that

Thistlewood had an affecting goodbye with his wife and children, although some sources say he only had one son.

Home Secretary Sidmouth was concerned about the reaction of the crowd at the execution. He decided to dispense with the part of the process that involved dragging the condemned men through the streets on a wooden hurdle, claiming that it would inconvenience traffic. The scaffold was also enlarged and a fence built around it to stop the pressure of the crowd prejudicing the process. The crowd started to build up the day before the execution as the contractors put up triple lines of poles between the scaffold and the people.

On the morning of the day of execution, crowds began to gather at 4 am, with the best seats costing three guineas. At 6 am the Horse Guards formed a line protecting the Old Bailey from possible rioters. A large banner had been produced saying 'The Riot Act has been read – disperse!' The authorities were clearly worried that they might lose control of the mob.

The four were executed at Newgate Prison on May Day, 1820. The men were led to the scaffold sucking oranges, looking brave and unapologetic. Thistlewood refused a blindfold and bowed when somebody shouted 'God bless you'. His last full sentence before an efficient hanging was: 'I hope that you will report to the world that I died a sincere friend of liberty.' They died well, with the grudging respect of the many thousands who still opposed their actions.

Half an hour later Thistlewood was decapitated, his face clearly bright purple and his body kept in a position that would prevent blood spurting from his body. His head was held up with the traditional cry – 'This is the head of a traitor!' The petitions of the families were ignored; the bodies had already been covered in quick lime and buried in the Newgate grounds. The bodies of traitors were never handed over in any case.

It is easy to see the Cato Street conspiracy as a hair-brained scheme. Cobbett thought it was, but admired their courage even if he did not condone their actions. Cobbett did notice that the ruling classes were never quite so insolent and arrogant again. Lord Castlereagh never recovered from the fact that people were meant to rejoice at seeing his severed head on a pole. The establishment clearly believed that there was enough discontent for Thistlewood, or somebody like him, to provoke the miserable lower orders into revolution. By 1820 economic conditions improved and the government started to modify its unsympathetic attitudes towards the poor. Perhaps the deluded Arthur had not been a complete failure.

Chapter 12

1817 – The New Peasants' Revolt

The ruling classes knew what to expect when rural rioters demanded a reduction in the price of bread, or urban artisans challenged employers about working practices. Grievances were specific and local and concessions could be made through discussions with people who knew each other and had to live together in the same place afterwards. The protesters usually wanted a return to the old ways rather than innovation or reform, and things would get back to normal if concessions were made. The protestors, despite their violence, were challenging the system but not trying to overthrow it.

In 1816 and 1817 these 'bread or blood' riots were replaced by protests that worried the authorities more. They feared that the lower classes were conspiring, organising nationally, or creating military and political organisations. Instead of complaining about parts of the system, some of the lower orders wanted the end of the whole system – or were being duped by evil conspirators to think in that way.

The Luddite machine-breaking in 1811-12 bore some dangerous characteristics. The plan to destroy machines was in many ways a call to return to the past, but there was a degree of local and regional organisation in the attack on property that was only defeated by overwhelming military force. It was in the best interest of the government to exaggerate the threat of armed insurrection, but the way they moved the militia suggested some worries about the loyalty of the ordinary soldier. During the Luddite crisis in Nottinghamshire, local militias were sent to Ireland, and the West Essex militia were moved from Chelmsford to the East Midlands, along with military from Somerset, Edinburgh and Surrey.

The fear was of armed insurrection by mobs of people, organised by a political leadership who used economic misery to achieve political aims. The government probably feared more that revolution would be attempted under the guise of a traditional protest, and in 1817 their worries seemed to be realistic.

John Bagguley was a remarkably young Mancunian; an unlikely change-maker amongst the writers, politicians and intellectuals who normally dominated the reform movement. He was a weaver, an apprentice or servant (depending on the source used) who had managed to get the attention of both the starving families of Manchester and the hardened political reformers. He was 17 at the time, and before he turned 20 he would have endured two years in prison and five months in solitary confinement for his principles. By 1817 he was addressing political meetings all over Manchester and the surrounding towns.

He was very critical of Watson and the Spenceans, who, to his mind, had done nothing but organise a drunken riot at Spa Fields and had ruined the potential of mass petitioning to achieve change. The Spenceans had gone too quickly from using the frustration of a rejected petition to an attempted coup, and Bagguley wanted to introduce more subtlety. He may not really have believed in petitions, but he was prepared to use them as a lever to get change.

In March 1817 it seemed clear that the government were about to suspend *habeas corpus* to allow mass arrests of suspects. This was as response to Spa Fields and the 'assassination attempt' on the Prince Regent, and Bagguley and his associates, Samuel Drummond and John Johnson, organised a meeting to draw up a petition to ask for help for distressed weavers and for the protection of *habeas corpus*. When protesters entwined economic distress with political demands, this rang alarm bells for the local magistrates.

Five thousand met at St Peter's Field on 11 March and about 400 were persuaded to march to London. The *Manchester Mercury*, being a local paper, was the first to describe the events. They noted with alarm that a group of Manchester weavers were planning to march and petition the Prince Regent. There had been, they reported, a series of seditious meetings in Manchester and now they would:

> *Proceed to the Metropolis ...to present a petition to the Prince Regent that they may be able to undeceive him!! Aware of these intentions, and the dangers of an immense influx of strangers, irritated by the inflammatory appeals of their fractious leaders, who under the pretence of promoting Parliamentary reform, have been agitating the minds of the labouring classes.*

The newspaper was showing its prejudices but there was a kernel of truth. There was a real worry that this was a new, more dangerous form of protest. In the past, these radical reformers had been active, but now they were trying to organise the 'deluded masses' in a form of political action. The fact that they were going to visit the Prince Regent personally was an alarm; the normal thing to do was to petition the Prince Regent indirectly and then be ignored. Parliament, Lords and Commons, were being bypassed, and the monarch was being threatened by a mob who merely masqueraded as petitioners.

Bagguley's strategy was to work hard to avoid breaking any law, especially at the beginning of the protest. He told the marchers to remain peaceable, promising that the magistrate would be called if people misbehaved. It was not illegal to walk from Manchester to London, but considering that it was more than a day by stagecoach, it was perhaps ridiculous. Only 400 of the 5,000 could be persuaded to leave Manchester, and because they were on the move they did not fall foul of the new Seditious Meeting Act; by moving in groups of ten or less they stayed on the right side of the Riot Laws, which were in any case still invoked when the military caught up with them. It was the deliberation by which laws had *not* been broken that convinced the authorities that treason was afoot and drastic action was needed.

The small group, armed only with knapsacks and blankets – hence the name 'Blanketeers' – set out from Manchester to go down to London; they were to be joined by more at Stockport and Birmingham. Bagguley, Johnson and Drummond had clearly offered the crowd something in addition to a long march to Carlton House. They expected reinforcements at every crossroads as they went. It was an organised version of Spa Fields, with a deliberate strategy to accumulate large numbers and confront the monarch directly, while blaming his advisors to avoid a charge of sedition. It was an attempt to repeat the events of 1381 when hundreds of thousands of labourers surrounded the king, killed his religious and political advisors, and tore up feudal contracts as they passed through villages. Bagguley was trying to organise a new peasants' revolt with weavers instead of peasants, and the Prince Regent instead of Richard II.

Drummond, Johnson and Bagguley had created a historical philosophy that they were going to use to incite a rebellion. Government spies reported that Johnson told meetings that if the prince did not listen to them, then the fate of Charles I awaited him. Bagguley told crowds that ancient law gave the monarch forty days to respond to petitions and then he could be imprisoned. It was common to use the analogy of the Peasants' Revolt; and the key here is that the peasants by-passed the aristocracy and appealed to the monarch in great numbers, the numbers being an implicit threat. Drummond seems to have told them this too – by the time they arrived in London, they could not be ignored, he told them.

There was never a chance for numbers to increase. The marchers were no match for the military; the Blanketeers were stopped at Ardwick and Stockport. There were some injuries through sabre charges and 200 arrests. Most were held in gaol for a few weeks without any evidence against them, and some were prosecuted using the vagrancy laws.

As the 'migratory reformers' left Manchester on that morning, the twenty-seven local radicals who had agitated them into action were themselves arrested. A few weeks later, in the so called 'Ardwick conspiracy' an attempt to rescue the prisoners and burn Manchester to the ground, almost certainly organised by government spies and agents, allowed more suspects to be rounded up.

Bagguley was kept in solitary confinement for five months due – ironically – to the suspension of *habeas corpus* that the original protest was ostensibly about. He was moved to the New Bailey in Salford, then in chains to Coldbath Fields, then to Horsemonger Gaol and finally to Gloucester and kept in near solitary confinement until 13 November when he was given leave to visit his dying mother. In September 1818 he was given two years' imprisonment for another incident in Stockport. He was not yet 20 years old.

In 1817 there was another attempt, in the view of Lord Sidmouth, 'maliciously and traitorously…by force of arms, to subvert and destroy the Government and the Constitution', which bore some real comparisons to the Blanketeers' march. This was Pentrich Rising, organised by a group of about forty framework knitters, stonemasons, miners and labourers from the Derbyshire villages of Pentrich, Heanor, Alfreton and South Wingfield, who believed that they could organise an armed revolt that would be picked up and strengthened by disaffected workers in the North and Midlands. Clearly this is not the same as having a drunken riot, attacking bakers and shopkeepers waving pieces of bread on pointed sticks.

Rebel leader Jeremiah Brandreth and his supporters were arraigned for treason in Derby in October 1817, after the inevitable failure of the insurrection of a few hundred poorly armed people. There were too many to hold in one prison, so they were split – twenty-six in Derby and fifteen in Nottingham. On 3 October they were charged with treason in Derby. The Nottingham prisoners were shipped into town on the top of a coach still all chained together, except the two who had become sick while in prison. The newspapers reported that they were of various ages and states, but having in common that they wore the blue smock frocks of 'the lowest and labouring classes of the community'.

George Weightman and his three brothers were amongst the prisoners. Their mother, Nanny Weightman, ran the White Horse public house where a planning meeting had been held on 8 June. Nanny was the sister of Thomas and John Bacon. Thomas Bacon ('an aged man, charged with having planned the insurrection') and his relative John had been captured in St Ives, either by the excellent work of the Derby prison officials, or by a reward of £100 that no poor person would be able to resist, depending on whether the newspapers could be believed. There were also four Ludlams and three Taylors among the prisoners.

The first day of the trial was 17 October, when the procession of prisoners from Derby and Nottingham happened again. The prisoners were once again in good humour, but the omens for their trial were not good. Behind the procession was a coach full of pikes and other sharpened agricultural implements that had been found after the attempted insurrection. This rather prejudiced the result of the trial.

Before proceedings started, the bias continued. The judges attended a sermon at Derby All Saints Church with a sermon by the Reverend Foxglove based on Isaiah 5:20, 'Woe unto them who call evil good and good evil.' The Reverend Foxglove compared the treasons of the accused to the evils of Oliver Cromwell. He probably did not get as far as Isaiah 8:21, which was much more popular with the reformers, 'and it shall come to pass, that when they shall be hungry, they shall fret themselves, and curse their king and their God, and look upward'.

The newspapers were dismissive of the accused; they were in rags, they were inane and ignorant, and they addressed a clerk of the court as 'My Lord'– so even when being deferential, it was not good enough.

The Grand Jury consisted of the usual gentlemen and baronets who would have no sympathy for the accused – it included the aristocratic Lord George Cavendish, MP for Derbyshire, and his third son, the Honourable Henry Cavendish, the MP for Derby. Another member of the jury was Richard Arkwright junior, a man who had inherited his fortune from the mechanisation of textiles, who was not naturally inclined to favour framework knitters. It was their job to decide whether there was a 'true bill' – i.e., a real case to answer. They decided that there was.

Derby County Hall was crowded on the outside and full on the inside. The patriotic newspapers gave no indication of the mood of the crowd, but even inside the building, it could take thirty minutes to get order on some days. All pleaded not guilty. Jeremiah Brandreth, who had led the insurrection, appeared wearing a ragged sailor suit and with a long, straggled beard.

Thomas Bacon was indicted first and it was fully expected that the prosecution would lead with his trial. Bacon was a political activist and conspirator in the new model, a follower of Thomas Paine, a republican, and a peripatetic agitator who wanted the end of the system rather than to wring concessions from it. He had a long track record of radicalism. He had been in contact with Oliver, another apparent radical agitator for a few months beforehand.

In April 1817 Oliver had arrived at the Talbot Inn, Derby, a well known meeting point for the disaffected, and declared that force and organisation were needed to make the government see sense. It was Oliver who had convinced people that they could rely on the resentment of the lower classes all over the North if they started an insurrection at Pentrich. However, Oliver himself was an agent provocateur in the same style as John Stones, whose dubious background had helped to acquit James Watson and made the trial of Thistlewood, Preston and Hooper collapse.

Bacon now knew that Oliver was a spy, and the government knew that Bacon was aware of it. He took no part in the insurrection, fearing (rightly) that he was about to be set up. The government had no idea what Thomas Bacon would say. Perhaps for this reason the authorities tried to stop real-time reporting of the trial in the newspapers.

Bacon was left in reserve and it was decided to start the process with the trial of Jeremiah Brandreth. It was still a surprise to many that Brandreth appeared on day two of the trial. It was suggested by the press that this was because the others did not want to be tainted by the charge of murder that stood against him and wished to be tried separately. The prosecution gave a narrative of the events:

> *a great number of persons had organised a plan for a rising in arms on Monday the 9th June last, at two or three villages and then proceed to Nottingham and that assistance was expected from Sheffield, Leeds, Wakefield etc…that the Nottingham Captain [Brandreth] was particularly active in organising the measures – that pikes and guns and swords had been collected and were to have been distributed – that they went to several farmers houses, compelling them to either give them arms or join them, then on demanding arms at the house of Mr Epworth, and being refused admission, the Nottingham Captain was said to have broken the window and fired a shot at one of the servants, who died in consequence.*

Despite a clear-cut case for the killing of the servant, Robert Walters, Brandreth was accused of high treason instead. Thomas Denman, defence for Brandreth, asked why the charge was treason and not riot. Denman argued that it was very uncommon for ignorant members of the lower orders to be indicted for treason in this way. Lord Chief Justice Baron ruled that they were armed not for a personal grievance but to alter the government. They acted in the belief that their numbers would swell. Their poverty, ignorance, and utter wrongness about their chances of success were not relevant. The absence of Bacon at this point meant that nobody would mention Oliver, the person who had created these unreasonable expectations in the first place.

The next day it was William Turner who was on trial, again for treason. He was seen by the prosecution as the second in command, the main procurer of weapons and the organiser of the men into military-like groups, creating ranks and a hierarchy as if they were an army. Thomas Denman and John Cross once again argued that this pathetic set of actions could not be treason – they had thrown down their weapons at the first appearance of resistance. The prosecution reiterated the difference between violence for a personal end and organised violence to change the government. The Treason Act of Edward III referred to 'rebelliously plotting' to kill the monarch, and the prosecution continued to argue that this is exactly what the Pentrich rebels were doing. The government had used the same arguments in the 1790s to accuse intellectuals and activists of treason, but this attempt to use it against the pike wielding lower orders was different.

Turner was found guilty; so were Isaac Ludlum and George Weightman on the same evidence. There was still no sign of Thomas Bacon. When he did appear, with eighteen others, it was only to change his plea to guilty and throw himself on the mercy of the court. He clearly knew which way the wind was blowing.

The remaining men were acquitted when no evidence was produced against them. The prosecution said that enough had been done to put down the spirit of disaffection that had been excited, and some of these were young and impressionable men who needed the chance to mend their ways. The prosecution felt the need to stress the legitimacy of the trial; the men, they asserted, had had their choice of defence counsel. They failed to mention that the accused had sold all of their possessions to pay for their defence. It was stressed that it was a jury trial; it was not mentioned that it was packed with prosperous farmers, and the trial had been delayed until after the harvest to ensure their availability. Perhaps more realistically, the point had been made that the poor could successfully be accused of political crimes and that perhaps politics was not for the likes of them.

Jeremiah Brandreth, Isaac Ludlum and William Turner were sentenced to be hanged, drawn, and quartered. They were the last men in England to receive that sentence, but in the end clemency was shown and they were only hanged and beheaded. It was a botched job, causing unnecessary pain and humiliation. Thomas Bacon and thirteen others were transported.

What had they planned to do? Brandreth at the White House pub allegedly said that people 'must turn out and fight for bread. The time is come you plainly see, the Government opposed must be.' As they turfed the local farmers out of their beds, they claimed to some that they were going to abolish the national debt, so they had some kind of economic programme. At his trial, William Turner deposed that at the planning meeting at the White Horse, he had only called for bread and work.

Was this a time of revolution or not? The problem answering that question is that both the government and some radical reformers had good reasons for saying that it was, as they both gained politically from the idea. Clearly, from late 1816 there were active individuals who wanted to ferment revolution. By 1819 there was an interest in politics by those who had been excluded – it was to be a year of mass meeting and government repression worst than 1817. It also split the reform movement further and made the government suspicious of any kind of mass meeting or political reform, no matter how moderate it claimed to be. Then, in 1819, came Peterloo, and things got worse.

Chapter 13

Peterloo: Who Killed Joseph Lees?

John Lees was a 22-year-old cotton spinner from Oldham. He attended the St Peter's Field meeting on Monday 16 August 1819, where 80,000 people had come to hear Henry Hunt call for a reform of parliament. It was a peaceful and family-orientated crowd. John was near the front of the hustings. When the Manchester and Salford yeomanry cavalry received orders to arrest Hunt and the others on the platform, they galloped into a crowd that had no means of escape. John was slashed on the arm by a member of the cavalry, and then clubbed by more than one of the special constables that prevented the crowd exiting, and was then trampled by a horse. He died as a result of these wounds on 7 September 1819.

The authorities were determined that neither the government, magistrates nor soldiers would be blamed for the deaths of protesters at St Peter's Field-later, called 'Peterloo'. There were no plans for any official enquiries, so the radicals decided to employ sympathetic lawyers James Harmer and Henry Denison to represent the family at the inquest. It turned out to be much more combative than most courts on the cause of death. The representatives of the Lees family wanted to prove the cavalry culpable, and shine a spotlight on the behaviour of the Manchester magistrates, who they accused of incompetence and panic. The legally required inquest would be their only chance to make these points.

There was a lot wrong with the inquest, starting with the failure of the coroner to turn up for the first three days, which led to an adjournment. The radicals felt that the government was prevaricating, allowing enough time to pass for anger to subside. Mr Battye, the deputy coroner, barely managed to hide his contempt for Harmer and the inquest started each day with recriminations between the coroner and the newspapers, who were determined to report the proceedings. When he forbade publication of details, he was successfully ignored.

Harmer called the first witness – Robert Lees, John's father. Mr Lees senior reported that John had gone to the demonstration without his father's consent. Robert Lees was a successful cotton factory owner in Oldham, more interested in profit than protest. He tried to set his son to work the next day when he returned home injured, but sent him away angrily when he realised that his son was unable to work. He told John to report to the overseer. It was a strangely cold reaction to his son's bloody and bruised appearance, his inability to move freely, and the lack of a shoe. Mr Lees admitted that his indifference to his son's condition was due to his anger, but also his belief that John's stepmother would look after him.

His stepmother Hannah was more observant; he had come home on the Monday night with a cut that had gone foul, his shoulder was sore and could not be moved and he could not hold down food. However, he continued to live as normal. Despite his mother's comments that he was not a regular drinker, he was seen in various public houses over the next few days. The government offered up a witness to say that he was drinking on the Wednesday after the event and had even offered to show people the cut on his elbow.

As the week passed, his condition became progressively worse. By Wednesday the twenty-fifth, he was seeing the local doctor who dressed John's arm and cleaned his cuts. His left foot swelled and developed purple spots, and he lost the ability to use his left arm and eye. He took to his bed more or less permanently after Sunday 29 August and by Sunday 5 September, his father had changed his mind about his son getting better. John died on Tuesday morning after two days of cold, rigid, monosyllabic agony.

A surgeon at the inquest, Mr Basnett, agreed that the wounds were caused by external injuries, and that the loss of his left eye and left leg suggested a spinal injury; but it was still difficult to link it to the actions of the cavalry. It was caused, said the surgeon, by 'cutting and maiming' – but by whom? The cause of death did not seem to be linked to the elbow wound; the bruises seemed linked, but it was not the bruises he complained about. When witnesses were asked why Lees had not complained more, it was suggested that he was still afraid about how his father would react. Betty Ireland, who knew John and saw his injuries, agreed with the stepmother, but neither had the medical knowledge to testify that the wounds were caused by sabre cuts and crushing.

The government case was that Lees had not died as a result of his wounds at Peterloo, but that he had failed to look after himself, the mortification of his wounds was caused by his drinking and his apparent lack of concern showed the truth of this. There was also no evidence of a named or known individual attacking him, so murder was not a verdict that could be supported.

The government's case went badly. John's half brother, Thomas Whittaker, with whom he had shared a bed since John's demobilisation from the army in December 1818, never saw him drunk, or even drink spirits. Another eye-witness at Peterloo, John Wrigley, had been at St Peter's Field, close to the hustings surrounded by women and children, and he saw Lees slashed in the arm by a sabre. Lees had made no attempt to attack the cavalry. His walking stick was merely to help him with the cobbled streets between Oldham and Manchester. Three witnesses saw him cut; one saw him beaten by one of the local constables, who were regarded as the personal instrument of the dep-uty constable Joseph Nadin. The Manchester radicals called them 'Nadin's Runners', and regarded them with equal measures of fear and contempt.

Friends, acquaintances and strangers all gave the same evidence. John Lees had offered no violence, was sober, and was clearly not a revolution-ary. He had seen a doctor, he had carried on for a while – he had after all, joined the army aged 14 and fought at Waterloo aged 17 – he was a tough, resilient man – but he seemed to have died of wounds caused by cutting and maiming, and there were a considerable number of witnesses to this happening to others as well. The Riot Act, which would have legally privi-leged the cavalry's action, had not been heard by anybody. The Manchester and Salford cavalry had struck him down illegally. Such were his internal injuries that Betty Ireland said 'he was still bleeding when they put him in his coffin'.

The chaos of the events at Peterloo, and the dust caused by the out of control horses, meant that it was not going to be possible to identify the per-son who attacked John. Some witnesses were confused by the fact that yeo-manry were in blue and white, and the 15th Hussars were in blue and with smaller yellow facings. One witness, when asked why he could recall so little, pointed out that it was every person for themselves. But the evidence for deliberate killing was mounting up. Harmer was able to produce one Daniel Kennedy, who neither knew nor saw John Lees but, as a cutler, had received orders to sharpen the blades of the cavalry and had completed sixty-three by 17 July in time for the St Peters Field meeting, initially scheduled for 9 August. Another damning witness, who talked to Lees after the attack, was William Harrison: 'He told me he was at the Battle of Waterloo, but he was never in such danger as at this meeting, for at Waterloo it was man to man, but in Manchester it was downright murder.'

On 13 October the coroner ordered a long adjournment. He claimed to be worried about the health of the jury. During the six-week break it was dis-covered that the inquest was null and void due to the failings of the coroner.

In November 1819 the Court of King's Bench determined that the original inquest was illegal, because it was held not by the coroner (Ferrand), but by his deputy, and the coroner and jury had not seen the body at the same time. Sidmouth kindly forgave Ferrand and the inquest lapsed; no verdict was ever made. Lees' representatives had many more witnesses who were never heard. The government had realised that with new repressive laws, no admission of guilt, and the passage of time, Peterloo was a storm that could be seen out.

The soldiers who did the slashing were officially supported. The Prince Regent, feeling under pressure from Lord Liverpool's government, issued an unambiguous notice of thanks 'for their prompt, decisive, and efficient measures for the preservation of the public peace'. As Archibald Prentice, a Manchester reformer commented: 'This haste to thank the delinquents greatly added to the exacerbation of the public mind.'

The Manchester and Salford Yeomanry cavalry were a new, angry organisation. Most volunteer militias had been formed in the 1790s and had some experience of successful action. The Manchester cavalry was a much more recent militia force, formed in 1817 in a blind panic after the Blanketeers' meeting at St Peters Field and the social tensions in Manchester and Salford. Joseph Nadin, the Deputy Constable, was the force behind their formation. Why did they end up killing people who were neither rioting nor aggressively protesting? The yeomanry were created as a result of fear and class war, and were always in opposition to the lower orders rather than complementary to them. Their fear seemed real enough, although the sources were unreliable; Nadin, the corrupt Deputy Constable, used spies whose jobs depended on them reporting conspiracy and hostile insurrection and this fear was transmitted to the cavalry. They sincerely believed that revolution was afoot on that day and were determined to nip it in the bud.

The Manchester and Salford Yeomanry were less effective and less dispassionate than any other similar force. The government relied on the local and volunteer principle that was unchanged since the time of the Spanish Armada. It needed wise magistrates who knew the people and wished to both control and support them, and relied on a voluntary militia force that, while ready to use violence to restore order, was still part of the community. Members of the yeomanry had to supply their own horses, and needed spare time to drill and practise, and this, by definition, put them into a different social group to most of the lower orders; but they were still expected to behave as if the rioters belonged to the same community. This was not the case in Manchester. They were brought up to hate the weavers and factory workers and the radicals who were deluding them.

As they knew the local people and the area and its history, most yeomanry cavalry in other parts of the country had done a reasonable job up to the Peterloo massacre. Previously, the gentry on horseback knew why people were rioting and how the action would pan out, so they did not over-react, remembering to use the flats of their sword and not exploit the advantages that their skilled horsemanship gave them.

Of the 101 members of the Manchester yeomanry present on that day whose occupation is known, thirteen were publicans who needed the magistrates to renew their licences. Sixteen were involved in the upper echelons of the Manchester cotton trade and were therefore on the side of capital rather than labour, and the rest were high-class workmen and shopkeepers who depended on the patronage of the rich. There was only one labourer and one servant who may well have felt uneasy in the presence of their social superiors.

When Joseph Nadin gave the order to clear the way to arrest Hunt, it was tragic that the Manchester and Salford Yeomanry cavalry received the order before the professional soldiers. It was the volunteers who did the slashing and trampling. They were drunk, they were amateur, they were incompetent, they were afraid, and they were malicious. They were the ones who decided that, once all the people on the hustings had been arrested, they would take the flags and banners and burn them. The regular soldiers were there on professional business, not for an ideological war. It was they who tried to calm down the proceedings; they trampled people in the course of their work, but did not slash and attack the crowd. The 15th Hussars were called into action when the magistrates told them the crowd were attacking the yeomanry, but they mostly used their military skills to hold back the amateur horsemen whose animals would have been more used to chasing foxes. For the yeomanry, the anger came out. It can be heard in some of the shouted insults to the crowd, as reported at the John Lees inquest:

> *Damn you, I'll reform you!*
> *You'll come again, will you?*

And perhaps the most telling of all:

> *I'll let you know that I am a soldier today!*

The crowd hated the yeomanry as much as the yeomanry hated the crowd:

Feather bed soldiers
King and Guts men

A witness heard a professional soldier of the 15th Hussars plead with the cavalry:

For shame sir, won't you give the people time to get away? Don't you see that they are down?

Joseph Nadin ordered the cavalry to arrest Henry Hunt at Peterloo, knowing that the militia would have to force their way through the crowds. Without this order, there would have been no massacre on that day.

Nadin's career had first prospered in London by the simple expedient of framing and arresting innocent people and taking the rewards offered by the government. He moved to Manchester in 1802, and by 1812 was in charge of fighting the Manchester radicals. In 1816 he was offering rewards of 200 guineas for information about anonymous letters being sent out by local radicals to members of the establishment. However, most of his illegal activity never reached the newspapers. In 1812 he attacked a meeting of radical weavers with blunderbusses and constables with fixed bayonets. The radicals were preparing a legal petition to the Prince Regent, in a local public house, the ironically named Prince Regent's Arms. When told of the constitutional purpose of the meeting, Nadin's carefully nuanced legal argument was, 'I do not believe you – that is only pretence.' Thirty-seven were taken away in chains to prison. They were locked up for seditious meeting and administering illegal oaths, on the evidence of the Deputy Constable alone. They were not to be allowed to be witnesses for each other and therefore seemed doomed, but they were able to produce a witness who had escaped the dragnet by hiding under the stairs and was able to say on oath that nothing illegal had happened. Nadin probably succeeded in the end however, as most of the weavers left the radical movement after the terrible prospect of a treason trial. To the radicals he was 'this coarse man' and the 'real ruler of Manchester'.[1]

In 1820 Nadin gave his own account of the events at Peterloo. The town had been in a state of agitation for most of 1819 – that at least was correct. He had been present at another meeting in Manchester in January where Hunt was speaking. An attempt was made then to arrest Hunt at that time; Nadin believed him to be dangerous, a man of unbounded influence on the deluded. On the morning of Peterloo, Nadin got close to the hustings. The reformers recognised him – 'It is Joseph…he has got great guts…he has more meat in his belly than we have.' Nadin saw this as a comment about his well-built frame, and as a veiled threat. Nadin too claimed that he came under an attack of stones, some coming from a house owned by Quakers.

He believed the ring of constables around the hustings were in danger from the radicals. He thought he heard the words 'knock them down', and he thought it might have been Hunt himself who said them. He had also heard that one of his constables had already been trodden on so, on the basis of this speculation, he decided that the civil power could not cope and asked his good friend William Hulton for a warrant to arrest Hunt and the rest, to be enacted by the military. He was at the hustings, truncheon in hand, and arrested Hunt and another radical, Johnson, who was dragged off by his legs. Nadin's reputation did not suffer at the time. Indeed, he gained some credit when it became clear that he had saved Hunt's life on the hustings rather than assaulting him. Hunt accepted this proposition, and it became clear that the yeomanry was out of control and Nadin prevented a physical attack, although it did not stop Hunt being dragged to prison.

Nadin died in 1848 but the passage of time did at least allow the media to be honest about him. His obituaries pointed out that he had accumulated a lot of money in Manchester, had bought the Queen's Theatre and owned a great number of public houses, which may strike us today as remarkably corrupt considering that he was in charge of issuing licences to sell alcohol in the city.

The man who so readily gave the order for the military to help the civil power (a undated and untimed three line scribble) was William Hulton, the 29-year-old chair of the magistrates, known behind his back as 'Mrs Hulton' due to his affectations, effeminacy, and love of fine clothes, despite his marriage and five children. He may have lost his nerve that day; he had already confided in the other magistrates that he was not keen on seeing violence and injury. He didn't want it to happen, but his main concern is that he didn't actually witness it himself. He was genuinely alarmed by seeing working men entering St Peter's Field in apparent military formation; it was clearly done to show that the crowd was a disciplined protest movement, but to Hulton and others it looked like a revolutionary army.

After the horrid events unfolded, Hulton and the magistrates received the retrospective support of Lord Sidmouth and Lord Liverpool the prime minister. Liverpool described Hulton's decision as 'substantially correct'– hardly a ringing endorsement. Sidmouth had reminded the Manchester magistrates that they should judge a meeting not by their impressions alone, but by facts and evidence based on what actually happened, rather than on their fears. Hulton clearly ignored this and deserves some of the responsibility for the day.

Although it was hard to identify individuals, one person stood out as a perpetrator of violence at Peterloo. He was Edward Meagher, one of only two trumpeters on the day, and he was riding a very recognisable piebald horse. Witnesses singled him out as a particularly violent soldier during the meeting, and his behaviour did not improve after the demonstration had dispersed. In October there was an attempt to bring a prosecution against him by a William Cheetham. Cheetham and three other people he did not know were moving away from the meeting in an otherwise empty street. Meagher was reported to have said 'damn you! disperse!'. Meagher temporarily gave them room to pass, but then lunged at Cheetham, threatened to behead him, but instead cut 7in off his hat and made a 3in cut on his neck.

Charles Pearson, a newspaper correspondent who was present at the trial, noted that these cases, and four others of malicious cutting, were rejected by the jury. Pearson said that the witnesses were believed, but the jury seemed to be working from a fixed principle – perhaps that the Riot Act had been read and therefore the consequences were acceptable in law. Pearson was angry; whether they were in 'tottering old age, unsuspecting youth, manly spirit, defenceless womanhood or unoffending infancy', there was no point in requesting justice from the law.

However, there were other forms of revenge. On one evening of the Lees inquest in October, Meagher went drinking in Deansgate. He was in a blind fury over the comments made about him; he seems to have exposed his weapons in the public house and dared anybody to comment on him. He was pushed out by shouts of 'shame!' and the altercation seemed to have spilled out on to the street. The *Inverness Courier* and other newspapers carried the story in detail; it was a national issue, not just a local one.

When Meagher started to go home, he was noticed by a group of men who called him out as 'one of the bloody butchers'. Meagher drew a pistol and threatened two men with it. When he got home he barricaded himself in his house. A mob appeared, stones were thrown, windows were broken, and Meagher started firing into the crowd with his pistols, injuring two people severely. He was eventually rescued by the military, who escorted him to a local barracks.

The inquiry was told that the two injured men – Jones and Robinson – were too ill to be moved from the infirmary, but a witness recorded that he had indeed been shot by Meagher, who 'had his coat off', and fired at least twice.

At the same time, Meagher was being name-checked at the John Lees inquest. Nathan Broadhurst claimed that Meagher had cut him, and he was not the only one. Broadhurst went on to say that a regular officer of the 15th Hussars called out for Meagher to stop, which he did, but only for the time that the officer was there.

Meanwhile, on 9 October, the case against Meagher continued. When he arrived at the dock, he was 'assailed with general and loud hisses'. It was announced by the prosecution that the two men who were shot were still not able to walk; but as they had many more witnesses to the identity of the assailant, and as Meagher was therefore facing a capital crime, the proceeding should continue. The magistrate, Mr Wright, instead granted another adjournment, as he wished all witnesses to be present. On the third examination, it was concluded that the windows had been broken, that the stones were thrown first and the shooting done afterwards when Meagher felt he was in danger. Mr Wright, one of the Manchester magistrates of the same class as those responsible for the policing on the day of Peterloo, dismissed the complaint:

> *Here a little hissing was heard among the crowd collected below the bar, but it was silenced by threats of commitment to prison.*[2]

Meagher then left the court 'in high spirits' and with good reason. He was another beneficiary of the establishment cover up at Peterloo.

Chapter 14

Peterloo: The Radical Women

On 28 July 1828, the *Manchester Courier* published a brief death notice:

> *On 13th inst, aged 34, Mrs Mary Fildes of Heaton Norris. This is the person who bore the flag on the hustings, at the meeting in St Peter's Field, on 16 August 1819.*

Mary Fildes was indeed one of the women around the hustings at Peterloo, but she did not die in 1828. She lived on until 1875. The newspaper had made an error; and this error shows how obscure the women reformers had become a mere decade after the terrible events at Peterloo, and how far the radical movement had receded after the economy recovered around 1820. This relative obscurity in 1828 does not reflect their lack of importance ten years earlier; although there were not many, they were new and active, and the male establishment was afraid of them and the example they represented to others.

Mary Fildes was not the first female radical. Alice Kitchen was president of Blackburn Female Reformers, who were constituted for the first time on 5 July 1819. At a large meeting called by the men of Blackburn, Kitchen made a speech supporting political liberty and parliamentary reform and promised that female reformers 'pledged themselves to instil in the minds of their children a hatred of civil and religious tyranny'. She went on to say: 'Our homes … which once bore ample testimony of industry and cleanliness are now alas, robbed of all their ornaments. Behold our innocent children! How appalling are their cries for bread!'

Her speech suggests a lot about the female reformers. None of the women involved actively supported votes for women. Whatever their private thoughts might have been, they saw their public role as supporting their husbands and providing a kind of 'radical childcare' for their family – it was very much the traditional role of the wife, but slightly modified by the economic and political crisis they now found themselves in.

Despite couching her radicalism within the traditional division of labour, Kitchen was known to the establishment as an enemy of the system. She was dangerous enough to be satirised. One example is a piece of heavy handed anti-radical propaganda of 1820 by George Buxton, based loosely on the story of Don Quixote in which every British reformer receives a satirical assault, Alice is the only female radical mentioned by name.[1] She is portrayed as the 'Lancasterian Thalestris' – the Queen of the Amazons in Greek philosophy – thus suggesting her as the pre-eminent female radical of the Regency period.

In what looks like a fear that women's rights would lead to role reversal, 'Dame Alice' beats up her husband. The husband, in his powerlessness, interprets this as an indication of love and a sacrifice for the greater cause. The 'happy husband considered it a trifle of matron-like attention in comparison to the blessings we might expect under the auspices of radical reform'. Later in the story, Dame Alice suggests that she has sex with the radical hero Don Dwarfino to produce children that, in an echo of Kitchen's Blackburn speech, might 'instil a hatred of religion, of nobility, of royalty, and of all rulers'. In the view of the establishment, radicalism produced promiscuity; her desire to bring down governments includes the government of men and the rules which respectable women follow. It was a completely inaccurate interpretation of Kitchen's ideas but an accurate representation of men's anger, fear, and lack of understanding.

George Cruikshank, often a friend of reform in his other caricatures, also took a hostile line in his satirical print '*The Belle-alliance, or the female reformers of Blackburn!!!*' The women on the hustings lift their dresses to show breeches underneath; some female reformers on the platform are large, armed, and aggressive while others are pretty and demure, and the object of the male crowd's condescension and lust. One woman winks towards the men below, saying, 'we are some of the right sort my lads!' The appreciative audience are poor and chaotic – suggesting the same poverty and chaos that would happen under a government ruled by women.

The *Nottingham Review* of July 1819 made a little joke about petticoat government, while their radical husbands would 'damn' the constitution, it was implied, the best the women could do was 'darn' it.

The *Bath Chronicle* of 22 June 1819 despaired of Alice:

Another Female Union Society has been formed. Some wretched creatures who disgrace their sex at Stockport, have followed the example of Mrs Alice Kitchen and her associates at Blackburn.

She disappears from the political records at this point. It would be hard to blame her.

Another early organisation, the Stockport Female Reform Society, was led by a Mrs Hallsworth. Her first name has not been discovered, partly due to the lack of coverage and partly because many newspapers made it a deliberate policy to simply use the title 'Mrs,' with the implication that they should be elsewhere as they were married. On the very morning of Peterloo, the *Morning Post* had some acid words for these ladies. Perhaps, instead of republican toasts, the ladies should take notice of what the women in the USA toasted on the previous Fourth of July: 'The Rights of Women – Innocence, Modesty and Prudence – may she be satisfied with those, without investigating any others.'

The article also names Mrs Hodgson and Mrs Hambleton as leaders and it is known that Hallsworth was in charge of one meeting where she suggested that the women meet separately. This had clearly rattled the newspapers, which saw female political independence as an aberration and a terrible precedent. Mrs Hallsworth went on to say that they were meeting separately because the women were new to the idea of political discussion and did not want to embarrass themselves; but it is still true that women were meeting and talking independently about radical politics for the first time since the civil war in the 1640s.

The newspaper also pointed out that a proclamation of Henry VIII in 1547 ordered that 'women should not meet together to babble and talk, and men should keep them in their houses.' On the basis that the establishment only make laws forbidding what people do, rather than do not do, this was a real political change, even if it did not last.

The Stockport women radicals were present at Peterloo. We do not know if Alice Kitchen was there too, although there was a contingent from Blackburn on that August afternoon. There were processions from the Stockport and Oldham Female Reform Unions, and this clear message from the women of Royton: 'Let us die like Men, and not be sold as slaves.' It is a great pity that the names of most of these brave women have been lost to history.

The chapter opened with Mary Fildes, another important female radical present at Peterloo. Mary and four others were members of the Manchester Female Reform Society (formed in July 1819, a month after the Female Reform Union in Blackburn). The women stayed in a barouche – a four-wheeled horse-drawn carriage – while Mary, as president, was on the hustings with her friends Henry Hunt and Richard Carlile, a radical reformer, a republican, and a deist who rejected the divinity of Christ and made Hunt look like a moderate. Carlile also had a history of working with women reformers such as Mary Fildes.

Mary had a drum and a large standard, with a figure of a woman holding a flag in her hand, surmounted by a cap of liberty – 'Joan of Arc could not be more interesting' thought Richard Carlile, slightly condescendingly. Mary was calm. We know this as Carlile, next to her, reported as such. He was impressed by her bravery, even if he did imply that it was particularly courageous considering that she was a woman. The women in the crowd were calm too – the radical Archibald Prentice noticed many young women marching in step from all parts of Manchester. When he asked them if they were apprehensive they all replied: 'What have we to be afraid of?' Many of the commentators, both sympathetic and hostile, thought that the large number of relaxed looking women and children in the crowd guaranteed a safe and orderly outcome and good behaviour by both sides. Henry Hunt began his address with the one word – 'Gentlemen!' and then stopped. He perhaps looked at all the women and children in the crown and started again with 'Fellow Countrymen'. Within minutes the forces of law and order were launching themselves towards the hustings to arrest everybody on it.

When Mary Fildes was truncheoned by Joseph Nadin's constables, she refused to let go of her flag. She tried to leap to the ground, but a protruding nail caught her dress, leaving her suspended in mid-air. One of the mounted yeomanry slashed at her and seized her flag but miraculously she avoided serious injury and escaped.

Mary Fildes continued in her struggle in the years after Peterloo. She went on to be an activist for women's contraception and supported the Chartists in the 1840s in the fight for the vote once more. In later life she became the owner and landlady of a public house in Chester; an occupation that gives some clue about strength of character.

Nancy Prestwick was another well known female reformer who was at the head of about 300 women at Peterloo, and like many of the female groups, she seemed to have been deliberately put near the hustings. Nancy was 64, the mother of a wool worker, Henry Tully, and both gave evidence at the later trial for conspiracy of Henry Hunt in 1820. She was a rather frail 64-year-old, and according to her own evidence, she went to Peterloo with her son and his wife, attracting a dozen or so female supporters on the way.

The organisers placed Nancy at the head of a group of about 300 women near the hustings and made her the leader – partly due to her age and partly due to the fact that she was well known, although it perhaps needs to be remembered that Hunt was also trying to establish beyond doubt the peaceful intentions of the meeting. She missed Hunt's opening remarks as she had gone to buy herself a gill of beer – a half pint – on this very hot August afternoon. She did see the yeomanry cavalry assaulting people when she returned. Hunt, at his later trial, asked Prestwick: 'did you and the 300 women attempt to take the cavalry prisoners?' in a sarcastic attempt to show the asymmetry of power between the two sides.

Other female radicals were taken prisoner. Elizabeth Gaunt was arrested after the hustings were broken up. Her own report, accepted by the prosecution, was that she was lifted up after feeling unwell, fainted during the yeomanry attack, and suffered some blows from a sabre. She was removed with the other people on the hustings (all except Carlile and Fildes) and spent twelve days at the Salford New Bailey gaol. The newspapers described her as a 'thin pale woman of about 45, wife of a shoemaker', but this rather understated her condition. The radical Thomas ('TJ') Wooler, a supporter, described her as 'almost fainting with weaknesses, after the wounds she had received and the subsequent solitary confinement'.[2] She was the only one of the prisoners who was allowed to sit on a chair during the proceedings. The use of solitary confinement suggested an indictment for treason; but three days later Gaunt was free. She was discharged through lack of evidence on 27 August. The conditions she endured can only be inferred; the *Leeds Mercury* of 8 November reported that one male prisoner, after also being released without charge, tore off his filthy vermin-ridden clothes as he left the New Bailey.

Gaunt was still a friend of the Carlile family in 1822 and still active in the radical movement. While Carlile was imprisoned in Dorchester gaol for libel, his wife Jane continued to edit their newspaper *The Republican*. When Jane was imprisoned, her sister continued the struggle. Jane was pregnant in prison and Gaunt sent her a letter, a present for the baby, and a message: 'I was one of those who witnessed the blood stained fields of Peterloo and suffered 11 days imprisonment in one of the borough mongers bastilles because I was exposed to the sabres of the ferocious yeomanry cavalry.'[3]

Gaunt went on to hope that the 'God of Nature' (a deist view of God) would protect her from the awful disease ('an inflammation of the bowels') that had, according to the authorities, been the cause of death of all the people slashed and trampled at Peterloo.

Like Mary Fildes, Gaunt's reputation was attacked by a ditty produced at the time of Peterloo, in which she is described as 'Hunt's Whore' in a loyalist song. She had been in Hunt's carriage but that is all; Henry Hunt however, had left his wife a decade earlier and openly toured the country with his mistress. In this case it was Gaunt's reputation that suffered, as the link between political protester and unladylike behaviour seems to have been a fixed idea for the political establishment.

Another woman, Sarah Hargreaves, was arrested but her treason charge was dropped after a few days too. Female reformers Ann Coats and Mary Waterworth ('a profligate Amazon' – *Manchester Courier*) were also questioned by the authorities. Louisa Hough, her daughter Sarah, and husband Thomas, pleaded not guilty to publishing treasonable material about the soldiers and the Prince Regent.

It wasn't just satirists who knew about the female reformers and felt the need to be horrible to them. On 6 November 1819 the *Morning Post* published a breathtakingly rude satire about Henry Hunt and the amount of money he was making by publishing appalling stories about the victims of Peterloo. It presented 'pen pictures' of people such as Weavers, Irish protesters – and two women in particular. One was 'Squintalina Goggle', the one-eyed woman (presumably Irish) who had spent the morning in the 'Cat and Bagpipes' with her friend Dermot O' Wriggler, left 'perfectly sober' and went to Peter's Field to see her sweetheart and accidently had most of her body cut off by the yeomanry cavalry.

Squintalina was not a reformer, and she was being attacked for being poor, feckless and stupid, but there was a pen portrait of someone who was presented as an even greater monstrosity of female nature:

Mrs Dorothea Tear-Sheet (a female Reformer), had both her legs blown [off] *by a bomb, which was fired on the 16th at an unarmed and defenceless people, at the very moment that that unarmed and defenceless people were singing 'God save the King,' and 'Rule Britannia.' Her husband being in the turnery line, and she working at her business, and having occasion to turn a lathe with her feet, great distress has fallen on the family in consequence of their inability to raise a sufficient sum of money (which cannot be enacted without a subscription) to purchase a couple of wooden legs, to enable her to resume her industrious labours for the benefit of her children.*

It is not clear which woman is being referred to, but her fictional name, Tear–Sheet, tells us a lot. Although she is married, she does not represent the traditional virtues of women of the time. Most people reading the newspaper would recognise the reference to a women of debatable virtue from Shakespeare's Henry IV. Dorothea works at a lathe – a masculine occupation – and of course her claim to have had her legs blown off is ridiculous, her real aim is to take the money of a gullible population in the form of a subscription.

In reality, Hargreaves and Gaunt were given £10 for their trouble, and the other injured people in the crowd mostly less than £3, and none of that was from public funds; but the newspaper was clearly resentful and frightened of independent women radicals. In real life, most of the female radicals mentioned, as well as others like Susannah Saxton and 'Mrs Wroe', worked within the context of their husband's greater involvement. Mrs Wroe's first name has been hard to locate, despite her suffering and sacrifices for reform, but a Jane Eckersley married a James Wroe in Manchester around the correct time in 1813.

Female reformers were also out in force in Wigan in early November 1819. As the speeches started, reported the hostile *Morning Chronicle*, the crowds began to hurry away, having seen a few men on horseback and feared a repeat of Peterloo. The paper reported that it was the women who had noticed that they were harmless civilians on horseback – they shouted 'Be firm – remain where you are.' Once order was restored, a resolution written by the Female Reformers of Wigan was read out – by a man.

The Manchester Female Reform Union continued into the 1820s, despite less favourable political conditions and a continuing attack by the political establishment. Their Committee sent greetings to Henry Hunt in 1822, who was in his second year in prison for his 'conspiracy' after the Peterloo Massacre – 'our tyrants have immured you in a dungeon, and we have enshrined you in our hearts.' It was signed by six members of the committee, headed by Mary Fildes.

Susannah Saxton, the secretary, was the second name on the list. She was a journalist and present at Peterloo. She wrote pamphlets supporting the vote for men and condemning the present state of distress, laying the fault firmly at the politicians. Many of her pamphlets have been lost, but there is a very famous one with the title: 'Dear Sisters of the Earth'. She described the abject poverty and then showed her radical credentials:

We are convinced that under the present conditions, the day is now at hand, when nothing will be found but luxury, idleness, dissipations and tyranny on the one hand, and abject poverty slavery, wretchedness, misery and death on the other.

She condemned war against France, the treatment of veterans and the selfish laws that had lowered taxes for the rich and raised food prices for the poor. She declared that the poor could not 'bear the ponderous weight of our chains any longer', and that they were left with no choice 'but to tear them asunder and dash them in the face of our remorseless oppressor'. However, just like Kitchen and Fildes, she makes it clear that the female radical reformer was meant to work with men to get them the vote, not to fight for it themselves.

Many of the other names on the list, Mary Black, Ann Thompson, Nancy Wheeler, Mary Jackson, and Mary Thornber are hard to investigate due to the lack of sources, but we do have evidence of their importance from those who hated and feared them. George Buxton's heavy-handed satire of 1820, '*The political Quixote of Don Blackibo Dwarfino and his squire Seditiono*', which had contained such unflattering remarks about Alice Kitchen, also made anonymous comments about the other female reformers. There were six from Manchester; all given the title Donna, they are 'Rapina', 'Sanguina', 'Maloventa', 'Deista', 'Atheista', and 'Desolata'. They go on to have a vicious row about what gift to offer to their 'Spa Fields Orator'. When Henry Hunt arrives at the inn, they row equally furiously about who is to have the honour of emptying his chamber pot. Then there were the usual innuendoes that radical reform and promiscuity were linked. One of the Donnas is found in Hunt's room, such a poor and wretched creature that she seems to have no clothes on. Hunt's ego is gratified, while women behave in a chaotic, dangerous and unladylike way. That was the establishment view of the female reformers.

It seems that a disproportionate percentage of the injured at Peterloo were women. Of the 654 recorded casualties, at least 168 were women, four of whom died on the day, or later as a result of their wounds. It has been estimated that only ten per cent of the crowd were female, so the number of casualties suggests that women were at significantly greater risk of injury than men. This may have been due to the central position of the women – which was precisely where the yeomanry cut a path through to the hustings; some have attributed malice to the soldiers, claiming they showed less mercy to the women, whose radical protest was all the greater for them being the 'frail sex'. Archibald Prentice believed that many of those injured avoided medical help as they feared that this news would filter back to their employees. One of the reasons for a public subscription was that the injured could not expect help from the Poor Law authorities if the basis of their claim was injuries sustained at Peterloo. Prentice reports that Margaret Booth received £3 after being crushed by the crowd and being unable to work nine weeks later.

Martha Heys was trampled by the cavalry on the day, and complications caused by that injury meant that she died in childbirth two months later. Although reports are hard to locate, it seems that she suffered from fits after being trampled and gave birth two months prematurely. Margaret Downes, age unknown, bled to death when she was sabred by the yeomanry cavalry. Sarah Jones, of Silk Street, Salford, was fatally injured by a police truncheon blow. She had seven children. The lack of information speaks volumes for the importance of poor women in this period.

There is some surviving evidence relating to Martha Partington of Eccles, however. Martha was crushed to death when she was flung into a cellar in Bridge Street, Manchester. The information that survives is due to an apparent attempt to destroy her reputation. An unsympathetic newspaper report explained how Martha had been seen on the day by a 'gentleman of the utmost respectability'.[4] She was described as one of two noted reformers (the other was Judith Kilner) who, 'liqueur in hand', shouted to the whole pub that she was 'hoping to God she might never go back alive if the reformers did not carry their point that day'. Later that day a failure in the iron palisades meant that she fell into the basement and was crushed. The gentleman seemed aghast that Martha was attending the 'rebellious' meeting, being political and making oaths; the subtext being that her death was a form of divine retribution. Newspapers all over the country reprinted the story uncritically for the next fortnight and were part of a pattern that tried to blame the victims for the tragic outcome of the day.

One month later, long enough for a lie to spread, the truth got its boots on. A Manchester resident who knew the people involved, wrote a letter giving another side of the argument:

> *I saw Judith Kilner on Sunday and she was with two other women who accompanied Mrs Partington from Eccles on the morning of the 16th, declare solemnly, that they never went into any public house on the way, nor did they ever hear any such expression anywhere from Mrs Partington as the writer imputes to her. These women further state that they did not accompany their husbands to the meeting. But as the husband of Mrs Partington means to bring an action against the Journal in which this paragraph first appeared, the whole truth will be fully elicited.[5]*

No further information can be found about Mr Partington's attempt to clear his wife – but then the whole weight of the establishment was against him; poor men protesting was bad enough, but the punishment for women daring to demand a voice was even more severe.

Chapter 15

The Freeborn Englishman?

S ome of the freedoms cherished by the British 200 years ago do not seem like freedoms today. The freedom to be left alone by a government, no matter what the consequences, was greatly cherished. Personal property needed protection, even if this meant a harsh penal code. Radical reformers and members of the establishment were united against the idea of a professional police force that both feared would be a government spy. Freedom sometimes even meant the right to riot if traditional responsibilities were not being honoured.

However, we would recognise protection from arbitrary arrest, equality before the law, and a degree of free speech as important freedoms. These all existed in some form in the Regency. Britain, except Ireland, compared well with continental Europe, and while the British held foreign regimes in contempt, they did not primarily compare British freedoms with foreign despotism. British freedoms at any time were to be compared with British freedoms in the past; that might be Saxon England, the Levellers of the seventeenth century, or the freedoms gained after the 'glorious revolution' of 1688, but people in the Regency period were conscious that they had something precious that could be taken from them by the government, and they were all – radical and reactionary – on their guard to protect it.

One established liberty was the right of '*habeas corpus*' (literally, 'you may have this body'). This originated at the time of the Magna Carta and was written down for the first time in 1305. It prevented false imprisonment by allowing anybody, including the prisoner, to question the legality of confinement in the courts. *Habeas corpus* was used in 1772 to prove that slavery was not allowed in Britain. James Somersett, a black slave brought back to the UK from Jamaica, was freed partly by the application of *habeas corpus* to his case. It was a cherished freedom, rightly, and still is. Lord Mansfield, the judge who gave Somersett his freedom, may or may not have said that 'the air of England has long been too pure for a slave, and every man is free who breathes it', but most people subscribed to the sentiment.

After the 1816 Spa Fields demonstrations, and the apparent attack on the Prince Regent in January 1817, the government suspended *habeas corpus* in a panic on 3 March 1817, in order to prevent the revolutionary conspiracies that they feared were being planned.

Opposition MP Henry Grey Benett was a vocal opponent of suspension. He and others argued that so-called political conspiracies were rioting due to terrible economic circumstances. Benett objected to all people being abused for the illegal acts of the tiny minority, and the power given to the government by the law. In a debate with Lord Castlereagh, he claimed that when *habeas corpus* was suspended in Ireland in 1798, there were criminal acts committed under the shelter of legal indemnity. As Castlereagh was in charge of Ireland at that time, this comment caused a 'violent altercation' in the Commons, and Benett felt the need to clarify that he was talking generally, not about the actions of individuals.

Lord Sidmouth proceeded to use his new power to initiate mass arrests of people about whom he was worried, but had little evidence against. Thomas Evans was an early and obvious victim of the suspension of *habeas corpus*, even before its ratification by parliament. He was an active member of the radical Spencean Philanthropists, became their new leader when Thomas Spence died in 1814, and was still a major theorist in 1817. His day job was as a braces maker, and it was at his work premises that he was arrested on 9 February 1817 – at the same time that the Spa Field leaders, Preston and Watson, were apprehended. Evans knew the law after more than two decades of falling foul of it. He insisted that the arrest was illegal and that an official wax seal be put on his bags of papers to prevent the authorities planting incriminating documents. He refused to leave his house until force had been applied, so a constable obligingly hit him on the head. Thomas Evans and his son, Thomas John, were then conveyed to Bow Street, where refreshments were served.

Tea and polite conversation soon turned to a possible charge of high treason, being placed in irons in solitary confinement at Coldbath Fields House of Correction and being denied pen, paper, and ink; his flute was also confiscated. After 10 April, he did not leave his prison cell until finally released, but was allowed two meetings a week with his wife Janet. He claimed not to have any dealing with Thistlewood and the other Spenceans, or any hand in the Spa Fields riots. Both statements were untrue, but the authorities were using some very draconian methods to contradict him.

Evans senior was suspected of publishing a leaflet demanding the division of aristocratic land into 'People's Farms' for the use of everyone, and Evans junior was accused of planning to speak at the Spa Field demonstration. One newspaper used the expression 'People's Farm!!!!!!!' to show their derision, but the authorities were clearly worried enough to use the suspension of *habeas corpus* to take the two men out of circulation. There was no charge against them, just imprisonment for suspicions.

Evans's case was taken up in parliament by Henry Grey Benett and Sir Francis Burdett. Burdett bemoaned the paranoia of the lawmakers with the Spenceans and declared that corrupt members of the establishment who lived on taxpayers' money were more of a problem – he called these people 'Expensions'. Bennett explained that Evans was afraid that he would spend unlimited time in prison with no charges ever being brought. This was no idle worry. Evans had spent three years behind bars in 1798 when *habeas corpus* had last been suspended; he had been moved from prison to prison and denied visits from his family. No charges were brought then either.

In June 1817, Watson, Preston, Hooper and Thistlewood were acquitted of high treason, but the man who was supposed to have worked with them was still in prison. On 17 June another debate in the Commons was fractious. Joseph Barham MP, who had approved the suspensions of *habeas corpus* during the war with Napoleon, was against it now. He wondered how it was justified to put a person in prison for a long time, when an English jury might find him innocent? Barham believed that much of the popular unrest was the work of government agents or the exaggeration of Home Office spies. Castlereagh, the chief government spokesman in the Commons because the others were members of the House of Lords, replied that Evans had coal, candles, a new bed, and a generous gaoler. With no sense of irony, Castlereagh confided that Evans was not allowed to walk in the garden because he would have been obliged to pass convicted felons to get there. Bennet pointed out that the problem was not just the conditions in the prison, but the very existence of the new law against *habeas corpus*. From Evans's later petition it did seem that his life improved after this debate in parliament.

Despite these improvements, Evans still languished in Horsemonger Gaol at the end of July. Thistlewood, Preston and Watson were prepared to swear on oath that Evans had nothing to do with the Spa Fields Riots. This made no difference. Evans was still regularly interviewed by the Privy Council like an Elizabethan Jesuit and asked whether he had had any dealings with Thistlewood, which now seemed to be Sidmouth's new definition of treason.

In early 1818 Evans was still in prison. He was offered his freedom on 1 February on the understanding that he paid £100 bail and held himself ready to answer any further questions. He refused, demanding either to be tried, or unconditionally released. He may have guessed – correctly – that *habeas corpus* was about to be reintroduced and he would have to be released soon in any case.

On 20 February, Thomas Evans and his son (who he had not seen since his imprisonment) were indeed unconditionally released, without charge, apology or compensation. Evans went home and transformed his now struggling business into a 'Patriotic Coffee House', perhaps in the spirit of sarcasm. It was raided by the constables, perhaps in the spirit of retribution. Evans then disappears off the radar of radical politics. However, it did rather prove that arbitrary power did the trick. He was not on the scene in 1820 during the Cato Street Conspiracy and little is known about him after that date.

Joseph Mitchell, radical printer and publisher, was another victim of the suspension of *habeas corpus*. His first mistake was to make an enemy of Joseph Nadin, deputy constable of Manchester. In his petition to parliament, Liverpool-born Mitchell said he had been in Manchester on business when his lodging house was raided in the middle of the night by Nadin and two constables. His possessions were opened illegally and Nadin chased him when he fled to the house of a friend, forcibly gaining entry. Nadin followed him to Liverpool, Yorkshire, London, and then Liverpool again as Mitchell tried to escape British justice by fleeing to the USA with his family. He was told by Nadin that he was implicated in a conspiracy to forcibly rescue the Blanketeers, and then make Manchester a 'Second Moscow' by burning it down in a manner similar to Napoleon's attack on Russia in 1812. He spent nine months in prison without being charged on a conspiracy that was mostly the creation of government spies and agents provocateur.

William Ogden, another victim of the suspension of *habeas corpus* was 74 years old and had been heavily chained in Horsemonger Lane prison. A manacle of 30lbs had been put on his arm, creating fifteen hours of absolute agony. He was in prison for nine months without charge and, when released, was unable to work and support his seventeen children (he had married twice). Although he was not charged, he agreed that he was a supporter of parliamentary reform and implied that he was in prison because a corrupt constable wanted a reward. He was also worried that the Commons would pass an Act of Indemnity and that all mistreatments under the suspension of *habeas corpus* would go unpunished; they did indeed go on to do this.

Habeas corpus was reinstated in 1818 through a 'sunset clause' which limited the amount of time that such a political restriction could remain. Sidmouth's arguments in favour of the suspension was its temporary nature, the fact that it was in response to a political crisis, and that it had been suspended before and then re-instated after the emergency had passed. However, this does not hide the fact that freedom from arbitrary arrest was a freedom that had been denied – again. Speaking in the 1790s, when *habeas corpus* was under attack, Mary Wollstonecraft, the campaigner for women's rights, suggested that freedom of property was the only one that really mattered to the establishment. However, Britain was not despotism, and there were enough people who valued *habeas corpus* to make a long term suspension politically impossible. Britain was not equal or democratic, but it was, to a reasonable extent, 'free'.

The British had always had some freedom of speech; the envy of the continent, but the problem was (and possibly still is), how much was desirable? In the period after Peterloo, freedom of expression and assembly were severely curtailed. The monster meetings, lower-class discontent, and stories of military-type drillings really worried the government. Some believed that an armed insurrection was on the way, and some who did not believe it thought it was politically useful to say so. Parliament did not meet for three months after Peterloo and when they did, it was to introduce the repressive Six Acts, rather than institute an enquiry into the events at Manchester in August. In December 1819, Castlereagh told the Commons: 'I rise for the purpose of proposing to the House of Commons measures of severe coercion.'

One of the six new repressive laws – the Seditious Meetings Prevention Act – required official permission in order to have any meeting of more than fifty people if the topic was Church or state. Additional people could not attend such meetings unless they were local residents. At first this applied to any meeting, but parliamentary opposition changed this to outdoor meetings only; it was the likes of Peterloo that the government was trying to stop. Another part of the Six Acts was the Criminal Libel Act, which toughened the existing laws against 'subversive' material. After 1819, the state reserved the power to transport libellers to Botany Bay for fourteen years – in effect, silencing them into a Siberian-like political exile.

It was argued by the opponents of these new laws that the jury system was already strong enough to protect against blasphemy and sedition. Lots of individuals were tried for both during the darkness years; the reason for so much legal activity was that in Britain there was no pre-publication censorship, which is the way repressive regimes work. In Britain, you got into trouble *after* publication.

There had been victories as well as defeats. The right to parody was established in England by the victory of William Hone in his three-day trial for blasphemy and sedition in December 1817. He produced comic versions of the Catechisms, Litany and Creed of the Church of England to make pointed comments about contemporary life and politics, including some newly framed commandments:

> *Thou shalt have no other Patron but me*
> *Thou shalt not support any measure but mine*
> *Honour the Regent*
> *Thou shalt not call starving to death murder*
> *Thou shalt not call Royal gallivanting adultery*
> *Thou shalt not say that to rob the Public is to steal*
> *Thou shalt bear false witness against the people*

His argument was that such parodies had a long history. Hone seemed to have brought most of them into court with him. He agreed that he was making comment about the present state of things but he was not disrespecting the original sacred texts and practices. It was a victory for free speech and religious parodies were never really tested in the British courts again. The Lord Chief Justice, Lord Ellenborough, who presided over many famous trials in the Regency period, was humiliated by Hone and the decision of the jury, who ignored the judge's strong direction to find Hone guilty. Ellenborough was ill at the time of the trial, but the trial may well have hastened his death a year later.

In 1819, sedition and blasphemy trials increased again. Robert Wedderburn, 'a person of colour', was prosecuted – unsuccessfully on the first attempt in September 1819 – for blasphemy and sedition at his chapel in Hopkins Street, Soho. He was linked to the Spencean Philanthropists but had – inevitably – fallen out with them. He was now drawing enthusiastic crowds of hundreds to his rented chapel, each paying one shilling a month each to hear his views on slavery and the present form of government. He was vehemently and violently against both. He first came to prominence in June 1819, when he complained to the local magistrate that the brewery workers behind his chapel were disturbing his sermons. He was told in no uncertain terms that his seditious and blasphemous uttering deserved to be drowned out and he needed to quit while he was ahead.

Despite the brewers' labourers making a racket, somebody, possibly a spy, heard Wedderburn say in August 1819 'that potentates and rulers who did not do their duty towards their subjects should be destroyed'. On the morning of Peterloo, 16 August, Wedderburn was arrested and charged with sedition and blasphemy. In September, a grand jury came to the conclusion of 'No True Bill' – that there was no reason to believe that a crime had been committed. Juries often protected those who were prosecuted for sedition or blasphemy. The state conducted these trials with absolutely no certainty that they would get their own way, although they usually did.

Wedderburn stood out in 1819. He was of mixed heritage, with a slave mother and a slave owning father from Jamaica; in the ugly language of the day, he was a 'mulatto' (mule). His views explain why the government linked sedition and blasphemy together; an attack on established theology would undermine the justification for monarchical government. Lord Sidmouth also correctly believed that Wedderburn's chapel was the centre of the most violent insurrectionary group in the country. It was a magnet for illegal activity, seditious speeches and the possible collection of pikes and weapons for a planned insurrection. The landlord of the chapel was a known associate of Arthur Thistlewood. Both government and rebels believed, correctly, that the group was deliberately trying to exploit the anger over Peterloo to incite insurrection.

Wedderburn did not care what he said. He attended the monster Finsbury Park reform meeting in October 1819 and was severely reprimanded by the other radicals present for making a speech telling the crowd to arm themselves for an imminent battle with the authorities, and they could use iron rails if they ran short of pikes.

The government tried to silence Wedderburn again in May 1820, this time on a charge of blasphemy. The first witness was the government spy William Plush. Plush paid his shilling in October 1819 and noted what he saw and heard. Wedderburn did not disappoint. He started his sermon controversially: 'While Christianity had certainly been introduced in Britain, it had never yet been carried out.' He went on to claim that Moses was a liar; Moses's claim to see God was directly contradicted by Jesus. Paul had twisted Christianity to suit the establishment. Jesus was a reformer, even a revolutionary.

Plush saw about 200 in the audience who were the very lowest in society. He also noted strong support for Richard Carlile in the room. Carlile was a religious free thinker who had a Fleet Street shop – more like a kiosk in size – called the 'Temple of Reason', (the Tory paper the *Leeds Intelligencer* had suggested that he had forgotten the 'T' on the beginning of the last word). According to the trial report, Plush – who claimed to be a parish constable – was backed up by another witness:

> *The account which this witness gave of the defendant's speech harmonised remarkably with the report of the former witness. Indeed it was*

given almost in the same words even in the arrangement of the most
trifling expletives; there was a most striking coincidence.

Wedderburn implied that there had been collusion. He declined the chance
to cross-examine the witness – 'they have learnt their catechism too well'.
His defence was that blasphemy was a form of slander, and there could be no
defaming of God, who was all powerful and all knowing, but beyond man's
capabilities to understand Him; therefore no human could judge blasphemy.
He believed that he was essentially being accused of opposing the state religion. Wedderburn claimed that the greatest libel on Christianity was the
belief that it needed laws and threats to protect it, and that was what the
government was doing, not him.

The jury found him guilty but asked for clemency because of a lack
of parental care. In Wedderburn's case, this was because his father had
sold his mother back into slavery after his birth. Wedderburn was still to
spend two years in Dorchester gaol at the same time as Henry Hunt, who
had tried different methods to oppose the establishment but ended up
with the same result, although Hunt was able to buy much better prison
conditions.

There was a real attempt in 1819 to restrict freedom of speech by muz-
zling newspapers. Closing them down was out of the question, but restricting
circulation was possible by forcing price rises and increasing accountability.
Newspapers had never been cheap. They could be printed for about 2d but
cost nearer 6d; a 4d tax was added in 1815 in a deliberate attempt to put them
beyond the reach of the poor. The move may have reduced sales but it had
less effect on readership. Radical organisations would have reading groups
where the cost of newspapers could be pooled by subscription; Luddites and
other workers' groups would often publicly read out the news to their non
reading, poorer members.

William Cobbett and his journalism was the main target of the 1819
Newspaper and Stamp Duties Act. In 1816, he had produced a new version
of his *Political Register* with all recent news taken out, and in a pamphlet
rather than newspaper format. This could evade the newspaper tax; his enemies called it 'Tuppenny Trash' but it sold 40,000 copies a week when the
Times or a similar establishment newspaper like the *Morning Post* would sell
4,000 a day. John Hunt defended Cobbett in his *Political Examiner* (which
cost an eye-watering 10d). Why would the starving weavers of Manchester
buy it? Why would they give their hard earned tuppences? It was because
they believed him!

In 1819 the tax was extended to cover those publications which had previously escaped duty by publishing only opinions. Cobbett's cover price
went up, and his influence diminished, but this was also partly due to the
return of slightly better times in the 1820s. As Cobbett himself said: 'I defy
you to agitate a man with a full stomach.'

Booksellers and newspaper sellers were often the subject of government
anger, and many radicals were also printers and publishers. Crowds would
gather around the windows of print sellers to see the latest disrespectful
image of the Prince Regent or politicians. At least these people could be
traced and punished; the iterant newspaper seller was feared more.

Joseph Swann of Macclesfield was a hatter who had encountered hard
times in 1819 and given up his artisan profession to start hawking newspapers and periodicals around the North of England. In October 1819 he was
accused of publishing (in his case this meant merely selling) the works of
Richard Carlile and other political reformers. He was also accused of attending a reform meeting at Macclesfield in July 1819 where he had tried to
'excite in the minds of the King's liege subjects a spirit of discontent, dis-
satisfaction and sedition'. He was given bail, but spent eight weeks in prison
without charge. He was re-arrested in December 1819, and separated from
his pregnant wife.

Owning a poem that contained the following was one of the charges
against him:

> *Off with your fetters; spurn the slavish yoke*
> *Now, now or never, can your chain be broke*
> *Swift then rise and give the fatal stroke*

It was the last line that put Swann in prison. At his trial in January 1820,
Swann, 'a low, vulgar looking fellow' (*Staffordshire Advertiser*), 'this danger-
ous individual' (*Chester Courant*), showed no deference at all to the court.
When sentenced, he was defiant:

> *Swann with a vast deal of apparent sang froid, held up his Radical*
> *emblem – a white hat bound with crepe and exclaimed 'Han ye done?*
> *Is that all? Why I thowt ye'd a got a bit of hemp for me and hung me!'*

He received three punishments for seditious conspiracy, seditious writing
and blasphemy which were ordered to run concurrently at a staggering
four and half years. This sentence in Chester gaol was double the tariffs

received by William Cobbett (two years for libel in 1810), Henry Hunt (two and half years in Ilchester for sedition after Peterloo in 1820) or Richard Carlile (three years in Dorchester in 1819 for seditious libel). His wife and four children survived on 9s a week, and a one off payment of £10 from Richard Carlile, whose October 1819 edition, denying the divinity of Christ was being hawked by Swann when he was arrested.

Swann was to receive an unbelievably severe sentence for his crime of selling pamphlets – Cobbett suggested that it was two publications in total – and attending a meeting, at which he claimed never to have spoken. Incarcerated in Chester prison, he also suggested that he was a victim of an *agent provocateur* called Buckley. Swann had not even spoken at the 'treasonable' Macclesfield meeting, but Buckley, who had organised the gathering, was not arrested and had been seen regularly on the streets afterwards. Swann wondered why and left it to others to provide the answer. He was clearly a stubborn and sarcastic individual; it is equally clear why he was given a salutary lesson.

Swann also claimed the magistrates were ashamed of what had been done to him and tried to get the authorities to remit the rest of the sentence. The prisoner was reluctant to ask for clemency because he wanted to show 'the severity with which an individual might be treated under a free government which was said to be the envy of surrounding nations and the admiration of the world'.

In 1831, Swann was still active selling unlicensed radical newspapers. This time he received three months' incarceration in the Knutsford House of Correction and was dragged out of the court by force, declaring that he would not stop hawking these newspapers, and his next port of call would be the judge's house.[1]

Although Swann was clearly cantankerous and fanatical, permitting a political principle to allow his wife and four children to languish in poverty, Swann and thousands like him deserve to be remembered as a friend of liberty as much as any radical journalist or reforming member of parliament. Over 120 ordinary people suffered prison sentences for selling Carlile's *Republican* alone, some of whom were Swann's father, wife and son. The British were clearly freer than most nations; but it was a struggle to keep those freedoms during the darkness years of the Regency.

Chapter 16

The Punishment Didn't Fit The Crime

The criminal justice system, like the Poor Law, was not fit for purpose by the Regency period. Outside of London there was no adequate system for fighting crime, and nowhere in Britain was crime actively prevented. There was a crime wave in Britain after Waterloo, with 7,818 indictable offences in 1816 and 14,254 a mere three years later.[1] Most people got away with their crimes, and to compensate for the unlikelihood of apprehension, punishments for those caught were exceptionally severe.

Not only were the punishments draconian, the number of new capital crimes in the eighteenth century meant that there was little differentiation between crimes of extreme violence and minor property crime. Severe punishments meant that the law was brought into disrepute, to the extent that juries would not reach true judgements in order to spare victims the noose. Many of those committed to hang were pardoned, giving significant power to the Crown to use or withhold a royal pardon. In 1817, the total number of executions was 115, although 1,300 received the death sentence.[2] It was a random and capricious system.

The crime wave reached a peak because economic depression forced more people into crime – sometimes of a pathetic kind. In January 1816, Ann Jones, 59, came to London to claim some prize money payable to her husband who had been killed in the war. With, she claimed, only one penny in her pocket, she entered the house of John Croker, and stole two sheets and a coat, value £5. Even Catherine Rook, the servant, had some concern for her: 'I then asked her what possessed her… she said she was a poor deranged woman, and begged I would pardon her.'

In the same year, Harriet Skelton, 33, was found guilty of passing false banknotes in Clerkenwell. She tried to get the note changed into silver coin and real notes. A witness reported:

I am a confectioner, and live at No. 198, Piccadilly. On the 6th of January, which was Twelfth Day, about seven o'clock in the evening, the prisoner came to my shop, bought a 10s. 6d. twelfth-cake, and offered

*me a 5l. note. I asked her what address I was to put on it? She gave me
the name of 'Moore, No. 29, Bury-street, St. James's.'*

Banknotes were usually endorsed with the name and address of the person
passing it on; £5 was more than a year's pay for a domestic servant. Mr
Ragless the shopkeeper knew that address and knew that Harriet was lying.

In November of the same year, Francis Losch murdered his wife after an
argument in the street. He first called her a drunk. A witness reported what
happened next:

*'If I am drunk, it is by prostituting myself for an idle fellow like you' –
upon which he came forward with great violence, and forced something
to her side – I did not see what was in his hand. She staggered a little on
her left side, fell on her back, and called to me to take the knife out of
her two or three times, but I never moved, I was so alarmed. She pulled
her clothes up – I saw her bowels gush out. The prisoner never ran away,
but said, 'Here I am, to be taken as a prisoner, if you choose to take me.'*

Losch was a hard-headed, German born soldier who had forced his wife into
prostitution and killed her with four wounds to the stomach with a six inch
knife when she tried to escape him.

On the other hand, Skelton was made an orphan when she was 3 years
old, and in 1810 she married John Skelton, a vicious alcoholic who earned a
living as a painter. She persevered in an abusive relationship for eight years
until he abandoned her in 1818. She lodged with her brother, Mr Goodluck,
in Holborn, but found that he was also a criminal – he passed forged notes.
After six months of successfully resisting her brother's demands to join his
criminal activity, Harriet eventually took part out of loyalty to her brother
and in order to pay his £60 debt. Or that was her story afterwards. Her
defence at the Old Bailey trial was slightly different:

*I never had any notes but what came from my husband or brother. When
they gave them to me... I asked them what names and addresses were to
be put on them? I thought the names were those of the persons they took
them off. If I had known them to have been forged, I would not have
passed them.*

Some people have suggested that the first sentence implies some kind of link
between husband and brother that contradicted her story about running away

from one to the other. It is more possible that both men had the same criminal methods. Her claim of ignorance about countersigning the banknote was a poor defence; it did not prove her innocence, as both criminals and non-criminals understood the system well.

She had also refused a plea bargain with the Bank of England, which would have saved her life and transported her to Australia instead. She looked and behaved like an innocent 'woman of genteel address and deportment', said one newspaper, and she attracted the attention of Elizabeth Fry and others who were making long overdue moves to improve the prison system.

Despite the two cases being completely different, Losch and Skelton were both hanged at Newgate Prison. It seems remarkable today that they received the same punishment, with the important difference that Losch was handed over to the St Bartholomew's Hospital for dissection.

How well you went to your death mattered. Francis Losch 'went hard' into eternity. His only regret was that he was being hanged and he refused to admit to his real motives, claiming his wife's actions had made him jealous. He did not go meekly to the scaffold, requiring wine to quieten him and two people to forcibly point him in the right direction. There was insufficient penitence and resignation and no acceptance of the justice of his punishment.

Harriet Skelton died quite well, considering the circumstances. She had the support of the establishment, apart from Home Secretary Lord Sidmouth, the one person who really mattered. She was visited by the Duke of Gloucester, who listened to her story, shook her hand and 'instantly repaired to the seat of royalty itself' to try to respite her sentence. Harriet had also received religious instruction from Elizabeth Fry at Newgate, and her case was brought up at the House of Commons. However, the extensive and aggravated nature of the offence meant that no pardon was possible; she seems to have been passing forged notes in an organised way for five weeks.

Now her hopes were crushed. Her brother, Burnsley Goodluck, was not charged with a capital crime and was merely sent to the House of Correction. On the Thursday before her execution, she had a hysterical nervous attack and the attempt at administering the sacraments was aborted. Her criminal partner, James Ward, also fainted. The Reverend Horace Cotton of Newgate performed his condemned sermon to all prisoners awaiting death, with an open coffin the focus of the service. Harriet's negative reaction was understandable.

By the evening they were composed enough to spend the evening in religious consolation. On the morning of the execution she showed the utmost fortitude and resignation until she saw the scaffold and then had to be supported by four people towards the drop. This temporary failure to compose herself was seen as a manifestation of her truly penitent nature, rather than boastfulness and cowardice. She regained her composure at the last moment, and that was what usually mattered to commentators at executions. Her last words, according to her supporters were: 'God be merciful to me, a sinner.' Elizabeth Fry used the story of Harriet Skelton as instructional literature for young ladies; so her death was not in vain perhaps.

Ann Jones, the pathetic burglar, was reprieved, despite committing a capital crime like Losch and Skelton. There were over 200 capital crimes – too many for the system to dispense justice efficiently. Some of the odder ones are well known, such as impersonating a Chelsea pensioner or being in the company of gypsies for three months, but they were never used as a basis for execution. The bloody code was severe because it was the only way the establishment could protect property and keep order. It was a universal warning rather than an attempt to make the punishment fit the crime. In the words of the seventeenth-century aristocrat George Saville: 'Men are not hang'd for stealing Horses, but that Horses may not be stolen.'

Ann Jones would have been transported for seven years, with the death penalty if she dared to return before this time. Around 100 people were executed in Britain each year; the system could not bear many more. In the year of Jones's reprieve, thirteen people were executed for murder, but fourteen were hanged for stealing sheep. Crimes that damaged the confidence in the monetary system were punished mercilessly. Twenty-three of the ninety-six people executed in 1818 were guilty of either forgery of bank notes or passing of counterfeit coin.[3] Paper bank notes were easy to copy and the silver coinage was in such a terrible state that forgeries did not have to be very good. It was just too tempting.

While the elite knew that the severe system was no substitute for proper policing and detective work, they still did not want a paid police force. It was seen as a foreign idea, a tool of despots that would threaten Englishmen's liberty, especially in the hands of a government that had passed laws restricting *habeas corpus* and employed spies to provoke the lower orders into breaking the law. It was one notion that all classes in society were agreed on, if not always for the same reason.

There was a very approximate link between the crime and the punishment. Fines were used for minor crimes. Three people were fined 3s 4d in Newark in 1819 for drinking alcohol instead of attending divine service. Street vendors without licences selling luxuries like silk and jewellery could expect a fine of less than £1. A group of gentlemen were fined 22s for leaving their team of horses in the street while they went to the public house.

Violence against the person could also attract a fine of around £1, as John Hall found out when he assaulted Richard Towers and was convicted at Lincoln City Sessions in October 1818. At the same sessions, William Burley was fined £5 for assaulting a constable, and John Watkinson was fined £10 for assaulting the excise officer John Younghusband. Watkinson was caught selling French silk handkerchiefs and offered only minor resistance; he was warned that, had he been guilty of an aggravated assault that prevented the government official from doing his work, the punishment would have been three years hard labour in a house of correction.

'Poor on poor' serious violence was rewarded with a maximum six months' imprisonment. An Edinburgh man who lived with a woman who kept a brothel in Cowgate, Edinburgh, was given thirty days for striking a man and making him bleed because he had entered his house of ill repute while drunk.

There were several ways of being sentenced to seven years transportation to Australia. As with Ann Jones, it was often a reduced punishment after being respited for a capital offence. At the other end of the spectrum were cases like that of Samuel Robinson, who stole two books from a schoolmaster in Castle Douglas, Dumfries, and was transported. There are lots of examples of how easy it was to steal from a Georgian shop, when most goods were within reach. Mary McWilliams of Annan stole cotton from the linen shop of Mr Thomas Hewitt. She had form and Mr Hewitt was clearly fed up of Mary coming into his shop and waiting for his back to be turned. Transportation was more likely if the court saw the same face several times. Stealing from houses would attract transportation, as long as the house had not been broken into. In 1819 James Robinson stole a smock coat and a pair of breeches from James Barker of Nocton, Lincolnshire a fellow servant in the house of Robert Wright, and was transported.

Bigamy was regarded as a serious crime, as Mr Newcomen Edgeworth discovered in 1812 when he married Mrs Townend while his wife Elizabeth was still alive. He was sentenced to live with neither of them as he was sent to Botany Bay. Organising a trade union by administrating illegal oaths would attract a similar sentence, as Thomas Holden of Bolton found out in 1812. He was perplexed by the punishment – he regarded it as what today may be called a 'victimless' crime.

Sometimes punishments were exemplary – a warning to others even when the crime itself was not particularly heinous. Hannah Smith, a 54-year-old mother of eight seemed to have been singled out for stealing butter and a 'great deal' of potatoes. She forced Charles Walker of Ardwick, Manchester to sell the butter at 1s per lb, a discount of 3d on the market price. She made it clear that the alternative was to have it all taken away from him. Later she seemed to be involved in stealing potatoes, single-handedly intercepting a cart belonging to James Rawcliffe at Bank Top, Manchester and with a mob encouraging her, distributed the food.

Her crime was political. She was in the company of Luddites who burned down Westhoughton Mill near Bolton. The stealing and under-pricing was done under the pressure of a mob, which had gone on to destroy the machines and the building that housed them. She was executed for highway robbery alongside four men who attacked the mill. The *Morning Post* was pleased to announce that all of them, after initially showing no contrition and some indifference to their fate, finally became 'broken and contrite spirits [who] cried out to Heaven's throne to have mercy on them'.

It would be untrue to say that society did not care about the treatment of children. In 1810, Mary Godby, a slum dweller of Angel Street, Covent Garden, was found guilty of beating her child and leaving her in a locked room until 9pm when she went out to sell vegetables bought from Covent Garden. Local people had tried to feed the child through a window, but the poor mite had its hands tied behind its back. On other occasions the child had had its toes stamped on; its hair pulled out and had been placed under cold running water in the middle of winter. Mary had to be rescued from the London mob and in court she was called an 'unnatural' parent. However, local people had been witnessing these cruelties for three years and had done nothing themselves. The father, who was not implicated in the cruelty, told people to mind their own business, and they did.

The punishment for Mary Godby is not known but it's likely it would have been a prison sentence. This seems shocking when minor property crimes carried the death penalty. Anne Wright of Yorkshire received a twelve-month sentence for mistreating her 9-year-old daughter. In a coarse age, this crime was still regarded as being one of singular cruelty. Her neighbour, Stephen Lockington, could hear the child being beaten every day through the thin walls of their adjoining houses. She was severely beaten by her step-father for asking for a piece of cake, imprisoned in one room for five weeks, and died with a body full of bruises, cuts to the limbs, and in an emaciated state. Wright was found guilty of child cruelty and sentenced to fifty weeks in prison followed by two weeks of solitary confinement. A further charge of murder was added after this indictment but it was impossible to prove legally that this mistreatment was the actual cause of Ann's death.

To put this crime into context, there were other crimes at the same sessions that attracted one year's imprisonment: stealing a £1 note from the Post Office; highway robbery (both capital crimes, in theory), and bigamy. Attracting a death sentence were the crimes of horse stealing, sheep stealing, burglary, forgery of banknotes and rape.

In the case of the rape of Harriet Halliday, the judge, Baron Wood, indicated that all of these accused, apart from the rapist William Hodgson, could hope for a reprieve. Hodgson was told in no uncertain terms to prepare for a 'future state'. The court officials were aghast at these comments. It was expected that Hodgson would be respited and the legal establishment was very much perturbed by how the judge had behaved. It turned out to be a historic turning point in women's legal rights in cases of sexual assault. Halliday's evidence was strong, witnesses had seen her dragged into a stable by Hodgson, a local surgeon had heard her screams, rescued her, and financed the prosecution against Hodgson. Harriet was a servant, and would not have the £10 or so to pay for a trial – she was probably earning around £4 a year and the state provided no funds to prosecute. This was another weakness of the system.

In the face of such strong evidence, Hodgson's defence became aggressive. They called Halliday's former employer and were about to ask why she had discharged Harriet after a mere two weeks. They were then stopped by the judge, who ruled that this question was not relevant to the case. The defence then asked her whether she had had any 'connection' with any boys in the past. Judge Baron Wood then made a novel and important ruling: 'witness was not bound to answer these questions as they tend to criminate and disgrace herself and there was not any exception to the rule in the case of rape'.

The prisoner's counsel called a witness to prove that the girl had been caught in bed a year before this charge with a young man. This second piece of evidence was ruled inadmissible and Harriet's evidence stood. The rule was extended in 1817 to cover the crime of attempted rape and although it did not ban general questions about the woman's lifestyle, it did rule inadmissible specific ones, such as were asked in this case.

Sodomy was a capital crime in the Regency, usually reported in the newspapers as 'unnatural' or 'detestable'. It was rare to read about examples; it was only discovered if there was a complaint by one of the participants or, as in the special example of 1816, the crew of a whole ship was suspected.

Blackwood's Law Commentary said that sodomy was such a terrible crime, and so easy to fabricate, that only the very strongest proofs would be accepted.

John Eglerton was accused of sodomy with his groom in 1816, on the evidence of the young man himself. The judge condemned John's actions as 'a crime subversive of every idea of virtue and manliness', but his treatment was similar to others accused of capital crimes. However, the similarity ended when most of the people indicted with him were eventually pardoned. The draconian punishments of the Regency's bloody code were a pantomime of condemning people to death and then pardoning them. This did not apply to John. According to the *Morning Post* (15 July 1816)

> *The jury retired for ten minutes, and returned with a verdict of Guilty. – Death. When the Prisoner heard the verdict pronounced against him, he fell into tears, and begged the Judge to recommend him to mercy on account of his family.*

He was executed at Newgate on 23 September 1816, and the same conventions were used as with other prisoners. He was reported to have died with 'perfect resignation' (*Cambridge Chronicle*) and was fully penitent.

In the same year, the Reverend William Woodcock was sentenced to four years in the House of Correction. His young partner, aged 'around 16' according to the judicial proceeding, was sentenced to three years as a willing participant.

The crime of sodomy was never reported in detail. However, a particular event in 1816 allows more details to be gathered. The whole crew of the *Africaine* was suspected of being a centre of 'unnatural crime'. The naval authorities had difficulty in finding those who were guilty. By December 1815, their on-ship investigations had produced twenty-three suspects. This was far too many to be hanging from the yardarm in Portsmouth, so the numbers needed to be reduced.

It was difficult to find a reliable witness, who wasn't also implicated, to prove that a crime had taken place. Initial suspicion fell on four men: John Westerman, Joseph Tall, Ralph Serraco and Raphaelo Troyac. The last two men were Italian. Many in Britain called sodomy 'le vice italien' – it was believed to have originated from ancient Lombardy. The newspapers certainly thought that it was significant that half of the accused were foreigners. Four men, including the two Italians, were hanged; other sailors were found guilty of unclean acts, and received two years' solitary confinement in the Marshalsea prison.

As part of the random nature of punishments for crimes in the Regency period, many attracted an hour in the pillory; a spectacle that usually took place at lunchtime to encourage the crowds, and was used as an addition to imprisonment for crimes that demanded public humiliation. Arsonists, thieves, perjurers, and pimps were subject of the pillory, but increasingly it was used as a way of punishing acts of sodomy.

When Joshua Vigners (or Viggers) was pilloried as part of his punishment for sodomy in September 1810 at Cornhill, he was at first pelted with eggs, mud, and potatoes but later in the hour he was pelted with stones which blinded him. Spectators climbed on to a balustrade in Charlotte Row for a better view. It collapsed and many were rushed to St Bartholomew's hospital with cracked skulls. The streets in the surrounding areas of Poultry and Cornhill were blocked and their shops closed. There was no doubt who was in charge during these exemplary punishments, and it was certainly not the government.

As with public hangings, the ruling classes needed to control other spectacles of justice. While the pillory did offer an opportunity to provide a punishment that was feared, there was a problem that the nature of the process actually put more power in the hands of the mob, leading to a diminution in respect for the law.

Another objection to the pillory was one based on class distinction. Humiliation was more of a punishment for those with some social standing and something to lose. This is what one caring MP said in the 1816 abolition debate:

> *The punishment, he insisted, was unequal: to a man in the higher walks of life, it was worse than death: it drove him from society, and would not suffer him to return to respectability; while, to a more hardened offender, it could not be an object of much terror, and it could not affect his family or his prospects in the same degree.*

Reformers such as Cobbett and traditionalists such as the reactionary Lord Ellenborough agreed that the pillory brought an unwanted degree of inequality and uncertainty. It was abolished for general use and reserved for perjurers until 1830, but this was not an act of humanitarianism, merely political pragmatism. That would also be a good description of the whole system of punishment and justice in the Regency.

Chapter 17

Retribution

In 1819, James Bilsham was found guilty of stealing ten bushels of rape-seed from the Great Ellingham estate of Nathaniel Weston of Norfolk. His crime was 'grand larceny'– theft of items worth more than one shilling. This was not very much money even then, but it was an indication of how seriously property crime was regarded. He was unlucky to be caught; most people were not. His luck deteriorated when he discovered that his twelve-month incarceration was to be at one of the worst houses of correction in Norfolk, and possibly the country.

Aylsham gaol was a poor and ill-favoured place. Although officially a House of Correction, such institutions were often called Bridewells, after the original prison in London of that name. Aylsham was constructed in the 1780s, just as prison building and reform stopped for the war emergency; it was built by private contractors for their own profit and the build quality reflected this. When Bilsham arrived in November 1819 there were about a dozen inmates, although a year earlier the number was nearer thirty. There were fourteen useable cells and he may have had one of these to himself, due to the unusual lack of overcrowding. There were also four new cells built to accommodate the wave of crime since 1815, but they were poorly built and some had windows on the external wall which allowed contraband to be passed through – and criminals to pass out. The governor of the prison, who had been there for twenty-three years, admitted during the 1819 visitation by the magistrate that a cripple had escaped from the establishment a year earlier after just an hour's incarceration. James was one of the prisoners during the inspection.

There were no baths, no infirmary and only two privies for the eighteen cells. Every morning, James would have taken a stone pitcher to the single water pump in the yard, washed, breakfasted, and then taken his container of water back to his cell. James would spend the day either in solitary confinement or walking around the small rubbish-strewn yard. There was no segregation of prisoners, either by sex or nature of crime. James probably didn't find prison a corrupting experience; most of the inmates were there for property crime of a similar level to his. The youngest inmate, Charles

Rennet, was a 14-year-old illiterate burglar who had received no trade or education, and had no family. At the end of the two years, young Rennet would simply leave prison a better criminal, with new connections and no alternative but more crime. He was one of thousands in this situation.

Neither James nor young Charles worked in prison, contrary to an Act of Parliament. There was corn-grinding equipment in the prison but no corn. The prisoners made shoes and did a little tailoring for each other – out of necessity, as they did not receive a fresh shirt every week as the rules demanded. They did not even whitewash their own cells. It was done by outside contractors, not that it would take long as most cells were 9ft x 6ins. They slept on straw in vermin infested wooden beds and subsisted on broth and 2lbs of bread per day.

Even if they wanted to be penitent, they had little opportunity. The chapel was a 9ft high hut with two perfunctory services a week and no individual pastoral care for the inmates. For this service a local cleric earned £50 a year. There were only three bibles available to the prisoners, which was not too much of a problem because only four prisoners were literate. Of the fourteen basic rules laid down by parliament, eleven were broken.

Not all prisons were terrible, but even those with a good reputation were getting worse. Things had certainly got worse at Bodmin gaol. Before 1815 it would have one of the best in the country. It was one of the few new prisons built in the period after 1780. Unlike Aylsham, it was not built by private enterprise, but by the local community:

> It was light & airy and therefore healthy; it had different isolated areas for felons, misdemeanants and debtors. Males & females were totally segregated. There was hot water, a chapel, an infirmary for sick prisoners and individual sleeping cells. Prisoners were paid for their work from the profits from the products sold by the governor.[1]

After the post-war crime wave, the prison became disease ridden, and overcrowded, with many more prisoners in each cell. It started to look more like Aylsham. It was now a place to be avoided at all costs.

When the corrupt MP Sir Massanah Lopes was convicted of bribery in 1819, his special pleading – he had asthma – got him a stint in Exeter while his poorer fellow criminals were crammed into Bodmin.

Improvements continued, but not ones that we would recognise as a step forward today. In November 1818, additions to the Hampshire County Gaol and Bridewell were completed. They had succeeded in meeting the government's standards. A new drop was built at the gaol to execute people more effectively, and chapels were built and repaired. The chair of the Committee for Improvements had some strong words for those rebuilding the prisons. He commented 'on the structure of some prisons, which instead of being loathsome dungeons were built like palaces'. He also understood that 'it was generally admitted that vice should be hidden from the public view'. He went on to say that £7,500 paid for the new door of Maidstone prison suggested that people now glorified in crime; and that care should be taken not to make the prisons as attractive as the workhouses.

Relying on religion and the noose was the philosophy of the whole prison system in the late Georgian period. Religion provided moral guidance and penitence for crimes, and a conveniently placed public gallows provided exemplary lessons in the fate of convicted criminals.

The system was held back by the fact the British did not really like the idea of prisons very much. It was preferable to launch the criminal either into eternity, or into Botany Bay – hanging or transportation. When it was reluctantly accepted that criminals would remain in prison, the debate began about what to do with them. Deterrence and punishment was taken as read; reform was accepted as an aim, but the method was not agreed. As more criminals spent more time behind bars, there needed to be experiments with different types of punishment.

Solitary confinement was new, and was in use after Coldbath Fields opened in 1794. The poets Coleridge and Southey condemned it:

> *As he went through Coldbath Fields he saw*
> *A solitary cell;*
> *And the Devil was pleased, for it gave him a hint*
> *For improving his prisons in hell.*

Coldbath Fields became perhaps the most feared and hated prison in the country, and the one used by the Spencean Philanthropists to agitate the population before the Spa Fields riots of 1816 as it could be seen in the distance, looming over them.

Complete isolation was used in many prisons for minor property offences; stealing oats or eggs would attract a month or two in solitary confinement – twenty-three hours a day in a cell on your own with nothing to distract you. It was originally introduced as a method of moral improvement; it would remove the prisoner from the corrupting influence of others, but it was now clear to many that even the briefest period could lead to mental instability.

Sir Francis Burdett was, inevitably, against solitary confinement. In a debate where a debtor was locked up on his own for eleven days in Lincoln castle in 1812, Burdett pointed out that there was a difference between isolating people from bad influences and driving them mad with loneliness. Henry Grey Benett brought up the situation in 1816 at Petworth House of Correction in Sussex where prisoners had a mere fifteen minutes association a day, and one woman had been in solitary confinement for three years, eventually going insane. Benett's opponents pointed out that she had been disturbed prior to this having threatened arson to the house of a local gentlemen, and that the isolation at Petworth was due to lack of communal facilities, which were now being built. It did seem that it was the buildings that were deciding the policies rather than the policies dictating what type of prisons were built.

Benett finished with a strong warning and an accidental prediction:

the system of solitary was carried to such an extent that even during divine service they were cooped in wooden boxes that no prisoner could see another.

He did not know that by the 1830s this type of isolation was to become a policy not a criticism.

It was a constant struggle to inflict a just measure of pain on prisoners. Part of this involved work – work was meant to be redemptive, but it was as difficult to arrange in the prisons as it was in the workhouse. The most common activity was the picking of wet and dry oakum, an activity that was common to both workhouse and prison. It involved teasing the fibres from large tarred ropes, with the raw material extracted being used in shipbuilding to fill in the gaps between the wooden planks of ships. In 1818 a ton of dry oakum could fetch £4 and an 1818 report into the Middlesex House of Correction suggested that the actual value of the work done by prisoners was less than 1d a day. It was one of the few activities that was so uneconomic that free labour on the outside would be extremely reluctant to do it. It destroyed the hands and posture, and was tiring and tedious. Kezia King, committed to Coldbath Fields for passing false shillings at a West End Fair in Hampstead, told a government report in 1818 that she appreciated her post as yard warden, washing and guarding new vagrants, prostitutes, and violent women, because 'she did not pick the oakum'.

Another solution to the problem of providing disciplined work and correction was the treadmill or tread wheel. It was first used in the Surrey

House of Correction at Brixton in 1816 and was usually called the tread wheel, because it rarely had any milling or grinding apparatus attached it. It was tedious, degrading work that, unlike oakum picking, did not make conversation easy, or encroach on proper work done outside the institution by free labour. No time was needed in teaching new skills and no materials could be stolen. It could be made more difficult by chaining prisoners together or running the wheel for longer. Some wheels could be modified to make physically stronger prisoners work harder. Those who opposed it saw it as an extra punishment rather than a legitimate prison activity, and unjust because it had not been specifically prescribed as part of their punishment. Those who refused to take part at Brixton were put in solitary confinement in the 'dark cell', which suggests that solitary was regarded as an even worse punishment.

Newgate was the Regency prison that has attracted the most attention however, both then and now. On Thursday, 22 October 1818, Newgate contained 376 prisoners; it was normally much more overcrowded. On 7 September the number had been 578.

In October, there were thirty-six prisoners in the forty condemned cells on the lower ground floor waiting to be executed, or more likely, waiting to see if the punishment would be respited. The condemned cells had been built in the 1770s on the understanding that this was more than enough, but they were regularly full after 1815.

Two of these condemned cells were occupied by James Higgins and William Mitchell, both 24 years old. They were found guilty of breaking and entering; stealing clothes, shoe buckles, watches, sugar ladles, a wine strainer, and anything else they could carry out of the prosperous household of Edward Dawson in Bloomsbury in September 1818. They would have waited for a reprieve; it could be hoped for, but not expected, and would have been agony. On 19 May 1820 they were transported to Australia. That was a long time on death row. There were twenty-six men and forty-one women imprisoned on 22 October 1818 who knew for a fact that they were going to be transported. Some would be moved to a prison hulk first; a prospect that was even more worrying than Newgate. Those with a fourteen-year or life sentence would have had little to lose and no reason to behave well. There were 114 women in total in Newgate, and the official capacity was sixty. The women were mostly guilty of petty property crimes rather than acts of violence or extensive theft.

There were thirty female and twenty male prisoners actually serving a sentence for misdemeanours, but by far the greatest number were the transient population of those awaiting trial at the Old Bailey. On 7 September 1818, the newspapers reported the biggest number of prisoners awaiting trial that had been known for many decades. Amongst the murderers and habitual prisoners was gardener William Hayward, who was accused of stealing a cucumber. As there was no classification or separation of prisoners, William would have had to take his chances with hardened criminals. He was 77.

Lawrence Halloran was in Newgate for forging the handwriting of a member of parliament to fraudulently claim the free postage for letters. His stay at Newgate was short; in December he and 300 other prisoners sailed on the *Baring* to New South Wales and arrived there six months later. Halloran was a doctor of divinity with a large family, who wrote poems and stories and had, in total, defrauded the state of 10d. He subsequently established a school at Sydney, which he conducted very successfully and, presumably, honestly. He died there in March 1831, aged a respectable 75.

Laurence Halloran and William Hayward would have been in a gaol at the same time as the pimp Francis Losch, awaiting trial for murdering his wife with a vicious slash to the stomach when she refused to continue being a prostitute. The pimp, the crooked cleric, and the aged gardener would all have been in the same position. They may have shared a kitchen, which had been recently opened to prevent prisoners cooking their own food in any corner of the prison with the subsequent mess and dirt that was produced. Prisoners received no bedding or clothes – rich inmates would buy them, the most powerful would steal them, and the weaker ones would soon be naked. There was no supply of soap. If you had no money of your own, there was no supply of anything.

Perhaps Losch or another hardened criminal could have scared or corrupted Samuel Dukes and John Jones, both 15, who had stolen some teaspoons, beer and cheese and were also transported to Australia.

Also living with no soap was John Fitzgerald, found guilty of 'stealing from the person' on 9 September and was in Newgate awaiting transportation. We know for a fact that Lawrence Halloran and John Fitzgerald did not have a conversation in prison, for John was deaf and dumb. It did not stop him receiving a life sentence in Australia. The two men went out on the same convict ship, from possibly the same hulk.

Hulks were floating prisons, usually a pensioned off Royal Navy vessel, anchored off the south of England in places such as Portsmouth, Sheerness, and Woolwich. They were used for temporarily holding prisoners before transportation to Australia. They were not the same as convict ships, which still had the ability to sail. The hulk was usually not part of the sentence, and was merely a place to wait until a ship was ready to sail. Most prisoners spent more than three months there, although much longer periods were not unknown and the prospect was terrifying for even the most hardened criminal. If you could bribe the gaoler, it could be arranged for you to spend longer in prison and less time on the ship. If your conviction coincided with the departure of a convict ship, you could avoid the hulk completely.

The petty criminal James Hardy Vaux was different to most Georgian criminals as he was intelligent enough to leave a biography, and charming enough to be given lots of chances by the gullible.[2] In 1809 he was convicted of the theft of jewellery. He had originally been sentenced to death, but like most in the Regency, was respited and given seven years transportation. He tried and failed to get himself aboard the *Anne*, which was just about to leave for Australia. Instead, he was sent in chains to the hulk *Retribution* at Woolwich to await the next sailing ship. He left the prison by cart with the eleven others; family would be allowed to say goodbye at this point, their grief made worse by the fact that the transportation of the main breadwinner would mean destitution for the family.

Like all Regency prisons, *Retribution* was overcrowded, with 600 men, mostly double ironed. Unless it was a stinking low tide on the Thames, convicts in chains would have rowed Vaux across the river. Vaux was then stripped and washed in cold water, given a coarse, cheap suit to wear and put in irons. Each ankle would have an iron fetter attached by a chain, shackled in the middle to a belt around the waist to stop the chain dragging on the ground. Some men were physically deformed for life by this double chaining; not so much when it was worn as when it was taken off. In theory their old clothes were kept to allow them to sell later; what they did not know was that when they finally got on the convict ship, their clothes would all be thrown overboard.

Most inmates would be expected to work, mostly at government owned military bases at the Woolwich Arsenal. Ten working hours a day was common in summer. They would perform various labouring jobs in groups of twenty, overseen by prison wardens who were 'most commonly of the lowest class of human beings, wretches devoid of all feeling, ignorant in the extreme, brutal by nature and rendered tyrannical and cruel by the consciousness of the power they possess'.[3] Vaux also reported that prisoners on the hulks were beaten unconscious in a way that did not happen in the prisons.

The diet was as cruel as the workload. The hulks were run by private enterprise contractors who bought the cheapest provisions they could find to feed the inmates. Vaux reported that breakfast was boiled barley which was so bad that there was often some left to feed pigs; there was meat four days a week but it was from animals that had died of old age. On days when no meat was served (banyan days in navy parlance) there was a vegetable or corn bread stew called burgoo; when there was cheese, it was an inferior type made with skimmed milk.

Thomas Holden, who was sent to the hulk *Portland* in 1812, agrees about the food in this letter to his wife:

> *We have nothing but oatmeal and barley boiled for our breakfast and supper night and morning for our whole time; and we have about half a pound of very bad beef and a pound and a quarter of brown bread four days a week for dinner, and the other three days we have the same bread and seven ounces of very bad cheese.*

Prisoners were not allowed visitors and letters were censored; when Vaux was there for a few months he claimed to have witnessed one murder, one suicide and many 'unnatural acts'. The aspect of the hulks that really terrified Vaux was the fact that bonds of solidarity and camaraderie that he enjoyed in prison dissolved immediately on the hulks; Vaux noticed that former friends would rob and cheat one another and that it was every man for himself on the prison ships.

On 15 June 1810, his memoirs suggest that he was highly delighted to be put on a convict ship of 200 prisoners and transported to Botany Bay. He preferred it to the hulk, but probably would not agree with Lord Chief Justice Ellenborough, who suggested that transportation was akin to 'a summer airing by an easy migration to a milder climate'.

Life continued on the *Retribution* after James Vaux had left for New South Wales. The contractors were offered an extra 3d per day to feed the prisoners in October 1810. In 1811, the authorities spent money bringing the *Retribution* up to the standard of the other hulks by building wooden barriers to separate the decks, stopping the prisoners on the three decks from communicating at night. The inmates rioted and tore them down and they were not rebuilt. At that time, inmates were sleeping on straw, and the stench caused by the hundreds of dirty men sleeping on three crowded decks would make the most hardened prison officer wretch. There was so little oxygen in the ship that candles would not light. At night the inmates were left to their own devices.[4] It was commented in the 1814 report that morale on the *Retribution* was higher than the *Captivity* at Portsmouth and the *Laurel* at Gosport because there was work for all inmates at the Woolwich

Ordnance and this was not the case on the Solent, where too many people were left unsupervised during the day.

By 1814, *Retribution* was the only hulk with no purpose-built chapel. The guns had gone, and instead of sails there were ramshackle workshops, chimneys, and drying washing. Death rates remained higher than on any other ship. In 1816 dysentery struck, but in 1817 the Pentrich prisoners noted that it had a chapel and was not as bad as was reputed. In *Great Expectations*, set in 1812, the desperate criminal Abel Magwitch escaped from a hulk on the Thames – described by Dickens as 'a black hulk lying out a little way from the mud of the shore, like a wicked Noah's ark. Cribbed and barred and moored by massive rusty chains.' This sounds like the *Retribution*, and the whole prison system sounded like retribution.

Chapter 18

Child Labour

Even before industrialisation, children worked and were expected to earn money for their parents. Labour was the obligation of all; in a very religious age, the fourth commandment, by the very act of allowing one day of rest implied six days of labour a week. Young children working was not a problem to people at the time and it would be anachronistic for us to see it in that way. The only real difficulty with child labour was that there often was not enough of it.

Children in the rural areas would start work when they were physically able to do it. Their work consisted of bird scaring, weeding, sowing crops, feeding animals, and driving horses or working in gangs to bring in the harvest. If domestic textile work was being done, the children could assist by cleaning and carding wool, flax or cotton.

Thomas Bachelor reported on child labour in his native Bedfordshire in 1808. In a good year there was plenty of work for children. Non-working children were a cause of poverty, and Bachelor believed that the low poor rate and general prosperity of Bedfordshire was due to the wide availability of children's work.

Bedfordshire was unusual in this period because it had two expanding rural industries when most others were declining. Straw plait making was a major industry, thanks to the local wheat that produced straw of distinctive colour and high strength for the production of hats in nearby Luton. It was an easy task for children, although adults did it as well. Picking and grading of straw for plaiting could begin at 4 years of age; plaiting began at 6 or 7. Some believed that many girls failed to go to school and learn to read due to the easy availability of work.

Lace making was also an option for girls. They would start about 6 or 7 years old and learn the trade in lace-making schools and two years later were adept enough to make lace commercially. This would earn their families about 2s per week. They would work a fourteen-hour day in both summer and winter, starting at 6 am in summer and a few hours later in winter. So, when these families migrated to towns and encountered the working conditions in cotton mills, the hours of work would not surprise them.

Boys in Bedfordshire worked in agriculture. A 'boy of all work', aged about 12, would live in the farmer's household for £2 to £3 a year. He would receive board and lodging, usually eat at the same table as the family and be treated like one of them. Other agricultural jobs would be ploughing and harrowing, and other transport work that involved guiding a horse or an ox under the supervision of an adult.

In non-agricultural work, children around 14 were apprenticed to trades such as upholstering, gun making, haberdashery, goldsmithing, carpentry, gardening, linen drapery, carving and gilding, baking, coopering, grocering, soap-making, sail-making, trunk-making, brass plate working, stationers, stockbrokers, builders, and surveyors. Apprenticeships were meant to be a regulated market. There was a fixed term of seven years, during which the apprentice would normally live with the master. Apprenticeships were the same length for all trades, and an apprentice could usually expect better conditions in the second half of his time, with perhaps half pay and some accommodation paid for. This had been the system since Tudor times.

Upfront premiums were payable in theory, but by the early nineteenth century these were becoming rarer; a London surgeon, an upmarket grocer, or a lady's wig maker in London or a fashionable seaside town ('Margate Ornamental Hair Empororium, 10 Queen Street') would certainly ask for one. Apprenticeship premiums were sometimes burdensome (a law of 1768 allowed parents to pay in instalments), but they did give the vital right to carry on that profession after successful completion of the seven years. More to the point, it banned untrained people from taking up that trade. It was a privilege held by the poor, and a protection of their livelihood.

This protection was abolished in 1814. From then on, anybody could take up these trades without an apprenticeship. It was a free-market solution for an establishment that now believed that such restrictions were bad for the economy; once again it was noticed by Cobbett and others that it was always the protection of the poor that was first to be legislated away.

Petitions supporting apprenticeships (one with 300,000 signatures) flooded into parliament with the usual degree of success. Supporters viewed apprenticeships as a moral good; during the most turbulent years of their life, ages 14 to 21, children were subject to discipline and the good example of a master. A large proportion of advertisements for apprentices in the paper assured parents that 'they would be treated as one of the family'. They learnt domestication and subordination and came out the other end as mature men (and it was mostly men) with a trade.

It was also argued that after the abolition of apprenticeships, nobody would pay a premium or do the full term of seven years and that the job market would be become ultra competitive and wages would fall. Others who supported the change did so for the exactly the same reason.

The workhouse was one source of apprenticeships. They differed a little from normal ones; they often concentrated on lower-skilled manual jobs, and would often offer opportunities for girls. This example comes from the *Kentish Chronicle*:

Apprentices

Wanted by the Parish of New Romney, Masters and Trades for four poor boys. For John Dussler, aged 15 to a baker, James Chittenden, fourteen and a half, to a cordwainer, Robert Puiles fourteen to a carpenter or bricklayer and Henry Warrington, to a painter or glazier.

Child labour such as chimney sweeping was more like child cruelty than job training. Being a 'climbing boy' was a perverse sort of apprenticeship. Normal apprentice children were indentured to a master at 14; that is when climbing boys started to lose their job, as they were now too large to scramble up chimney flues that were on average a foot square. Undernourished 6 year olds were used − if they were not already undersized, they could be starved.

Most came from the workhouses as pauper apprentices or from the streets, and would end their life there too. The only advantage was that they had money at an early age; Henry Mayhew in *London Street Life* suggested they had 2d a day to spend as they wished; however, after age 14, penury and unskilled labour was the norm. By 14 the climbing boy had learnt a trade that had no transferable skills and had stunted his physical development so much that other employment was impossible.

William Moles of Spitalfields was an exploiter of this mockery of the apprenticeship system. He would employ climbing boys to clean the flues of the rich for 1s a time. We know for a fact that one of his apprentices was a boy called John Hewley.

John would probably have lived in the same house as William and his wife Sarah. He would subsist in one soot-infested room of their house, sleeping on a black mattress. There were laws protecting climbing boys that William would have been aware of − these dated from the humanitarian efforts of Jonas Hanway in 1788. Under that law, sweep apprentices had to be at least 8 years old; John was only 6. They had to attend church every Sunday and be washed every week. Moles almost certainly ignored this part of the law as well, given what happened to John afterwards.

On 2 April 1816, Moles and John went to the house of Elizabeth Ware in Fashion Street, Spitalfields. Ware later gave evidence that John was beaten about the legs by his master, presumably as a punishment for his reluctance to go up the flue. On 23 April, at Chick-end in Spitalfields, John was sent up the chimney of Ann Chandler. John was already up the chimney when the witness saw him assaulted, although some details are unclear. While up the chimney he might have panicked and cried out that he was stuck. Then the master would try to 'buff it' – pushing the boy upwards by using his shoulders on the poor boy's feet, forcing the lad to try 'slanting' – altering his body to fit the shape of the flue. John clearly got fully stuck; Moles tried to pull him down, but in the process the boy fell on to the marble hearth, breaking his legs and dying a few days later. Staff at the London Hospital tried to save the boy by amputating a leg but it may have been in vain anyway; there would have been traumatic damage to John's head as he was pulled out and that could have been the cause of death.

Mole's legal team claimed that it was an accident and the judge decided that murder could not be proven. Moles was found guilty of mistreatment of John. The apprentice's body had previous marks of abuse, especially around the feet and legs. Moles was imprisoned for two years. Sarah Moles needed protection from a mob of 200 when she left the court.

Child apprentices generally were vulnerable to cruelty and mistreatment, perhaps even more that factory children. Those without parents, or without family nearby, were most at risk. This case is from 1817:

> *G. Barber, of York Street Bethnal Green, was charged with a series of the most horrid cruelties to his apprentice Mary Elder, a child apparently 11 years of age. His counsel was so disgusted with the recital that he threw up his brief…the jury sentenced him to two years imprisonment.*

Her indenture – an apprenticeship agreement – was annulled. She was also rather young for her apprenticeship; the 'apparently' in the report shows either disbelief or uncertainty, neither were good. Two years was quite a harsh sentence for the time. Other, less squeamish, newspapers reported that she had been beaten with a stick, caned on her legs, starved to a skeletal state, kicked and punched and dashed against stone floors. When George Barber's wife complained, the cruelty to the child was redoubled.

Mary's young age and gender suggest she was a workhouse placement. The workhouse of St John Hackney paid for the prosecution, and it was the overseer who rescued her from death. These were the most vulnerable working children of all, whether they were found in a mill, a weaver's house, or working for a sweep. The only good news was that the large hostile crowd at the Middlesex sessions showed that this was not a typical case. Mary was nursed back to health at the workhouse.

Domestic service for young people was common before industrialisation and young girls would often take up the role of 'maid of all work'. By the beginning of the nineteenth century there were many middle-class families whose income was precarious, but liked to advertise their new status by employing a girl to do all the work in the house. Girls were often in their twenties, but those aged 12 or 13 would do this as their first job. From the many advertisements it seems that food preparation – 'plain cooking' – is the most often mentioned role. Regency ladies of any ambition did not cook for their own family. Mrs Bennet from Austen's *Pride and Prejudice*, for example, is offended when the socially inept Mr Collins asks which daughter he should compliment after a nice meal.

The second requirement in the advertisements is that they should be able to cope with loneliness. One advertisement plainly pointed out that they should be able to bear confinement; older servants were meant to have no followers. Cleaning is the next requirement, and many hinted that the maid would need to answer the door to guests as the household would have no footman, but would have social pretensions to want a servant to greet visitors at the door.

It was an open-ended job between 6 am and 11 pm with the option of being turfed out of bed at any other time if necessary – one advertisement asking for washing and ironing, and 'willingness to do anything required of her'. In the best households, she would be treated as one of the family in the same style as an apprentice; in the Regency this would have been the most common domestic arrangement in the rural areas, but slightly less likely among the urban elites.

Young girl servants often came straight from the countryside, pushed out of agricultural work by enclosure and the new technology that was destroying their casual and seasonal work. One advertisement from a townhouse in Salisbury indicates what part of the job was least liked by promising none of it: 'No cows, no washing, no brewing.' Slightly less respectable ways of being a maid were to go to an agency, or apply to a kitchen or public house. There would also be young boys working in the pub as waiters, potboys and errand boys – a step below the level of apprentice.

Eleanor Cooper was a typical maid of all work in this situation. She was working at the Tavistock Arms in St Giles, London, in October 1814 when the barrels at the nearby Meux Brewery exploded and flooded the streets with beer. She was scouring pots and pans at a water pump when she was drowned by the incoming wave, or crushed by a collapsing wall. The newspapers added to the distress by lamenting that sixty pans were smashed beyond recognition. Early newspaper reports gave Eleanor's age as 10; while this turned out to be incorrect, it did not seem implausible to the newspapers that a 10-year-old would be working as a servant in a public house. Other reports suggest she was nearer 16; again the lack of certainty shows how unimportant a young woman like this was to Regency society. Her body was sent to the local workhouse and her age was settled at a guess of 14.

Nobody in Regency Britain doubted that children working in textile factories were a new phenomenon; but there was some disagreement about whether it was worthy of worry or new laws. In 1818, Sir Robert Peel the elder, the father of a future prime minister, and a factory owner himself, laid out the crucial differences between the old and new patterns of children's work. Nowhere else were children working a fourteen hour day in 70°F of heat and sticky humidity. All children were doing the same punishing hours with no regard to their individual physical and mental strength. Unlike apprentices, who were worked hard and similarly treated, there were no long-term benefits or career path for factory children. There was no paternal or maternal connection between child and employers; indeed if children sickened, died, or ran away, the master would simply go back into the over-supplied market and replace them. This was not regulated rural work or traditional family labour – from our view, this was red-in-tooth-and-claw capitalism, and it was being applied to children first because they were much more likely to put up with it.

Peel eventually managed to get his bill into law, but there was some serious opposition. Lord Stanley, who approved of the protection of pauper apprentice children introduced in 1802, felt he could not support a bill that interfered with the rights of 'free labour'. It is hard to understand in what ways Lord Stanley thought a factory child was a free agent. Many MPs in the debate were concerned for the parents – it was they who were having their economic rights infringed by the law limiting the economic value of their children. If children's work was restricted, the same would happen to adults. It is easy to understand these reluctant attitudes to reform when it is remembered that children were meant to be an asset for the present and an investment for the future. What other security did poor people have?

Lord Lascelles elaborated on his free market philosophy: who was to say which other industries would need regulation? Why should the law say how much a worker should endure? If the working hours of children under 16 were regulated they would be sacked and the burden placed on the poor rates or the poor parents. How would mills, some of which shared the same water-power source (Lord Lascelles knew of such in York), manage to keep going if hours were restricted? How would British exports remain competitive?

Other arguments were from the same mind-set: if hours were reduced, children would not be improved but ruined by the extra opportunities for vice; the demand for short hours was coming from adult workers in seditious meetings in smoke-filled public houses, and they were doing it to increase their own pay by removing cheaper labour – there was some truth in this.

Other voices in the debate were the cotton mill owners of Manchester who petitioned parliament, claiming to have the names of hundreds of doctors and surgeons who would depose that children working in factories came to no harm. No less a person than Prime Minister Lord Liverpool, not well known for his sympathy for the poor, stated 'emphatically' that: 'If all the medical staff of Manchester ... stated that the working of children for 15 hours a day was not injurious to their health, he would not believe them.'

It was the unusual and novel nature of the work, with perhaps a hint of patrician disdain for middle-class manufacturers, that led Lord Liverpool to this conclusion.

The Bill that passed in 1819 forbade child labour under the age of 9 in cotton mills. It was only passed by the Lords with the understanding that the cotton mills were a special case and that there would be no more interference with private industry. In order to protect the competitiveness of the industry, Peel relented and allowed children to continue to work twelve hours a day. This was despite the fact that evidence suggested overproduction and consequent lower prices were more of a problem than failure to reach production targets. Some factory owners actually supported the 1819 Act, as it enforced minimum standards against unscrupulous owners who would use exploitation of children to undercut them. A bigger problem than this was that the law was never enforced properly anyway.

Children working in cotton mills have become a 'textbook' example of cruelty and exploitation. Debate rages about how bad it actually was. The main problem, shared by all other child workers away from home, was that their treatment depended on the whim of the individuals who owned or ran the factory. Robert Blincoe, who produced his own account of child labour in a water-powered cotton mill in the early 1810s, described the capricious cruelties of individual overseers against the pauper apprentices, made worse by the fact that, unlike steam-powered mills in Manchester, the magistrate was a long way away and was more likely to be the mill owner's dining companion, and less concerned about enforcing the new regulations.[1] The 1819 Law did not allow for a proper inspection regime; obeying the law almost became a personal choice.

What can be said with certainty is that work in cotton mills was hot, tedious, and repetitive, and mostly unskilled and dead-end. It was dangerous; but then children who worked elsewhere suffered accidents. The main objection at the time was not just the nature of the work, but also the moral implications of the separation from family. The Manchester weavers petitioned parliament with these complaints in 1823:

> *There, uninformed, unrestrained youth of both sexes mingle ... absent from any parental vigilance ... confined in the artificial heart to the injury of health – the mind exposed to corruption and life and limb exposed to machinery.*

It was the novelty of this type of work that parents objected to; it lacked the basic definition of work for children: natural conditions, parental supervision, and moral improvement. There would be no more training up of children to take their parent's place at the loom. The family as a working and social unit had been seriously undermined.

The new factories did not have the monopoly on treating children badly. In 1824, a report on Sligo Protestant Charter School suggested that it was as horrible as any dark satanic mill. Although it was supposed to be a school, most of the time was spent learning handloom weaving – a dying occupation at the time. Robert Robinson was seven in 1811. He deposed that his teacher 'used to get hold of their neck and knock their heads against the boards or any thing in the way and I often saw him give them clouts on the jaw... A slap on the jaw with the hand.'

He was one of a series of masters, ushers, and overseers who were completely unaccountable to any moderating power. The rot started at the top. Mr Hines, the master in 1824, was accused by the subsequent investigation of serving the children his diseased cow for Sunday lunch. Hines also used vicious, and sometimes random, violence against boys, mostly for not working hard enough in the weaving shop. Mr Hines's son, Richard, attacked Terence Gallagher with the butt of a rifle for a trifling problem with work. Lawrence French, 13, was strangled by Mr Hines and was unable to eat for three days. His crime was having insufficiently clean shoes. Thomas

Fullerton ('twelve, very small') was locked up in a potato shed and fed on bread and water for not letting out his tight clothes and for weaving badly. Mr Hines survived the scandal:

> the master in the ebullition of momentary passion...in which he unfortunately allowed his better judgment to be overcome. He has adopted a mode of punishment extremely objectionable and unjustifiable however...the complaints of the boys are greatly exaggerated and proceed more from a desire to criminate the master.

You did not need to be a factory child to be abused, and then not believed.

One of the arguments against reform of factories in 1818 was that other industries were worse. Lord Stanley, elected (unopposed) for the coal-rich county of Lancashire, thought that collieries were worse, although he had no plans to bring forward new regulations. He had a point. Mines created less excitement as they were less novel, and children continued to work in coal mines without too much comment beyond the era of the Regency. Scottish coalmines still employed 9 year olds in the 1840s.

The Board of Agriculture, ever ready to collect data to improve the productivity of the local industries, published a description of the work of children in collieries in 1817. Both boys and girls were employed to guide a corf (a wagon) out of the mine – using iron rails. It was clear that this was dangerous. It was cramped, dirty, poisonous, and full of dangerous equipment. However, the authors were more concerned with the asses – 'fine beasts, fourteen hands high':

> I have several times shuddered to witness...the conduct of a brutal Girl employed in driving a poor Ass that dragged the corves from the top of the Pit to the Stack at Ballyfield Colliery in Hansworth in Yorkshire which she incessantly cudgelled with a truncheon two inches or more diameter. It excites horror even now by its recollection.

It was clear that asses were in shorter supply than children, and therefore the law of the market demanded better treatment. The report then explained how it was best practice not to shackle their legs when they were grazing in the sunshine. This referred to the animals, not the children. A large stick attached to a chain is enough to stop them leaping hedges or straying. Children were stopped from leaping in fields by spending twelve hours in a 4ft high tunnel of a coal seam.

Young children died in coalmines regularly during this period. On Friday 2 June 1815 there was an explosion caused by firedamp (methane) at the 'Success' pit of the Newbottle Colliery in County Durham. Seventy-two bodies were brought to the surface, including twenty–eight boys, the youngest of whom, John Stout, was 6 years old. His father, John Stout senior, also died. There were at least seventeen boys under 13, and seven were 10 years old or younger.

John Stout was a trapper – the most junior of the children's jobs. It seemed a simple task, to open and close the wooden doors that allowed fresh air to provide ventilation. They would sit in total darkness for up to twelve hours at a time, waiting to let the coal tub through the door. It was not hard work but it was boring and could be very dangerous. If they fell asleep or kept their doors open when they should have been closed, the safety of the whole workings could be affected – poor ventilation would lead to explosions. John was quite near the entrance to the pit and was pulled out after the explosion; he died on the surface. When people were rescued alive by heroic efforts, it was often their first breath of fresh air at normal atmospheric pressure that killed them.

There were attempts to stop the carnage. Sir Humphrey Davy's lamp was being used in mines to detect flammable gases before they could cause an explosion. A Society for the Prevention of Accidents in Coal Mines was formed in Sunderland 1813, with Davy and the young engineer George Stephenson as members. The mine owners were more worried about petitioning the government to reduce the coal duties, although the rising alarm about casualties, and a natural desire to protect their mines meant that they supported Davy's efforts. His safety lamp was in use at Harraton Colliery, south of Newcastle, in June 1817. A hewer (coal digger) by the name of John Moody refused to use one however, and lit candles instead. His reward was to be incinerated in a massive explosion. It happened at 11.30 am when the mine was as full as it could be. This was the biggest coalmine explosion of the period, with two miners being blown out of the shaft; the body parts of one were found in a neighbouring corn field. Ten members of the Hill family were killed, including the grandfather, father and eight children, the three youngest being 8, 9 and 10.

Robert Langley was working in Plain pit, Rainton, County Durham at 3 am on the morning of 17 December 1817. The importance of Davy's safety lamp was well known but it was thought that it was not needed in this particular seam. On that morning, 10-year-old Robert was killed in an explosion, along with fifteen boys.

In July 1819, three poor boys from Whitehaven were forced into employment at the Sheriff Hill mine near Gateshead. Their desperate parents would have known that the mine had had two serious accidents in the last four years with the loss of sixteen lives. When the three children lost their job for reasons unknown, their parents begged – successfully – for their boys to be reinstated. They were there on 19 July 1819 when another accident killed them and another twenty-eight boys. It happened towards the end of the day. Most of the adult male coal hewers had left, which explains the disproportionate number of youngsters. The average age of the victims was 14.

Chapter 19

Currency Crisis

In January 1810, a man who claimed to be called Mr Wright ordered dinner in the near-empty George Inn in Sittingbourne, Kent. Travelling alone and wanting some company, he asked the landlord if there were other single gentlemen in the inn who would like to share a glass of wine with him. This was a common thing to do for the single male traveller in Georgian times, and would have caused no suspicion in itself. The waiter pointed out a Captain Sanderson, and Mr Wright sent him over a glass of wine and request for his company. Sanderson, noting a member of his own class (Wright was a navy officer), accepted the invitation. One glass of wine led to one too many, and at the end of the evening the obliging Wright helped his new friend to bed. In the meantime, he stole the drunken man's pocket book. He then made his escape; in the language of the time, he 'decamped'.

Wright stole 'ten pounds and three Bank of England pound notes'. This was not, in the eyes of the newspaper, the same as £13. His £10 would have been in gold and silver. In the early nineteenth century, most money for daily use was in the form of coins, not paper. The expression 'having deep pockets' was not always a metaphor.

Captain Sanderson and the whole country were using paper money because they had to, not because they wanted to. During the late Georgian period, the now meaningless statement: 'I promise to pay the bearer on demand the sum of...' first appeared – and still appears on every British banknote today. Before the abolition of the 'gold standard' in 1797, all notes were exchangeable for gold of the same value, but gold was running out in the 1790s, and it was needed to pay for the war with Napoleon.

His bank notes would therefore be less valuable than his gold and silver, and the metal was worth more than the face value of the coin. The gold in a guinea was worth a guinea and a half by 1812. In 1810 there was a severe shortage of gold coins in general circulation; they were being melted down into bullion and exported. If 'Mr Wright' had been a criminal, he could have sold the guineas for more than their face value if they were in a reasonable condition.

It was clear that others were doing the same, because in 1811 the law was changed to make it legal to pay debts in paper, and fix the value of the guinea at 21s, making the sale of guineas at a higher price illegal.

This law was passed because of the criminal market for the gold guinea. In 1812 a man called Hodgson, a mail coach driver, was found guilty at the Old Bailey of exchanging eight guineas (£8 8s) for £10 in Bank of England notes. A coachman was always a good bet for criminal currency activity. He could move about the country without comment. He mingled with dubious characters in coaching houses and could fence currency. He could also steal notes that were regularly hidden in luggage by wary passengers, or smuggle them himself using the same method.

Unless Captain Sanderson was more careful with his finances than his social life, he could not be sure that his banknotes were real. Forgery was not difficult as the banknote was only a part-printed document. The amount and the name of the bank were pre-printed but the note number, name of payee, and the chief clerk, were handwritten. The simple design also made forgery easily.

The original process by which the note was produced was the same copper engraving process that was practised by thousands of artisans all over the country. Unlike today, the technological skill needed to be a forger was limited, and many of the tools and materials required – apart from crudely watermarked paper – could be obtained in any urban street of artisans. In the decade before 1811, the Bank of England had refused payment on £101,000 worth of notes, and banknote forgery continued to rise until 1818.

If Captain Sanderson had been the original recipient of the note, his name would be on it. If not, it would contain the names of all the people through whose hands it had passed. This was not a legal requirement, but it would add to the confidence that the notes were genuine, unless of course, the names on the note were also forged. If they were originally his banknotes and he had recorded the number, then he could have them stopped at the bank. Otherwise, genuine small denomination notes that had been stolen would be very easy to spend. Highwaymen and robbers were often quite disappointed if they were to steal a £50 or £40 note (they were issued for lots of different amounts), because they would be hard to dispose of. Jewellery was preferable as it could be more easily fenced. However, since the smaller notes were issued, they were increasingly in the hands of criminals, and this helped forgeries circulate.

As a gentleman, Sanderson would not have used banknotes to pay small debts. He would be extended a long line of credit by suppliers and would pay back a large amount at a later date, perhaps with an individual banker's draft. He would certainly not pay a debt with gold if he could help it.

If Captain Sanderson had banknotes from an obscure minor bank on the other side of the country, then they were more or less worthless in Sittingbourne. Similarly, assuming he was just passing through, if Captain Sanderson had been able to pay his bill, he would have waited to the end of his stay and paid in such a way as to avoid any banknotes from the Sittingbourne and Ashford bank in his change; a highly respected Kentish bank, but useful only in that area.

If Captain Sanderson had been robbed of a large denomination note at home, he would have put an advertisement like this in the newspaper:

TWO GUINEAS REWARD – Lost, in the neighbourhood of Chancery Lane or Holborn, a forty pound Bank of England note Number 5385, dated 15th January 1810 with the name Hoare written in the right hand corner. Whoever has found the same, and will bring it to Mr Warrens China Shop, Chancery Lane, shall receive the above reward. Payment is stopped at the bank.

Whether lost or stolen, a £40 note would be hard to cash without drawing attention, or questions being asked. Passing stolen notes was a capital crime and a guaranteed £2 would be enough compensation. If you had stolen the note, it would be better to send a third party to pick up the reward. As the note came straight from the bank, the number would be known. It was usually better to settle for a sum that would be two weeks wages for a skilled man rather than risk the noose.

The Bank of England and its notes were guaranteed by the government, but county banks were unregulated. Anybody could open a bank and issue promissory notes. There were 800 banks in Britain by 1811. In January 1810 a group of businessmen with money to lend formed the Northampton Town and County Bank. On the same page of the newspaper announcement, the Percival Bank announced that contrary to rumours, the bank was in good shape. The system was based on reputation and trust, and not much else.

Both banks thrived, despite the Percival Bank's panicky advertisement. On 2 June 1811, the Society for the Relief of British Prisoners in France announced that they had £359 in the Percival bank, and £504 in the Northampton Town and County Bank. They split their money partly for safety. Unlike the Bank of England, there was no guarantee that money lodged with the bank was safe; if there was a panic, a 'run' on the bank meant it would run out of money and those at the back of the queue would lose everything, which would cause yet more panic.

The Town and County Bank must have been a success, as in 1811 Antoine Roche Orasion was found guilty of forging one of its £1 notes.[1] The fact that the forger was a French prisoner of war languishing in a damp cell shows how easy it was. In 1813, General Warde had thirty £1 notes of that bank stolen by a John Goodman, who then hid them in a parcel and sent them to an accomplice on a stage coach.

In the provinces, local notes from banks that were known were often more acceptable than Bank of England notes. 'Known' was the key word. Some social events that charged admission would state which banks' notes were acceptable in their newspaper advertisements. Ambitious county banks would link with London banks for the benefit of their more mobile clients – the Town and County, for example, was linked with Praed's Bank of 71, Fleet Street, where their notes could be swapped for Bank of England notes.

The collapse of county banks was a common occurrence. In December 1825, both Northampton banks suspended payments as part of the banking crash partly caused by the great number of unregulated institutions. Jane Austen's brother George was a partner in the bank of Austen, Maunde and Tilson, which closed its doors in March 1816 with Jane losing only £13, a portion of her profits from *Mansfield Park*.

Many people lost everything. The county banking system was another aspect of Regency life that was waiting for reform; although the banks provided credit for businesses and extra currency for transactions, by 1820 there were too many of them and they could not be relied upon. When banks failed they destroyed trade, savings, and created instant misery. When the Portsmouth bank of Goodwin, Minchin and Carter failed in November 1818 it destroyed £200,000 of assets, ruined businesses who deposited there and created mass poverty because their £1 notes were held by the poor as far as Gosport and Portsea. County Banks were strictly limited in the denominations they could offer; mostly £1 or £2, so when they crashed the poor suffered as much as the rich. When the Melverton and Taunton bank failed on a market Saturday in September 1814, local traders were in great distress and panic as they tried to offload their notes for whatever price they could get. On most occasions however, bank failures turned hard-earned wealth into useless pieces of paper.

Captain Sanderson would have probably had silver coins in his pocket. They would have been a sorry sight compared to today's. Many of the coins were in a very poor state, especially those of a lower denomination, which circulated quickly. Two of the nicknames for the 6d piece were the 'crip-ple' and the 'crook back' giving some hint of their condition.[2] Therefore, even when they could be found, silver coins could be damaged, completely smooth disks that might have come from anywhere. A letter in the newspa-per suggested that only one in thirty sixpences had any monarch's head on at all.[3] Many were blank discs, some were actually foreign coins that had been over stamped.

There had been a crisis in England's currency for almost 100 years. The silver coinage contained silver with an intrinsic value as a precious metal. For most of the eighteenth century the silver content was worth more than the face value of the coin. This led to shortages. In the Regency period, adver-tisements appeared offering to buy old silver coins. Coins were melted down and exported or turned into silverware. Others were clipped by those wishing to pass the coin on and still gain a profit from some of the precious metal in it.

Any silver coins that Captain Sanderson owned would need to be checked for clipping and 'sweating'. Silver was relatively soft, so it could also be 'sweated'; that is, placed in a bag with other coins and shaken vigorously, this caused friction and created silver dust which was collected and sold. In an age when thinking people claimed to detect a reduction in anti-Semitic feel-ing, this activity was still linked in the popular mind with the small Jewish population.

Clipping was also an easy process. Some of the coins would have been in circulation for a century and would already be in a poor condition. Clipping was done on an industrial scale and was a simple operation using files. When completed, the slightly lighter coins would often be used to buy banknotes, and then the whole operation would begin again.

It was a major criminal industry and the criminals took great efforts to avoid detection. In June 1813, Birmingham constables, lead by High Constable William Payne, smashed a note and coin-counterfeiting ring that had moved from Warwick. The factory was deep inside a slum area, with barricaded doors in the house, and the factory itself in the cellar, with secret trap doors and burly men guarding them. Luckily, the constables had ham-mers to smash through doors and anything else that got in their way.

There was a vast army of poor, desperate, 'utterers' who tried to pass the coin in the local area. Armed with a genuine note, they would make a pur-chase or ask for change and slip a bad shilling into their own change, show it to the shopkeeper or publican, and demand a real one. It's hard to appreciate today that when dealing with money in the Regency, you had to be on your guard all the time.

Captain Sanderson would probably have had no copper coins, being too rich to use them. By 1811 there was a shortage of copper coinage as well, as prices were rising and they, too, were being melted down. He would not have made purchases using pennies and smaller coins, but the poor would need them. Employers often could not find enough small coins to pay their workers. Many took the opportunity to produce their own coins, especially if they were in the metal industries themselves.

If the captain had worked in the Hull Lead Factory of John Kirby Picard, he would have been partly paid in the owner's own currency. Picard made a fortune producing the lead that was the dangerous main ingredient of paint but he could not rely on a constant supply of copper coin. Tokens with patriotic images – the Duke of Wellington and rampant British lions, as well as others showing his lead works and family crest – circulated in Hull as currency. As a substantial manufacturer he had enough credibility to do this. In 1813, criminals started to forge his 'Wellington' token, so he called them all in by appointment and swapped them for Bank of Hull or Bank of England notes. This would apply to shopkeepers rather than his poor workers, as you would need a minimum of 240 tokens to make £1. His confident newspaper advertisements suggested that he would issue more tokens, 'as long as they were of benefit to the public'.

In January 1818, copper tokens were banned by parliament as part of an attempt to reform the whole currency. Not all issuers were as scrupulous as John Pickard – some issued anonymous tokens that were seriously underweight; other companies demanded that debts to them were paid in their own coin, and due to the small denominations, large numbers of them ended up in the hands of the poor. In the wrong hands, it was no more than half a step from forgery.

By 1816 the system was a jumble of copper, copper tokens, fake copper tokens, debased silver, clipped gold, over-stamped foreign coins, and bank paper from eight hundred banks. Something had to be done, and quite unusually when something needed to be done in the Regency period, it was done!

It seems odd that a laissez-faire government, one that did little more than collect taxes, wage war and run a moderately efficient post office, should intervene to change the whole basis of money. However, the soundness of the monetary system was the very basis of the nation's prosperity.

The preamble to the new 1816 law describes the problem

Whereas the silver coins of the realm have, by long use and other circumstances, become greatly diminished in number and deteriorated in value,

so as not to be sufficient for the payments required in dealings under the
value of the current gold coins, by reason whereof a great quantity of
light and counterfeit silver coin and foreign coin has been introduced
into circulation within this realm, and the evils resulting there from can
only be remedied by a new coinage of silver money

The Coinage Act of June 1816 created a gold sovereign of 20s to replace the guinea of 21s. New silver sixpences and shillings were planned for February 1817, and silver crown and half crown coins were introduced. All silver coins were of a higher face value than the value of the metal; there was now nothing to gain from sweating or clipping them. On 16 September, Prime Minister Lord Liverpool approved the plan to take in the old silver coins and to distribute the new ones via the banks. This was kept secret, and like many secrets, caused panic when the news leaked out.

The first panic was in June when the Bill was passed. It started when the local banks showed some reluctance to take in the debased silver currency. It then spread to local businesses and then would cause distress to the poor who could not spend their money in the shops. This happened in Norwich in June; the Bank of England had to step in to guarantee the exchange of any silver that had not been debased or was not French or Irish.

In September, panic started again. Businesses all over the country had stopped accepting the old debased silver currency. A rumour had spread that the Bank of England would not accept the old coins, despite the Chancellor of the Exchequer, Nicholas Vansittart, stating the opposite in parliament in June 1816. By September, old coins were not being accepted in Smithfield Market and this spread throughout London. London pawnbrokers were not prepared to redeem the small pledges it had, to the disadvantage of both sides.

The Lord Mayor of London, Francis Hobler, stopped the panic by announcing that all silver coinage that was not foreign was still legal tender, and there was a controlled tumult as the Bank of England exchanged the silver coins for Bills of Exchange. It did not help in the building of confidence that the replacement coins were not ready until February 1817. However, the whole operation went relatively well; unlike many economic and social problems of the Regency, this one was solved with administrative efficiency and a lot of government intervention. This certainly explained where their priorities lay.

Chapter 20

Adultery

In July 1816, Lord George Thomas Beresford sued for damages from his erstwhile friend, the Honourable Thomas Taylour, the Earl of Bective. Beresford accused Taylour of the successful seduction of his wife, Harriet Beresford, and demanded the sum of £30,000 in compensation.

This was no twenty-first-century quickie divorce or twentieth-century legal court case with witnesses and co-respondents. It wasn't a divorce at all; merely a demand for compensation as a prelude to a legal state known as '*Divortium a menia et thro*' –'separation from bed and board'. Under these conditions, neither party could remarry and any children would stay with the father. The wife would receive no financial support, and her future would range somewhere between uncertain and ignominious.

These legal separations were, in the parlance of Georgian times, 'Crim. Con.' cases; criminal conversation being the euphemism for sexual intercourse outside of marriage. The case of Beresford versus Taylour is not a well-known case, largely because it was not contested and there were no lurid details for the press to report. But these cases tell you a lot about the state of marriage in the Regency.

Because it was uncontested, no witnesses were called in this proceeding. However, the wife was never called even if there was a dispute about the facts. As a married woman, she had no separate legal identity. The aim of the hearing was to assess damages. Beresford was asking for more that he was ever likely to receive – by that time in history, £30,000 had only been awarded once. The compensation amount was more of a statement of social pretension than a realistic demand. It could only go down from this point. The prosecution would try to maintain the level of compensation and the defence would try to reduce it.

Beresford's representative recounted the marriage history at the Sheriff's Court at Bedford Row on 17 June 1816. George had married Harriet Schultz, daughter of John Bacon Schultz, in 1808. She was 'a lady of high connection, immense fortune and was endowed with every accomplishment'. This may or not have been true, but it was not meant as a compliment. This was a compensation case about loss of amenity, so it was very much in the interest of Beresford to portray his wife as something valuable.

After their first child, Harriet had fallen into a 'derangement' that today we would identify as post-natal depression. However, it was spun to George's advantage; he had not abandoned her, he was a good man, later to be betrayed. He could possibly feel the compensation rising as Sergeant Best spoke on his behalf.

Another factor in assessing the compensation was the social standing of the people concerned; the higher the status, the more compensation. Nearness in social class would reduce it, as it would lessen the shame and humiliation. So there was little scope there to make money on the latter point; both were the sons of important aristocratic landowners in Ireland. Instead, Beresford's representative went to great pains to point out how close the two families were. If Crim. Con. involved betrayal and calculation, the compensation would rise accordingly.

The successful seduction took place in the summer of 1815. George was, it was strongly pointed out, away from home only because he was a major general fighting for king and country. On receiving reports of the further derangement of his wife, he rushed home to care for her. However, acting on reports received, he obtained a key from her writing desk, which contained a letter, 'couched in the most passionate language' from Thomas Taylour, Earl of Bective, son of the Marquis of Headfort. It was a long and declamatory missive about a set of events that had already happened. In the letter, the Earl tried to qualm her fears about her reputation. 'No man, presumptuous, confident or artful, would think you lightly won.' He tried to reconfirm their love: 'Search now that bosom, and see that it still loves Bective.'

This was the prosecution case. He had been the seducer. The seduction had been calculated. He had exploited her illness and the friendship of the families. How was Beresford going to bring up their three daughters without their mother? Before this, their life had been one of domestic harmony. George brought forward no less than five witnesses to prove it. And even now, George took care of her, rather than abandon her to 'The London World', a cauldron of vicious gossip about those who were caught defying convention or failing to be discreet about it.

Bective's defence was brief. He was far from rich (this was not regarded in law as a relevant defence – when the aristocracy claimed for high Crim. Con. damages, bankrupting the defendant was part of the plan). He was young and naive. (The papers reported that he was '[a]n agreeable young man, born in the same year as her ladyship'.) He was sorry.

The jury took thirty minutes to agree compensation to George Beresford of £10,000.

Regency Crim. Con. cases varied in compensation and the starting figure was normally about £50, as in this example of two London skilled tradesmen in an uncontested case. Mr Atherton, a London goldbeater of Long Acre, was awarded £100 in compensation after his wife was seduced by another goldbeater of the same street, a 'Mr W------------N'. It was a mere three lines in the newspaper. With no aristocratic interest or prurient detail, the papers were not interested. Other papers were more forthcoming. His name was Mr Willshen; Mrs Atherton had been free and frequent in her unlawful conferences with him. This marriage was clearly not worth much. Lord Ellenborough considered that 'the loss of such a wife could not have injured him materially'.[1]

The quality of the marriage affected the compensation considerably. Despite Francis Lee being a clergyman and friend of the Prince of Wales, he was offered a mere £500 in compensation when his wife was seduced by Captain Blaquire in Ramsgate. However, Lee was 40 when he married his 16-year-old wife. 'It was a clandestine marriage…she being very beautiful.' He had left her unprotected when he went to Spain for two years and his wife spent the time quietly cohabiting with her new lover. Lord Ellenborough, who presided over a lot of these cases, did not consider it an aggravated case, and the jury took the hint by offering the lowest possible figure that was commensurate with social acceptability for a member of the aristocracy.

A reduction to £50 from a much higher claim would be a slap in the face, no matter what the social standing of the plaintiff. In the case of *Jones v Houlton*, Jones wanted £1,000 for the loss of the amenity of his wife, but the defendant was awarded £50 when the judge noted that Jones, observing his wife in the horse stables with Houlton, had 'remained outside at the door with a relative, not like an exasperated husband at all, but as a limb of the law who was anxious to bring this action'. The judge also commented that Jones hardly knew Houlton, so there was no real betrayal of trust, and that Jones could not be sure that Mr Houlton was the first seducer. When offered the paltry sum, Jones, an attorney, went on to prosecute one of his own witnesses for perjury, or perhaps not saying what he had been paid to say, which in this case was probably the same thing.[2]

At the same Shrewsbury assizes, the case of *Evans v Hughes* was dismissed due to lack of evidence. There were two letters, suggesting a relationship between the defendant and the plaintiff's wife. One was anonymous. It wasn't enough for a separation, but the *Chester Courant* took the opportunity to provide its readers with other details; the couple's child had been born a few days after their marriage in 1810; Mr Evans was spending a lot of time with a former intimate friend, Miss Emma Jones, who had recently suffered an unfortunate miscarriage. Readers were clearly expected to fill in the gaps. If illegal intercourse had been proved, it seems unlikely that Mr Evans would have been awarded more than £50. As it was, he remained married.

Illegal intercourse had to be proved for any compensation to be issued. By the nature of the deed it was largely done in private. Husbands with suspicions could hire a spy. For the aristocracy, it was the husband's servants who provided the evidence. In the 1811 case of *Verelist v Staples*, this evidence was offered:

> *John Preston, the gardener, stated that, happening to attend in doors instead of the footman, he chanced to have business in the drawing room, where the defendant Major Staple and his mistress were together. She was standing against a table under the pier glass and the Major was standing with her. He had his left hand round her waist,____(here the witnesses gave a description of the exact attitudes of the respective parties but we must forebear to follow him). He said a great confusion was manifest, and left the room.*

Sometimes there would be evidence of criminal intercourse that was simply not believed by the judge and jury. In the case of *Holland v Lupton* (September 1815) the defendant, a brewer, accused his wife of sexual intercourse in the cellar of one of his public houses. An employee of Mr Lupton, a Mark Osborne, reported that he had been in the habit of sleeping on the job next to the beer barrels in the basement. On one occasion he was interrupted by the wife and her lover creeping into the cellar in the pitch darkness. The paper went on to report that 'the remaining part of his testimony afforded the most unequivocal proof of the depravity and the indelicacy of the criminal parties'. However, the defendant's lawyer was not having this. Did Osborne really spend an hour, in the darkness, a yard away from the two criminal parties? Would two rich people choose three stretched out barrels to engage in their criminal conversation?

Mr Topping, the defendant's lawyer, had done research on Mr Osborne. Osborne had lied about working for the London brewer Barclay Perkins; he had lied about his apprenticeship and credentials and had fabricated his personal background. Topping asked the jury for only nominal criminal damages. He brought witnesses to prove that it had not been a particularly happy marriage. For example, Holland had struck his wife in a public Manchester Street when Mrs Holland had an infant in her arms. Mr Topping's expensive investigations repaid the investment. Mr Holland was compensated to the amount of a mere £100 after the jury considered the matter for ten minutes. It was likely that the jury would have just talked amongst themselves in the court rather than retire to consider seriously a verdict.

If the defence could prove that a wife had been complicit, then the compensation would fall dramatically. In the case of *Mellis v Baker* the judge instructed the jury that the compensation should not be large as the 'plaintiff's wife was not the most prudent or chaste of women'. Much to the disgust of the newspaper, the plaintiff was still awarded £750.[3]

If the woman was the seducer, compensation would still be due but would fall to almost nothing and the social shame would be unbearable. In the case of *Haslam v Burn* (1812), Lord Ellenborough pointed out to the jury that the 'violation of the marriage contract meant some compensation must be given', no matter what the moral weaknesses of the woman. In December 1812, a Mr Mortimer of the Militia Regiment received only £100 when his wife, aged 30, had an amour in Cheltenham. However, 'the evidence suggested that the wife had beguiled him, rather than the defendant her'. The defendant was 20 years old.

Pleas of mitigation were various but predictable. Naivety was one. Mr Holden, accused of Crim. Con. with a Mrs Defries in 1810 'was in his minority when he became acquainted with the highly interesting and universally admired Mrs Defries'. His legal team added that this was in no way an indictment of her reputation, which seems hard to believe. If the husband himself had made improper connexions, this would reduce the amount of compensation, not because he had committed adultery himself, but because his behaviour showed, in the flowery language of the court reporters that 'the plaintiff did no longer set a value on his jewel'.

It was not possible to receive nothing if Crim. Con. was proved; but it was possible to receive next to nothing. In the 1813 case of *Green v Marden*, the plaintiff was a modest army paymaster and the defendant was an even more modest navy clerk. There were no reputations to pay for here. Mr and Mrs Green had managed a mere two years in Sicily before she was sent away. She had flitted from lodging house to lodging house, spending money so quickly that Mr Green had to put a notice in the newspaper saying that he was not responsible for her debts. There was no betrayal of trust; the plaintiff did not even know the string of lovers she had seduced, one of whom jumped out of the window when challenged. She was said to have claimed that her second child was not her husband's.

Compensation was set at one farthing.

Chapter 21

Regency Body Snatchers

During 1816, the Anatomy School of Great Marlborough Street in London advertised dissections of the human body 'every Thursday, as usual'. These lectures were attended by medical students who needed the experience of dissecting bodies to obtain a medical degree. Such bodies were hard to obtain; apart from the corpses of executed murderers, there was no legal source. Hangings for murder brought in about fifty bodies a year; more were executed than that, but families would move heaven and earth to avoid their relatives being 'anatomised'. London teaching hospitals were using about 500 corpses a year in the Regency period. So the other bodies had to come from somewhere. Private enterprise provided the solution.

The Borough Gang were Britain's most famous 'sack 'em up men'. They operated between 1802 and 1825. Membership and leadership varied over time, but membership probably never exceeded six. The prominent individuals, moving in and out of the group over the years, were Ben and Joseph Crouch, Joseph Naples and Israel Chapman.

Private enterprise had a solution to the problem of body snatching too. Jarvis and Company of 139 Longacre in London had a range of coffins, including the patent 'unopenable' coffin at 3½ guineas, available at a few hours' notice. The coffins were essentially a set of steel and wooden boxes within boxes with no visible screws on the outside and no weak corners that could be prised open.

The poor were the main victims of the resurrection men. They could not use these metal-plated coffins even if they could afford them. Cemetery officials forbad their use, as it would make it impossible to reuse the ground for future burials. Iron coffins could only be used in family-owned ground. The poor could not afford to guard their loved ones either, knowing that after two weeks the body would be unusable anyway. The other was a practical problem; a witness at the 1828 select committee said that the body snatchers 'seldom took the rich…as they were buried so deep'.

Robbing corpses from graves was not an offence at this time, although stealing property associated with the burial was. Robbers would strip the body and carefully leave all the property behind. It was always naked bodies that were placed in sacks – hence the name 'sack 'em up men'. There was only a moderate sense of outrage about this activity in the newspapers. While the ghastly subject was not referred to very much, when it was talked about, it was treated in a jocular and almost childish way. After a bout of robberies, one newspaper announced that 'the resurrection men have risen again'. In another newspaper, grave-robbery news was sandwiched between an article about curing chilblains and a new bridge in Galashiels.

The Borough Gang were the leading Regency grave robbers because they aimed to control the market in all corpses. They saw themselves as professionals and looked down on amateurs. The job involved more than stealing from graveyards. It meant controlling demand and supply.

In November 1816, a group of six resurrectionists attacked the home of a Mr Millard. Millard was the beadle (overseer) to the dissecting room at Guy's Hospital. They believed – correctly – that Millard was responsible for hiring private contractors to steal bodies in order to bring down the price. A mob opposed to the six men gathered around the house and the *Morning Chronicle* announced that it was only the intervention of Mr Milliard that stopped these people attacking the resurrectionists. This seems unlikely. The men intimidating Millard, and by implication the whole staff at Guy's, were hardened criminals who could have handled the situation easily. They merely threatened the beadle with unspecified punishments if he did not stop organising competition. They asked for six guineas, not four, per body and gave Millard a fortnight to think about it. A spinner would be earning £1 per week and a weaver 12s at this time. Body snatching was a lucrative trade that was worth defending.

William Millard claimed complete ignorance of the gang, but he was lying. Millard was a major supplier of bodies to Sir Astley Cooper, President of the Royal College of Surgeons, and the gang knew it. The gang also had links with Sir Astley, and the attack on Millard was a proxy warning to a man too eminent for them to threaten directly.

The problem for the resurrectionists was that the London teaching hospitals were the only market for their goods; they partially got around the problem by sending bodies to the provinces (normally packed onto weekend coaches or ships), but it did not solve the problem of the hospitals trying to dictate the price.

Benjamin Crouch was a key member of the Borough Gang by 1811-12, as he is mentioned frequently in Joseph Naples's famous account of their work, *The Diary of a Resurrectionist*. By 1816 he was being described as the captain of the gang. He was formerly a porter at Guy's and would have known

Millard well. Ben was described as short, ugly, but more often sober than the rest of the gang, and their undoubted leader. He had a previous criminal record. In December 1814, a Ben Crouch was convicted of passing stolen bank notes. His address in Kent Road was one that he was known to live at, according to Millard's wife Ann, who later wrote a pamphlet explaining how her husband was found in a graveyard in the middle of the night, and while doing so gave out Crouch's home address.

Earlier, in January 1810, a Benjamin Crouch was accused of assaulting a guest at the wedding of a local man to a 'Daughter of Israel', having gate-crashed the celebrations at the 'London Hospital' public house. This was close to, and named after, the nearby hospital of the same name. It seems likely that Crouch was in the area doing some sort of business related to it – perhaps working there. There is no motive given for the attack, but through-out his career, Crouch was indignant about the role of Jews taking 'his' trade and this might explain the assault. This kind of intimidation was certainly part of Crouch's way of working.

Crouch had been to the Waterloo battlefield in 1816 with another resurrectionist, Jack Harnett. They had been collecting teeth from the corpses of those who had fallen, as well as the epaulettes from uniforms to sell as souvenirs. Later in the year Crouch was indicted for an attack on St Thomas's Hospital. He pointed out that teeth were just as profitable as corpses and that, if push came to shove, he would concentrate on that. Indeed it seems that Crouch was to move away from body snatching and spent more time cutting the jaws out of corpses in the years after 1816. Ben went on to buy a hotel in Margate, which failed because his reputation preceded him – hospitality and grave robbery not being complementary ideas in the minds of most hotel guests.[6]

The Borough Gang continued their intimidation in 1816. In November four resurrection men entered St Thomas's Hospital during a dissection. It may be that they had been organising a kind of strike to push the price of bodies up to six guineas and the surgeons had responded by encouraging others to enter the profession. As with other workers, trade unionism was illegal for employees in 1816. The *Chester Courant*, killing two birds with a ghastly pun and a reactionary attitude, announced that the 'spirit of combination' had even spread to the grave robbers. The gang mutilated the corpses that were being dissected; they had a good attempt at turning the young surgeons into future business too.

The leader of the mob was Israel 'Easy' Chapman, a noted resurrectionist, according to the papers, although perhaps his Jewish background was the reason for his top billing. When they were finally apprehended they complained that they were badly treated by the surgeons, who could not survive without them. The judge asked them to find bail; the paper, in an aside, noted that 'the sums that these men make are immense'. It seems clear that the teaching hospital paid their bail and negotiations were restarted.

Israel Chapman was born in 1794, in Chelsea, and died in the Jewish poor house in Australia on 4 July 1868. Little can be worked out from his early life – the lack of compulsory state records and his Jewish background put him outside the normal system. However, he had a young brother, Noel, born 1809, and both boys were coach drivers – a job that could put you in contact with body snatchers.

Israel Chapman was well known to the legal establishment. In the mid 1810s he was living first in Haymarket, and later at Vine Street, Covent Garden. The *Morning Post* of 27 August 1816 reported that the 'well known character Israel Chapman' had been indicted at Hatton Garden magistrates' court for stealing a watch. In April of the same year, it was reported by the papers that the 'Jew resurrection man' was accused of carrying off a wounded man from a site of attempted murder in Newton's Court. It is clear that Chapman had not kidnapped the wounded man to administer first aid.

Chapman was well known to the magistrate John Nares, who worked at both Bow Street and Covent Garden. Chapman once told him that, should Nares die first, he would be after his dead body. Nares died on 16 December 1816, and the Bow Street Patrol guarded his body for three weeks. There was no sign of Israel – he was at war with the London anatomy hospitals at the time.

In December 1817, Israel's life changed forever. Chapman and his partner George Scott were accused of the highway robbery of a half sovereign in gold and four shillings in silver. The victim was James Palmer. Palmer was from Southall, had been drinking in the Seven Stars public house in Star Court, Whitechapel, and had been violently beaten and robbed by a gang, of whom only Scott and Chapman were captured by the watchmen.

Scott – a 'tall athletic type', probably in contradistinction to the 'Jew Chapman', was also convicted of a similar crime committed the same day – waiting around in public houses for people to leave drunk, although Chapman's victim claimed to have only had two pints of porter and some tea. This was the turning point of Chapman's life in England; this attack on the property of a gentleman was much more serious than taking the dead bodies (and dignity) of the poor.

Scott and Chapman were given the death penalty in January 1818, later commuted to transportation.

Scott and Chapman were given the death penalty in January 1818, later commuted to transportation. Chapman arrived in New South Wales on 14 September 1818. His life improved almost immediately – he became a poacher-turned-gamekeeper in a very profound way. He became a police officer and a local businessman, clearly using skills learned on the other side of the law in Britain.[1]

Joseph Naples was another member of the gang who kept a diary of his activities in 1811-12; by 1816, he was the bookkeeper for the group. Naples was born in Deptford in about 1773 and was a sailor during the Napoleonic Wars. He worked both as a gravedigger at Spa Fields in Clerkenwell, and a servant at the dissecting rooms of St Thomas's, so he had the perfect CV for a body snatcher. From around 1802, Naples was an important ally of Sir Astley Cooper as a valuable source of cadavers. It is clear that Cooper used his influence to keep many of the Borough Gang members out of prison and paid their bail and sureties.

Naples was caught many times by the authorities. In May 1802, when he was a gravedigger at St James in Clerkenwell, he received two years in the Coldbath Fields House of Correction for stealing bodies to order from the Spa Fields burial ground. His mistake was to pilfer other property from the coffins. He upset people as well. A local paper reported:

> *George Windsor and Edward King were next called. They swore that, having heard of the last mentioned circumstances, and that the bodies were lying in the vault under Clerkenwell Church, they went there, when the former recognised the body of the woman to be that of his wife, and the latter that of the child to be his son, both which had been buried by them a short time before. They were much agitated during the delivery of their testimony.*

The authorities put him to work picking oakum by unravelling old rope; in May of the same year the *Morning Post* reported that he and an accomplice had made a new rope and scaled the walls and escaped. By December 1804 he was back in prison, pleading clemency for his good character and the need to support his two children and his wife Jane.

In September 1813 he was apprehended at the St Pancras graveyard, and in April 1819, he and an accomplice (George Marden) were caught stealing bodies from Sutton graveyard. A few months later the same two were accused of stealing the recently interred body of Ann Johnson from a grave in Guildford, and hiding it under a dunghill.

Joseph seemed to be living in Reigate at the time and was clearly operating in Surrey rather than London. Joseph seemed to prefer burial places that were recently opened. In the case of Sutton, the *Windsor and Eton Express* reported that only twenty people had been interred there, and sixteen had been stolen. Joseph went back to work in the local hospitals when his trade was abolished by the 1832 Anatomy Act. A man of that name died in Southwark in 1843.

The final leading resurrectionist of the Regency period was Joseph Crouch, a relative of Benjamin, but the details are sketchy. Joseph Crouch was fortunate in his timing when he was eventually brought to justice. His career was over anyway; the new Anatomy Act of 1832 was to provide the anatomy schools with a regular supply of bodies and body snatching as an organised, lucrative trade was about to come to an end. He and his accomplice David Baker were found guilty of stealing the shroud from one of the bodies that they had taken from St John's Horsleydown in Southwark. They were intercepted with two bodies still lying on the ground, one without a shroud, on 8 April 1832. Crouch's last words before arrest were: 'Don't hurt me. I will go with you quietly; this way I have got my living for the last twenty years.'

There is no reason to doubt the claim. Joseph had body snatching in the family, and Joseph himself had made headlines on at least three occasions. In January 1832 he was accused by a William Dunelly of stealing his rope and ladders. Dunelly had been away for the weekend and found his equipment missing when he returned. Crouch had a solid defence. Dunnelly was, like him, a body snatcher. It was by no means a coincidence that Dunelly's lodging had a view of St George's burial grounds in Southwark. They were in a gang of six – a plausible number. Crouch explained that it took two to carefully remove the body, and four to take it away to a teaching hospital. The rope and ladders were owned in common, according to the defendant. Crouch was dismissive. Dunnelly was such a bad character that 'ne'er a decent body snatcher would 'sociate with him'.[2]

Joseph appears in the newspapers in 1828, but before that had what we must presume to be a decade of not getting caught. There are a few possible reasons for this; it seems that he was a professional, full-time body snatcher rather than an occasional one, as his own admission proves. He was a known associate of Patrick Murphy, who took over the Borough Gang when Ben Crouch retired to run his hotel in Margate. This was well-organised criminality.

It was also very easy to evade arrest. The graveyard watch was designed to deter rather than to catch; with a gang of six it would take only two to remove the body, the rest could scarper. Gravediggers and church deacons were poor and could be bribed. At the worst, a surgeon at the anatomical hospital could give them bail. Unless property was damaged or stolen, they were safe from serious punishment.

In 1828, Joseph Crouch was involved in an abortive attempt at raiding the mortuary of St Mary's church workhouse in Newington. The gang had forced an entrance and removed two male and four female bodies. An Irishman called Fitzgerald seems to have been sub-contracted to move the bodies to St Bartholomew's and Guy's in his pea green cart. He claimed to have no idea about the possible contents of the six unwieldy sacks. Even his admission that he had dropped the two sacks off at the famous anatomical hospital had not given him any clues. By the time the authorities had tracked down the bodies they had been dissected to the point of being unrecognisable. The police tried to use Crouch's accomplice, Kent, to point the finger at Crouch, which he duly did. The judge was not impressed by the police admission that Kent was certainly drunk. The judge asked them to find bail. As usual, this was not a problem.

Body snatching was a treacherous world, with little loyalty. According to the *Morning Chronicle* (February 1820), Joseph Crouch appeared as a witness for the prosecution. Crouch explained that he had seen Patrick Murphy, Michael Wood and a man named Wild, remove three bodies from the St Clement Danes burial ground near Portugal Street. Crouch shows his high level of knowledge:

Joseph Crouch stated, that on Monday morning last, about two o'clock, he saw all the prisoners enter the burying-ground in Portugal street, Lincoln's-inn-fields, by a wicket gate, and afterwards he watched them, having no doubt what their object was, when he saw a large sack thrown over the wall, which he had no doubt contained two bodies, and they brought out a small sack through the wicker gate, which he had no doubt contained one body. Both the sacks were put into a hackney coach, which was waiting and drove away by the prisoner Wood, whom he knew to be a hackney coachman: the prisoners Wild and Murphy, rode in the coach with the sacks.

He followed the coach to St. Thomas's Hospital, in the Borough, where the sacks were taken in. On the following day he gave information to the parish officers of St. Clement Danes, of what he had seen, when an examination of the burying ground took place; it was ascertained that the bodies of three old people, which had been interred on the

*Sunday, had been stolen, one of them 82 years of age, and the youngest
was 72: they were two women and a man. Only the bodies were taken,
the coffins and shrouds remain. A number of other bodies it was ascertained had been stolen, particularly in what was called the poor vault.*

Crouch had been a body snatcher 'since being a child'. He was presenting
this evidence due to motives of revenge. This all sounds very plausible –
perhaps the gang had fallen out over the distribution of money, or Crouch
had been cut out of a deal. It could have been that Murphy supplanting his
relative as the leader of Borough Gang was the problem.

They were told by the judge to find bail.

Whatever the situation, it is clear that Crouch, a major criminal (he
would need to be very brave to take on Patrick Murphy), was associated
with the leading resurrection gang, and was able to act with near impunity
in Regency England.

Chapter 22

Being Irish

Ireland was part of the United Kingdom during the Regency, but the Irish were treated like potential traitors. Mostly Roman Catholic, they were regarded as rootless foreigners whose real loyalties lay elsewhere. In the 1790s there had been revolts against British rule, and Irish movements had links with France that were seen as trouble at best and treason at worst.

The fact that they were enthusiastic about coming to England and Scotland spoke volumes for the dismal quality of their life in Ireland. Those Irish who left their miserable, landlord-infested life in Ireland – a country essentially under military occupation – would migrate to London, or new slums in Liverpool, Manchester or Glasgow, hoping for the best, but rarely experiencing it.

Before permanent settlement there was seasonal migration. Irish families went to England every summer to help to bring in the harvest – up to 100,000 people per year by the 1820s. They were often invited by landowners for whom an oversupply of unskilled labour in summer was a positive advantage when negotiating pay rates with the native labourers. Their presence was resented – they undercut the English labourer, for which at least the landlords were grateful, although it did increase their poor rate contributions that prevented the underemployed English from starving. There was no Poor Law in Ireland similar to that of England, which further encouraged migration in the summer. Calculations were made in the hostile press about how much money was lost to England by paying wages to the Irish. There seemed to have been an element of having it both ways in regard to Irish migration – accepting the advantages but resenting the extra call on resources.

The prejudice towards the Irish could be seen in the newspapers. Many of the lower classes lived in a similar way as them but did not suffer the same prejudice. The Irish poor were studied hard by concerned Georgians, but mostly in an effort to condemn. Newspaper reports of the period suggest that they were prone to violence; that they were under the control of Catholic priests and that by definition, their loyalty to the protestant state was in doubt. When violence happened and Irish immigrants died, the amount of coverage could be insultingly small. This was the complete article on 25 June 1815 in the *Leicester Chronicle*, buried on an inside page:

> *An alarming riot took place on Monday afternoon, among a party of the lower orders of Irish in St Giles, in which several have been killed and wounded.*

When violence was sectarian, the newspapers were particularly scathing, although they were exactly the same divisions that had been deliberately stirred up in Ireland to allow the protestant minority to rule.

There was a view that violence happened because they were, fatally for them, both Irish and a member of the lower orders. The stereotype was the 'stout Hibernian':

> *Seven stout Hibernians were indicted for assaulting a watchman, and for creating a tremendous row in St Giles, by which that celebrated neighbourhood was thrown into the utmost terror and dismay. Two of the parties were found guilty and sentenced to imprisonment.*

Like many groups in society that were regarded as the 'other', the Irish were either condemned or treated like a joke. Often corners of local papers were filled with jokes or apocryphal stories about the Irish which made them villainous or simple minded, or sometimes both:

> *A TRUE PROPHET*
>
> *A Hibernian who was tried and convicted during the last Western Circuit for burglary, on being asked his age...replied that he was pretty well as old as he'd ever be and declined to give any other answer. He was executed on the Wednesday following.*
>
> *A gentlemen going out one morning, bade his Hibernian servant tell Mr T (if he called) that he should be back at dinner; very well, says the servant, but what must I tell him if he doesn't call?*

One of the first permanent areas of Irish settlement was St Giles, London. The Irish had already been living there for 150 years by 1815. They were poor and therefore occupied the worst houses and lived in the least salubrious parts of town. They were as demoralised and poor as migrant English rural labourers or Scottish handloom weavers. Due to the suspicious attitude of the establishment we have a fair amount of data about the Irish that was collected by people who vacillated between fear and contempt, with the occasional flash of compassion when something was clearly not their fault.

Thomas Finigan, master of the Irish Free School told a commission on the education of the lower orders in 1816 that there were 6,000 poor Irish adults in St Giles and Bloomsbury who had 3,000 children. The children spent their Sundays either in the public house with their parents, or playing on the streets. Many children were kept away from school by the lack of clothes to wear, and the fact that women had irregular work and used their children for begging. Girls of 13 or 14 were convicted of prostitution, and other children were affected by seeing criminal activity. Finigan claimed to be organising a non-sectarian school for the Irish Catholics but was under great pressure from the local priests, who would occasionally burst into classrooms, shouting protests. He was an Irish protestant himself, but claimed that this was unimportant. The morals of the English protestant poor, he said, were far better, and his implication was clear. His pupils and their parents were from rural Catholic Ireland and that was always going to be a problem.

In 1814 something happened to the Irish that could not be blamed on their religion or habits. Ironically it was an accident at one of the many British businesses that the Irish supported with their exploited labour. At 5.30 pm on Monday 17 October, a clerk inspected the huge vat of porter – a strong black beer – at Meux's Brewery, near the Tottenham Court Road. A large iron hoop supporting the outsize barrel had fallen off an hour earlier; however, there was no real concern – this had happened before. The barrel was huge – the size of a two storey building. And, as it turned out, was rotting away.

The huge fermenting barrel then exploded, and a million pints of beer, mixed with bricks and timber, streamed through the brewery at waist height and spread into nearby New Street and George Street. The lethal stream of beer, bricks and wood filled the basement cellars where people were having their tea, and destroyed three houses in George Street. Bricks from the brew house also rained down on New Street. The explosion weakened the facades of the houses and the inundation destroyed the walls, partitions and roof supports. The newspapers reported that people living on ground or upper storeys had to stand on their furniture until help arrived. However, this was not a possibility if you lived in a cellar with only sticks of furniture, as many of the Irish did.

One Irish cellar inhabitant was Mary Mulvay, a widow whose first husband had died a few years earlier. She had remarried and had a 3-year-old son, Thomas, from her first marriage, and an unnamed daughter. Her mother, Catherine Butler, was 65 and lodged with them. They all lived in New Street, in the cellar of a house that had once been the residence of a rich family. Mary had a friend who lived locally called Ann Saville, who had a child called John, and a husband, also called John. Most of the Irish in St Giles had unskilled jobs in labouring or the building trade. John was a bricklayer; he would be lucky to earn 12s a week, which would put their standard of living below that of a weaver. Many others laboured at the gigantic brewery of Henry Meux, which adjoined the street where many of them lived. Most Irish women did irregular and seasonal work such as portering at Covent Garden or hawking vegetables.

Ann's child John had died the day before. Ann, Mary, Thomas, Catherine and another friend, Elizabeth Smith, were holding a wake when the accident happened. Ann Saville was found drowned in the brew house at 7.30 pm, and Elizabeth Smith on the first floor of her house at midnight. Mary Mulvay, Thomas Mulvay, and Catherine Butler, were also drowned in the cellar while keeping vigil for Ann's dead child.

These were poor people, living day-to-day, and would have not put aside the £3 or so needed to avoid a pauper's funeral. However, their cruel death meant that they would be buried decently. The victims were placed in the Ship Inn in Banbury Street, and they were visited by their male family members. No adult men died because at the time of the explosion, they were at work; this would not have been the case if the explosion had taken place two hours later. John Saville, Ann's husband, and Thomas Smith, husband of Elizabeth, were present at the coffins of their loved ones. They formed, according to the papers, 'a doleful group'. The unnamed daughter of Mary Mulvay was taken in by Mrs Finigan, wife of the master of the local school, where she was a pupil.

Ann and her child were buried at St Giles churchyard on 21 October in the same coffin and the others lay a bit longer at the Ship, until £33 was raised for their burial. This was more than enough money for pauper funerals; however the money was extorted from the crowd rather than being a charitable donation. It was more of an entrance fee; two constables were stationed at the door with plates in hand to collect sixpences and shillings. The money was to be used for the general welfare of the local poor too, who had lost an estimated £3,000 in property – which puts the £33 into some perspective.

The local working poor who survived were soon forgotten, and the backlash began. In late October, one hostile newspaper reported that the 'lower class of Irish' who lived in the area were seen by Wednesday 'busy employed putting their claim to their share ... every vessel from kettle to cask were used ... many were seen enjoying their share at the expense of the proprietor'. This is a ludicrous smear; the beer was polluted with the blown up building materials of a factory and a slum; nobody would be drinking it.[1]

Many of the reports of drunkenness and beer looting do not appear in the early descriptions of the tragedy. A few weeks later, identically written reports appeared in a few places only. The newspaper could – shock horror! – have invented the story to pander to the prejudices of its readership. Much more likely to be true are the many reports of heroic efforts by the local people to pull people alive out of the rubble, with whole streets going silent in order to detect the cries of the injured.

Other press created myths were the belief that somebody died of alcoholic poisoning having drunk too much beer flowing from the street, and that the floor collapsed under the weight of sightseers to the coffins of the Irish dead, although it is true that there was a lot of disrespectful gawping and disaster tourism going on for the few days afterwards.

By November, the emphasis turned away from the victims. The inquest jury at St Giles workhouse had taken only a few moments to declare that the eight were killed 'accidently, and by misfortune'. The newspapers reported with relief that the Horseshoe Brewery of Henry Meux was insured, and that in November 1814 the company successfully asked the Treasury for the rebate of £7,664 of excise duties that had already been paid. Another £800 in aid was raised in the next two months from local people, including a donation from Young's Brewery at Wandsworth. Meux's brewery made almost no contribution. The victims were, after all, merely the poor, and the Irish poor at that.

By 1816, high bread prices, unemployment, and terrible weather had hit poor people hard, and none more so than the poor Irish. However, no subscription society sprung up to help them; instead the master of the school had to write to the newspapers to ask for help directly. It was Thomas Finigan again, who despite some of his views, which were very much reflective of the time, seemed to want to help:

DISTRESS OF THE POOR IRISH AT ST GILES

To the editor of the MORNING CHRONICLE

Sir

In the name of the one hundred and forty poor Irish children, now in the St Giles Free School in Bloomsbury, most of whom are in an absolutely

starving condition, in consequence of the parents being out of employ
and this inclement season, I solicit some relief from a benevolent public.
I beg to assure you that some of the children fainted in the school room,
this day, for want of food!

The school had long since stopped charging children to attend the school – a
nominal amount was usually required – and now the children were starving.
Much of the unskilled work done by the lower orders in St Giles was out
of doors – labourers, paviors, costermongers, and the work had dried up in
the terrible winter of 1816. Later in the year, Finigan reported that £40 had
been raised, which was not a lot. As 'foreigners', Catholics, and people with
a reputation for spending money on drink, compassion was hard to find.

A petition to the House of Commons was fruitless. The MPs were
contemptuous:

The Irish in St Giles – Mr W. Williams said, as he rose to present a
Petition from the Poor Irish Inhabitants of the Parish of St. Giles. He
had not long had the Petition in his possession – indeed he had only
been able cursorily to glance it over; he however, had not found in it
any thing disrespectful to the House. There was some peculiar language
to be sure – such as that 'one good turn deserves another' – 'a great
bother' was made about minor matters – and 'charity begins at home.'
– (A laugh.) But notwithstanding such peculiarities, he considered the
Petition to merit the attention of the House.

The Petition was then brought up and read, and its characteristic
phraseology occasioned a good deal of mirth. It set forth the difficulties
of these petitioning labouring Irish, as they were without the means of
subsistence, and unable to get work.... Their present difficulties were
increased from the circumstance of English labourers being preferred,
where any labourers were wanted. This they did not complain of, as
charity began at home. But relying on the wisdom of Parliament, they
could not but implore the House to take their case into consideration,
as they felt that work for the labouring poor would be the best barrier
against the insinuations of the Radical Reformers, about whom there
was so much bother.

The Irish were often a burden on the Poor Law. The simple explanation
was that they were poor, but that was often too simple for hostile commentators. By 1818 the Manchester districts of Ancoats and New Cross had a

considerable Irish population. The *Morning Chronicle* article in 1818, *The Mischievous Effects of the English Poor Law*, pointed out that in 1817 the Poor Law cost £65,912 in Manchester, mostly in the topping up of wages for poor weavers, but that the local Scottish community were quite unknown as receivers of poor relief:

> *A Scotsman is taught from infancy to trust to himself, and when he finds himself unsuccessful in one quarter he betakes himself to another. For the Irish however, a separate list is kept of the Irish poor, who number nearly the same as the English.*

There must have been a reason for a separate Irish list – once again they seem to be keeping an eye on a problem. The criticism of the Irish for showing insufficient labour mobility is unfair; as the poor Irish arrived in Manchester they moved rapidly into the only job that was available – the handloom weaving which made them poor in the first place.

Also in 1818, perhaps not accidently, the law was changed so that the poor Irish could be sent back to Ireland, sometimes under distressing circumstances. By 1819 many Irish were lying about where they came from. In that year, the Mendacity Society, which prosecuted beggars, brought Irish seaman John Lewis to court for begging in Southwark and claiming to be from Halifax, Canada, rather than his native Dublin. He had been in the British Navy for fourteen years, but was now finding it impossible to live on his 9d a day pension. The paper noted that lots of Irish were claiming to come from English speaking colonies to avoid a seven-day imprisonment and deportation. However, thanks to the work of the Mendacity Society, who were tough on poverty but not the causes of poverty, John received both punishments.

From 1818, the effect of this law was to remove many Irish families to places where they had no roots. One paper reported a 'wretched looking woman with three children with no stockings, almost naked', whose pauper husband had deserted the family after twenty years living in London. Now that he was missing, the family had no settlement in any English parish and were to be deported to Ireland as vagrants.

Mr Bodkin, an Overseer of the Clerkenwell parish, agreed with the Hatton Garden magistrate that this was an unjust law which made poverty a crime, although in practice it made poverty a crime specifically for the Irish. Mr Bodkin was reluctant to use the powers that the new act gave him, but felt he had to because if the other London parishes knew that Clerkenwell was being humane, all the burden of the iterant poor would fall on them.

Many Irish made the decision to leave the country completely and emigrate to the USA. In 1817 a group of exiled Irishmen in New York set up a society to resettle and aid Irish emigrants. The Society was lead by Thomas Addis Emmet, and offered charity to the poor migrant, who often landed friendless in a busy port, and who was therefore in great danger of being exploited. The implication was that the migrant could expect only a slightly warmer reception in New York than Liverpool or London. The society offered advice, credit, and protection from those who would prey on them, and the chance to start a new life farming in the American Midwest rather than settling in overcrowded US cities. The reaction of the British establishment was hostile. Many newspapers would aggressively publish accounts of Irish migrants suffering in the USA. The deep-down motivation was political. The implication that the USA could offer more was resented, mostly because there was truth in it. Emmet put forward a plan for the Irish to buy 'unworked' land in Illinois for two dollars an acre, payable over twelve years, where they could live a life without the protestant landlord, bailiff, and cleric watching over them and stealing the fruit of their labour.

Thomas Emmet was a highly controversial figure. He was a lawyer, born in Cork, and was a leading member of the United Irishmen, who fought against British rule and for a liberal, non-sectarian Ireland. It was a name that the newspapers would have recognised as an enemy of the British establishment. His brother Robert Emmet had been executed in 1803 for organising rebellions against British rule.

The newspapers were keen to play down the importance of Emmet's ambitions for Irish emigrants. It was page one news when Emmet's Illinois land plan was rejected by the US House of Representatives. At the same time, the press gleefully reported that migrant ships from Europe to New York were to be restricted in the number of passengers they could carry to prevent overcrowding and deaths. The danger was not a lie; in 1817, twenty per cent of the 5,000 migrants who had left from Antwerp bound for the USA had died en route.

Thomas Emmet was also a member of the New York Shamrock Society, which produced a book of hints and advice for British-based immigrants, published by the radical bookseller William Hone in London. It was as much a critique of Britain as a comment on the USA. The USA was a democracy, and that was a good thing:

> *You will soon perceive that the laws (and ours is a government of laws) are made by the will of the people through agents called Representatives. The will of a majority passes for, and requires, the consent of all.*

There is much more food than in Europe:

> *The European of the same condition who receive meat or fish and coffee*
> *at breakfast meat at dinner and meat or fish and tea at supper an abun-*
> *dance of animal food to which he was unaccustomed insensibly falls into*
> *a state of too great repletion which exposes him to the worst kind of fever*
> *during the heats of summer and autumn.*

While overeating could cause fever in the USA, in Ireland fever was caused
by the starvation harvest of 1817, and in Britain by freezing in a garret in
Manchester or London. Emmet claimed that labourers earned the dollar
equivalent of six shillings a day in the USA, not nine shillings a week like in
St Giles. Money went further as taxes were lower:

> *Our governments are more frugal they demand few taxes so that the*
> *earnings of the poor man are left to enrich himself they are nearly all*
> *his own and not expended on kings or their satellites. Idlers are out of*
> *their element here and the being who is technically called a man of rank*
> *in Europe is despicable in America.*

The new, young Republic was a different world from Regency Britain, and
for that reason, the Irish wanted to be there.

Chapter 23

A Rash and Melancholy Act?

The Regency was a rough and violent age. It had a hard, uncaring image and a bloody, vindictive set of punishments for criminals, but attitudes to suicide were gradually changing from condemnation to an attempt at understanding. The belief that it was up to the individual to choose whether life was worth living was not common in an age where eternal damnation was feared, but some changes can be seen in the Regency era – a softening of attitude in places, with perhaps a tendency to extend the search for mitigation, to members of the establishment if not the poor. Not all agreed. John Wesley believed that the English leniency towards suicide was the reason for its great frequency.

The traditional view of the crime of suicide – *'felo de se'* (felon of the self) – would mean that the person killing themselves would forfeit their property to the Crown and lose the right to be buried in consecrated ground. A busy crossroads, where traffic might drown out the activities of restless souls, was preferred. Burials had to take place at night. Often a stake would be put through the heart, which was as messy as it sounds.

Georgian inquests were quite ready to give a verdict of *felo de se* and then the coroner would order this humiliating form of internment. However, on occasions there would be a judgement of lunacy instead, when derangement, preferably over a long period of time, could be proved with examples. This would avoid the humiliating penalties.

The following cases were adjudged criminal acts in 1810, and there is a clearly discernible pattern. Esther Chapman of Chatteris took just enough arsenic to kill herself; she lingered in agony for twenty-four hours. Later in the same year an unnamed servant girl of Mr G. Uppleby took laudanum and expired after eight hours. She had been distressed by rumours about her reputation in the town. In May of the same year, a soldier who had recently deserted went to the White Hart public house near Clare Market and partly cut his head off with a penknife. Jan Fesh, another soldier proved that he was not insane when he destroyed himself by loading his musket with metal buttons from his tunic and used a string attached to the trigger to allow him to put the weapon into his mouth.

At Canterbury, in June 1810, a servant, James Lawman, shot himself in the head due to disappointment in love, 'the object of his affection having refused his advances', and lived just long enough to acknowledge that it was a rash act. Also in June 1810, Mrs Wraight of Chatham, the wife of a blacksmith, swallowed arsenic. No reason was given in the press, but it was noted that she was buried at a roadside just outside the town. In July, a Mr J. Widman hanged himself after being caught stealing boots from a shop in Fleet Street. In August, an unnamed carter in Islington hanged himself; he had two girlfriends, one of them was pregnant and he did not know what to do. John Thornton, aged 70, hanged himself using his garters in his room in October. He was declared perfectly sane as he had spent the day concluding some financial affairs and locking up his money securely. However, in the act of being so efficient with his cash, he denied it to his relatives.

All of these unfortunates were buried at the local crossroads. Another similarity was the low social class of most of the victims – they were mostly servants, soldiers and wives of the lower classes. They also showed the various methods of 'dispatching yourself into eternity', as the papers delicately put it. Hangings and shootings were used by men, and dangerous but easily available poisons were used by women. Drowning was also popular; another unnamed woman in 1810 was found sane when she drowned herself after calmly walking out of the marital home and telling her husband that she would never return.

The law did not regard all such deaths as a punishable offence. They were able to accept that individuals were not in their right mind. Another poor woman in 1810, this time from Portsmouth, killed herself with laudanum. However, she was known to have had periods of melancholia in the past and had tried to poison herself on other occasions – she was granted the verdict of lunacy. It seemed to some that one successful suicide made you a criminal, but a couple of failures followed by a success made you merely insane. Juries were of local composition, and if the locals knew the person and could put the suicide into context, there was more chance of it being viewed sympathetically.

Melancholia was an accepted reason for suicide, as was immaturity or mental derangement caused by domestic problems. Children were rarely adjudged *felo de se*. In February 1816 a 12-year-old girl from Smithfield tied lead weights to her feet and hanged herself after a disagreement with parents – it was a 'rash act' and a 'melancholy incident', but not suicide, despite the obvious planning. William Dumbell, a labourer, had twelve pots of beer and then hanged himself in a privy in Newhaven. He had been 'melancholy'. On the other end of the social spectrum, Edward Hussey, a magistrate in Lamberhurst, Sussex, had blown out his brains with a blunderbuss with exactly the same reason given. All were adjudged as being the result of lunacy. The law was democratic on this occasion, although that does not always seem to be the case.

The extremely religious and respectable often escaped a humiliating judgement by an odd logic. Mr G Lecke, a former soldier, hanged himself in May 1816. No reason could be found – 'he was a very religious man and it would have been thought of him one of the last men in the world who would have committed suicide had he been in senses.' Therefore, due to Mr Lecke's conviction that suicide was a mortal sin, by killing himself this proved that he was not in his right mind.

There was little mercy given when itinerant criminals committed suicide. In November 1816, the coroner gave a verdict of *felo de se* on a criminal called Brock who was never favoured with a first name. He had been apprehended during a robbery of a tallow chandler named Thompson and placed in the black hole of St James Watch House. Despite being handcuffed he had managed to strangle himself with his handkerchief. He was buried at two in the morning in unconsecrated ground near Great Pulteney Street. However, this was not the end of it:

> *MOST DISGRACEFUL EXPOSURE – We stated yesterday that Brock, who committed suicide at St James Watch House, was buried at the end of Bride Lane... The body was deposited about two feet from the surface of the ground, and there was much murmurings amongst the inhabitants at the body being committed to the earth before their doors, and at night the body was taken up by the people and left in the street. As might be expected, the place was a scene of riot and confusion, and the body was dragged around the street in a most disgraceful manner, to the amusement of some and the disgust of others.*

It was clear that the locals were not up in arms at the severity of the law, but the application of the law in their back yard; the lack of sympathy shown to Brock after his death would be the result of his criminal background, but due to this protest he was eventually reinterred at the local workhouse.

Some mob action against the law did show that different views were developing. In 1810, a young soldier called Thomas Tomlinson shot himself in the head in Leeds. Despite being a brave soldier in battle, he had confided to his comrades his fear of death, and this seemed the reason for his actions. There was an outraged reaction from his regiment when the lowly soldier was declared to be rational when he killed himself.

The corpse, in consequence, was seized by the civil power, and lodged in the prison until Monday night, when the remains of this unfortunate young man were taken at midnight... and buried in the lanes usually appropriated for this purpose. The body had scarcely been committed to its ignominious grave, when some of the military, impelled by their attachment to a brother soldier, and encouraged by the populace, jumped in the grave in the presence of the civil officials, and finding it impossible to get up the coffin entire, they lifted up the lid raised the corpse out of the grave...and carried him to the new burying ground at the parish church, where it was interred with military honours.[1]

It certainly did not help your chances if you were a soldier and you took your own life. However, it was a different matter if you were a foolish London gentleman, as seen in the example of Mr Charles Bradburn in February 1816. He had attended a masquerade at the Argyle Rooms in Regent Street. He met a woman of new acquaintance there and was about to take her home when two men, Wallace and Andrews, jumped into the coach. They went together to a hotel and Bradburn took up the invitation to play dice for champagne and claret that could be given to the young lady, who seemed to know the other men well. Gambling for drink turned to gambling for money; Bradburn won at first but eventually lost £2,000.

His friends rallied round and attempted to find the swindlers. His new female 'friend' was identified as Maria Bartram of Portland Square, a 'woman of the town', said the newspapers, with a meaning clear to all. Charles resisted the help of his friends, and when Wallace and Andrews arrived at his address a few days later, armed and noisy and demanding their money Bradburn blew his brains out. He was found insane by an inquest. His fortune and reputation were saved, although in the short term his story was repeated in dozens of newspapers all over the country to the disgrace of his family's reputation.

Not everybody agreed with the verdict. A letter to the paper pointed out the problem. The Argyle Rooms were the well-known haunt of prostitutes. The strumpet and the gamblers were in cahoots. Why did Bradburn use somebody else's dice? The writer went on to say that if Bradburn was mad, then he was mad at the beginning of the evening in showing his appalling judgement. He certainly had no history of melancholia to help his case; but he was a rich London gentleman, and that was enough to save his reputation.

It was clearly seen that people took their own lives from the derangement caused by economic distress. Mr Hollingsdale of Chailey, Sussex, was last seen tending to the cattle that were about to be sold to pay his rent and tithe debts. Richard Bishop of Exeter 'put a period to his own existence' in old age, having encouraged others to make unsuccessful investments.

There were some dissenting voices. Where, complained newspaper letter-writers, was the resignation to the will of God? Surely, it was the sin of pride that turned people to suicide? In September 1816, the *Cumberland Pacquet* referred to suicide as a crime that condemned the bereaved family to torment on earth and the deceased to torment in the afterlife. On 15 August, a person with the pen name 'HUMANITAS'[2] wrote to the *Morning Post* bemoaning the number of lunacy judgements, which were clearly designed to save people's feelings and protect inheritance rights. Without any irony at all, HUMANITAS commented that this had all gone too far, in an era of 'universal benevolence and philanthropy' he believed that the re-application of the proper judgement would discourage suicides; if this was not possible, perhaps the bodies could be dissected rather than buried at the crossroads in an unmarked grave? A slightly more constructive suggestion was the banning of arsenic; HUMANITAS claimed that the use of poison was under-reported as a method of suicide, and this may well have been the case. It is interesting that a commentator who had no sympathy for the suffering of suicides was nevertheless losing patience with the humiliating burial ritual that was associated with it.

Much of the disgust about the verdict of *felo de se* was the variable, and often disgraceful, way the punishment burial was carried out. Lancelet and John Younghusband of Alnwick were sober, respectable, and successful farmers. In November 1818 they were seen doing business in the market on Saturday and in church on Sunday, but two days later they killed themselves by cutting their throats with a razor. Their friends tried to convince the coroner that the two were insane, but their actions to the day of their death proved otherwise. It seemed premeditated – a hairdresser had been called in on the Saturday to sharpen the razors. Hours before their death, one brother was overhead to say 'Are you ready?' to the other. The popular brothers were buried in the pathway just away from the consecrated ground, but the next day it was ordered that they should be dug up and buried in the humiliating place dictated by law. Lancelot's bereaved wife and daughter were plunged into a life of grief and poverty, and some people were starting to believe that this was not morally correct.

In 1820, a Mr B Perceval hanged himself after going through some difficult situations. He suffered continued pain from an inflammation of the chest. He was in reduced circumstances and was refused relief both by the

Poor Law officers and private charities. He was declared to be in a state of derangement, and it was noted that his brother had 'put a period to his existence' a few years ago. Attitudes were changing slowly, despite complaints in the press that the poor needed more patience and resignation to God's will. It would have been the same argument that Mr Perceval would have heard when being denied outdoor relief.

On 12 August 1822, the most hated man in Britain, Viscount Castlereagh, carefully committed suicide by cutting his carotid artery with a penknife, having had all of the other sharp objects in his house removed by his concerned wife. He had come to believe that he was being persecuted. He knew he was hated by a large section of the community, and he was said to be particularly affected by the bag that the Thistlewood conspirators had prepared for his severed head – but this was sudden and more extreme. A few days before his death, Castlereagh's behaviour made the king lose sleep. The famously unemotional foreign secretary was weeping, kissing the king's hand, accusing himself of crimes, including being blackmailed for homosexuality. The king commented to Lord Liverpool 'either I am mad or Lord Castlereagh is mad'. Lord Liverpool agreed: 'There is greater danger in these cases from strong minds than weak ones.'

This seems to indicate a real discrimination in attitudes to suicide – it was thought that members of the establishment, by definition deep thinkers with great responsibilities, were more prone to suicide than the simple-minded lower orders. Castlereagh was declared insane, and buried with honour in Westminster Abbey to the sound of boos and hisses from the lower orders, and to the glee of the radical press.

The problem with the Castlereagh case was not the decision, which fitted in with other cases of lunacy, but the lack of condemnation of his actions in the newspapers. Others disagreed with the verdict, seeing his act as premeditated – Castlereagh's last words were: 'I have done for myself. I have opened my neck.' Cobbett was clear that there was no chance at all of such an important person being buried in such a humiliating way. Byron, who produced a poem inviting people to urinate on the dead man's grave, commented sarcastically that poor people 'slashed their throat', but you had to be a member of the ruling classes to 'cut your carotid artery':

> *Of the manner of his death little need be said, except that if a poor radical had cut his throat, he would have been buried in a cross-road, with the usual appurtenances of the stake and mallet.*

Cobbett also believed that, rather than being a deep thinker with all its attendant problems, the deceased was one the most empty-headed people in the government. His joy over Castlereagh's suicide seems unnerving to our gentler political age, but it was an emotion shared by many. The death of Margaret Thatcher in 2013 is the only modern event that bears similarity to the reactions to the death of Castlereagh.

In June 1823, less than a year after Castlereagh's suicide, Abel Griffiths, a 22-year-old student, was convicted of murdering his father Thomas, and then 'hurling himself into eternity', after an unexplained argument. Griffith's servant, William Wade ('a man of colour') reported that Abel had tried unsuccessfully to see his father a number of times that day, and that he was under orders to keep the son away from him. They only met because Abel arrived first and waited for his father to return. When they met, there was a brief low-level conversation which seemed to be about money. Thomas Griffiths was a plantation owner in Barbados who had financed his son's law education, but it was surmised by the inquest that this subsidy was being ended.

Those who knew Abel provided evidence of his escalating derangement. He had been taking mercury for an unknown, but probably socially embarrassing, illness and had been unpredictable and irritable with his friends. 'Pinborn, I have such depression of the brain, I cannot stand the pain. Will leeches do me good?' Witnesses attested to his unpredictable behaviour, illness, and deep derangement over the last few months of his life. The jury actually adjourned and met in private for ninety minutes – an extremely rare event at this period, where verdicts were often given while still in the chamber and after just the briefest of discussions – but the eventual verdict of *felo de se* astounded the audience in the court, and Griffiths was then prepared for a humiliating burial.

Crowds began to gather outside the father's house, 4 Maddox Street, on the Wednesday evening. Abel's friends were also there, still indignant, but the rain prevented the movement of the body. It was moved to St George's workhouse around 10 pm and the crowd followed. It was assumed by most of the crowd that the funeral procession would start from the back of the workhouse and most of the crowd placed themselves there to 'avoid disappointment'.[3] At 1.30 in the morning however, he was carried from the front door by four men. He was wearing no more than stocking socks and wrapped in a blood soaked sheet. He was then wrapped in matting with a rope to secure it and was interred at the cross-roads formed by Eaton Street, Grosvenor Place and the King's Road. He was dropped, rather than placed, into a hole about 5ft deep. Two hundred people surrounded the special constables and were largely disgusted by the spectacle (although the cynic might point out that they had taken great trouble to be so adversely affected), and because of this no stake was placed through the heart; but Abel had been buried in a unmarked hole in the ground, and there was growing feeling amongst all classes that this was inhumane, unnecessarily disruptive to society, and reeked of superstition rather than Christianity.

A few days later, persons unknown dug up the corpse at 5 am and hired a hackney carriage to transport it, which they abandoned at the end of the journey. The coach driver went to Bow Street with the body, and after a few days of wrangling about Abel's next place of burial, he ended up back at St George's workhouse and was finally laid to rest in their burial ground.

The law to abolish this practice had just started its passage through parliament; but it was the grotesque difference between the treatment of Castlereagh and Griffiths that gave the new humane view its impetus.

Some did not agree. In July some of the press were still trying to justify the horrid burial of Griffiths. The *Sussex Advertiser* published information, not available at the inquest, that Griffiths had bought, rationally and calmly, two guns from a reputed Holborn gunsmith two days before the event. They were trying to reintroduce some pre-planning into the death and justify the unpopular verdict. However, juries were more regularly giving people the benefit of the doubt. More examples appeared in the press of people carefully arranging their own death; on one occasion an unknown man bought a gun, retired to a hotel, went back twice to the gunsmith to fix the weapon, and then killed himself. He was still declared a lunatic.

When the law was changed in 1823 it was made illegal for coroners to issue a warrant for burial of a *felo de se* in a public highway. The suicide was to be interred in a churchyard or public burial place instead. This was a change in attitude and sensibility about the methods of burial and not a new acceptance of all forms of suicide. It was also a practical move to protect the integrity of the law; the punishment for *felo de se* was now regarded as unacceptable and juries were more regularly reaching verdicts of insanity, reducing the deterrent effect of the punishment. These changes did not change the religious concerns. A *felo de se* was still to be buried without Christian rites and at night, between the hours of 9 pm and midnight. Goods were also still subject to forfeiture, although that was regularly waived as long as the death had not been planned to prevent prosecution for unrelated crimes.

Postscript

So, why do we need to rethink the Regency?

It is quite remarkable that such a short period of time – strictly speaking a period of less than a decade – has such a strong historical identity. No matter how memorable this version of the Regency is, it leaves too many people out of the picture and over-emphasises the experience of the elite.

We shouldn't make the mistake of blaming the people at the time for the glossy romantic myth of the Regency. We invented it. The worship of the rich and glamorous comes easily to us, and we are still doing it in the twenty-first century.

Hollywood will always love the Regency elite; romantic novelists, quite rightly, use the Regency to produce books that their readers understand and want to read, but the poor and powerless needed their voice back. By the time of Queen Victoria, sufferings of the poor were being regularly documented by a political establishment who started to care a little more. There is no real Regency Dickens or late-Georgian Elizabeth Gaskell. Perhaps that is why there is no adulation of the Victorian elite.

This book has re-visited the poor without condescension or contempt. Jane Austen's character Emma did this, with some admirable motives and aims:

> *She understood their ways, could allow for their ignorance and temptations, had no romantic expectations of extraordinary virtue from those, for whom education had done so little; entered into their troubles with ready sympathy, and always gave her assistance with as much attention as good will.*

This book shares Emma's ambition, if not her motivation. She felt the desire to help them practically; this book writes them back into history. This bias is our fault, not the people who lived at the time. It is subsequent generations that have caused this imbalance. As this book shows, people knew that they lived in extremely difficult times, and it was only more recently that the fluffy and cosy view of the Regency prevailed.

Another reason to rethink the Regency is to prompt us to worry about the twenty-first century. When the structural weaknesses of the Regency are examined, they look quite frighteningly similar to our own. The good news was that the problems of the Regency were solved: painfully, but mostly resolved. Will we, in the twentieth-first century, be able to say the same?

We should be more appreciative of the reformers who risked prison, and the thousands who organised, protested and rioted. In 200 years time, will the historian comment that, in the face of misery, powerlessness, and exploitation, everybody in the twenty-first century signed a Facebook petition? Perhaps a book about the Regency should to do more than entertain and divert. The Regency needs to regain the power that it had at the time – the power to alarm, to make people worry about the future and to plan for a better one.

End Notes

Chapter 1

1. The currency at the time was pounds, shillings and pence (£ s d). £1 was 20s, a shilling was 12d; so there were 240d in £1. A newspaper cost 6d in 1816; a poor person's wage was around 12s per week, depending on their job. Dr Lucas was worried that the quartern loaf is 1/6; that was 1s 6d, or 18d. The 'd' is Latin (denarius).
2. Dr Lucas's diary courtesy of the Stirling Council Archives. Dr Lucas was more interested in money and the state of agriculture, but he could be relied on to get a bit reflective every New Year's Eve.
3. Most newspapers attributed the poor weather of the darkness years to bad luck. Recognising climate change needs long-term data, as we now know.
4. In 1816 there was a feeling amongst many that the world was about to end. Church attendances rose and there was a panic that the sun would go out on 18 July 1816. The most remarkable aspect of that day was the good weather in the afternoon.
5. *In Our Time* (BBC iPlayer) is a good description of the science behind the Tambora eruption. It explains the global impact of what is now called 'The Year Without A Summer'. The next few summers were not much better.
6. According to M. J. Trow, (*Enemies of the State*, Pen and Sword, 2010) Cobbett hated 'Pitt, his paper money, Robert Peel, Thomas Malthus, William Wilberforce, Americans, tea, corruption, Methodists, Quakers, Unitarians and the Landlord of the George Inn, Andover'.

Chapter 2

1. William Radcliffe: *Origin of the New System of Manufacture, commonly called Power Loom Weaving*, 1828.
2. Lots of sources suggest the Bolton weavers showed off like this but the details seem unlikely. A £5 banknote would be hard to find and hard to earn. It was a story often repeated by the Victorian establishment as criticism of workers' vanity.
3. *Lancaster Gazette*, 27 August 1808 and lots of other papers. There was a considerable amount of direct lifting of reports from one newspaper to another.
4. *Public Ledger and Daily Advertiser* 17 August 1812 – a more sympathetic source.
5. www.lancastercastle.com gives more information about Thomas Holden. He is an important example for the voice of the working man in the transportation system. Diary quotations from www.ludditebicentenary.com.

6. *The Morning Post* 16 November 1819; this was by far the most anti-reform newspaper in the capital; in the provinces that accolade would be for the *Stamford Post* or the *Carlisle Patriot*.

Chapter 3

1. *Morning Post* 10 January 1815, which, unusually, gave significant space to Hunt's view.
2. *Kentish Post* 29 March 1815. Newspaper reports constantly use the expression 'some of the persons called Quakers'.
3. After the abolition of the slave trade in 1807, Wilberforce was asked what needed to be abolished next, his reply was 'the Lottery'.
4. Byron *Don Juan* (1819), Canto Nine. Byron was a regular and trenchant critic of the Regency establishment, as they were of him.

Chapter 4

1. Eric Hobsbawn – the great historian of the mob from *The Machine Breakers* (1964)
2. *Bath Chronicle* 30 May 1816 has an extensive report. The fact that it was an event in Essex shows how important these riots were.
3. Charles Wilkins *History of Merthyr Tydfil* (1867).

Chapter 5

1. *Taunton Courier* 18 June 1814
2. John Saines of Masham *Royal Cornwall Gazette* 21 December 1816 and other newspapers.
3. *Morning Post* 9 August 1816. I believe this to have been a serious suggestion.
4. *Stamford Mercury* 6 December 1815. Many patriotic newspapers carried articles about how life was worse in France and the USA than Britain as a warning against emigration.
5. *Morning Post* 29 August 1817.
6. Cobbett *Rural Rides* (1830). Cobbett seems to be linking the potato with illness by associating it with the catholic last rites (extreme unction).
7. *Sussex Gazette* 11 December 1815.
8. *Morning Post* 26 August 1819.

Chapter 6

1. Huntington Quarter Sessions as reported in the *Stamford Mercury* (15 October 1815)
2. *Norfolk Chronicle*. Much of the anguished letters about the cost of the Poor Law were from the South and East Anglia. Pen names in papers were always capitalised.

Chapter 7

1. *Leeds Intelligencer* 1 November 1819; *Carlisle Patriot* 19 November, and others.
2. Online History of Parliament – historyofparliamentonline.org is full of wonderful stories of morally dubious members of parliament.

Chapter 8

1. Oldfield, Thomas: *A key to the House of Commons* (London, 1818) has a constituency-by-constituency report and a scathing commentary on the state of the system.
2. historyofparliamentonline.org is packed with dry descriptions of quite outrageous behaviour of politicians and is used throughout Chapter 8.

Chapter 9

1. Evidence of pluralism and absenteeism can be seen in the definitive database of the Anglican clergy – Clergy of the Church of England Database: theclergydatabase.org.uk.
2. You needed to be 5ft 4in to join the militia. Many advertisements asked for substitutes from 5ft 2in – they were clearly going to lie, or get them to stand up very straight.
3. John Wade, *Corruption Unmasked*.
4. historyofparliamentonline.org

Chapter 10

1. John Morley, *The Making of the Royal Pavilion Brighton*.

Chapter 11

1. A full, but often inaccurate account of Thistlewood's life is contained in GT Wilkinson, *Authentic history of the Cato Street Conspiracy* (1820).
2. *davidcsutton.com* (Spa Fields) and the *Dictionary of National Biography*, 1885-1900, both produce evidence that he joined the militia in Yorkshire in 1797.
3. There seems to be little doubt that this is the same Arthur Thistlewood. His wife held property in Lincoln; he lived there and the date of sale was the point at which he needed money (or gambled away the proceeds) and ran away.
4. *Thistlewood v Darley and Craycraft* as reported in the *Examiner*, 26 February 1815.
5. *Leeds Mercury* 16 March 1811 and other papers report a 20 February meeting chaired by Burdett with 'A Thistlewood' fulfilling a humble role as secretary. This looks like his earliest political activity in London.
6. *Examiner*, 8 February.
7. *European* Magazine Volume 77, 1820.

Chapter 13

1. Archibald Prentice – *Historical Sketches and Personal Reminiscences of Manchester*.
2. The pro-reform *Examiner*, but reported similarly in many papers.

Chapter 14

1. *The political Quixote of Don Blackibo Dwarfino and his squire Seditiono*, (1820)
2. Thomas ('TJ') Wooler's radical paper *Black Dwarf*. Wooler was another strong supporter of female participation in the reform movement.
3. Carlile, *Republican* Volume 22.
4. The *Morning Post* 19 August 1819. This paper could always be relied on to start a rumour, and actively sought hostile witnesses.
5. The *Morning Chronicle* 15 September 1819; more sympathetic than the *Morning Post*, but that was not difficult.

Chapter 15

1. Quoted from E.P. Thompson, *The making of the English working class*, which tells the story of Joseph Swann in loving detail.

Chapter 16

1. Meticulous statistics were kept by the state and they were regularly reported in the newspapers with alarm.
2. Information from oldbritishnews.com.
3. Information from capitalpunishmentuk.org.

Chapter 17

1. Quoted from bodmingaol.com, tells a story similar to many Georgian prisons, although Bodmin is one of the better ones.
2. James Hardy Vaux, *Memoirs* and his *Dictionary of the Criminal Slang*. Two remarkable pieces of primary evidence. The latter was written to aid magistrates to understand the language of criminal classes.
3. James Hardy Vaux, as above.
4. James Hardy Vaux, *Memoirs*.

Chapter 18

1. Blincoe's diary was reprinted in the 1820s by Richard Carlile and is now the mainstay of many key stage three British history textbooks.

Chapter 19

1. In 1867, this note was an exhibit in Northampton Museum. The idea of county bank notes disappeared very quickly and became a historical novelty.

2. *Dictionary of the Vulgar Tongue 1811*. Available as a free kindle book. It offers lots of insights into life in the Regency.
3. *Cambridge Chronicle* 27 September 1816.

Chapter 20

1. *Kentish Weekly Post* 10 August 1810. Local newspapers rarely published people's names. Newspapers further away had fewer inhibitions.
2. *Chester Courant*.
3. *Suffolk Chronicle*, August 1812.

Chapter 21

1. See the *Australian Dictionary of Biography* for more details of Chapman's life in Australia.
2. *Morning Post*, May 1832.

Chapter 22

1. *The Bury and Norwich Post* in October 1814 reported it first and this seems to be the only original source.

Chapter 23

1. *Aberdeen Journal* 10 January 1810.
2. Another letter to the papers with a capitalised pen name. Many of the names seem to us to be unintentionally ironic.
3. *Bell's Life in London*.

Bibliography

Websites

Bodmin Gaol: bodminjail.org
British History Online: british-history.ac.uk
Capital Punishment: capitalpunishmentuk.org
Diary of Dr Thomas Lucas of Stirling: thedrlucasdiaries.wordpress.com
Gay History and Literature: rictornorton.co.uk
Lancaster Castle: lancastercastle.com
Peterloo Witness Project: peterloowitness1819.weebly.com
Spa Fields 1816: davidcsutton.com
The History of Parliament: historyofparliamentonline.org
The Victorian Web: victorianweb.org

Primary Sources

Bachelor, Thomas, *General View of the Agriculture of the County of Bedford* (London 1813).
Bamford, Samuel, *Passages in the Life of A Radical* (Harper Collins, 1967).
Bigland, John, *Essays on Various Subjects* (Longman, Doncaster 1804).
Birkett, Norman, *The New Newgate Calendar* (Folio, 1960).
Butterworth, Edwin, *Historical Sketches of Oldham* (Oldham, 1856).
Buxton, George, *The political Quixote of Don Blackibo Dwarfino and his squire Seditiono* (London, 1820).
Carlile, Richard, *The Republican* (London, 1822).
Cobbett, William, *Cottage Economy* (1833).
Cobbett, William, *Rural Rides* (1830).
Dowling, Joseph, *The Whole Proceeding before the Coroner's Inquest on the body of John Lees* (London, 1820).
Fare, John, *General View of the Agriculture of Derbyshire* (London, 1817).
Followes, Robert, *The Rights of Property Vindicated Against the Claims of Universal Suffrage* (London, 1818).
Guizot, François, *Memoirs of Sir Robert Peel* (Bentley, London, 1856).
Gurney, William, *Trial of Arthur Thistlewood and others for High Treason* (London, 1820).

Hone, William, *Report on the Coroner's report on the Body of Edward Vyse and Jane Watson* (William Hone, London, 1815).

Hone, William, *The Whole Four Trials of the Thief Takers, and Their Confederates* (London, 1816).

Hunt, Henry, *The Trial of Henry Hunt, Esq. and others for High Treason* (London, 1820).

Hutton, William, *The Life of William Hutton* (Knight, 1841).

London Philological, *The European Magazine and London Review* (London, 1805).

Oldfield, Thomas, *A key to the House of Commons* (London, 1818).

Perkins, Erasmus, *The Trial of the Rev. Robert Wedderburn for Blasphemy* (London, 1820).

Philips, R., *The Monthly Magazine, or British Register* (London, 1815).

Prentice, Archibald, *Historical Sketches and Personal Recollections of Manchester* (Gilpin, Manchester 1856).

Radcliffe, William, *Origin of the New System of Manufacture, commonly called Power Loom Weaving* (1828).

The Baptist Magazine (London, 1818).

Thistlewood, Arthur, *Trials of Watson, Thistlewood, Hooper and Preston for High Treason* (London, 1817).

Urban, Sylvanus, *The Gentlemen's Magazine and Historical Register* (London, 1804).

Vaux, James Hardy, *Memoirs* (London, 1827).

Wade, John, *The Black Book, or Corruption Unmasked* (London, 1819).

Wilkinson, George Theodore, *An authentic history of the Cato-street conspiracy* (London, 1820).

Secondary Sources

Adkins, Roy and Adkins, Lesley, *Eavesdropping on Jane Austen's England* (Abacus, 2014).

Ashton, John, *Social England under the Regency* (Chatto and Windus, 1899).

Barnes, Donald, *A history of the Corn Laws* (Routledge, 2006).

Brown, Colin, *The Scum of the Earth* (History Press, 2014).

Burnett, John, *Plenty and Want* (Routledge, 2014).

Clark, Anna, *Scandal – the Sexual Politics of the British Constitution* (Princeton U.P., 2004).

George, Dorothy, *England in Transition* (Penguin, 1965).

Griffin, Emma, *Liberty's Dawn: A People's History of the Industrial Revolution* (Yale U.P. 2014).

Hibbert, Christopher, George IV (Penguin, 1988).

McCalman, Ian, *Radical Underworld: Prophets, Revolutionaries and Pornographers in London, 1795-1840* (CUP, 1988).

Mingay, G. E. (ed), *The Unquiet Countryside* (Routledge 1989).

Porter, Roy, *English Society in the Eighteenth Century* (Penguin, 1990).

Read, Donald, *Peterloo; The 'Massacre' and its Background* (Manchester University Press, 1973).

Reid, Robert, *The Peterloo Massacre* (Heinemann, 1989).

Rickward, Edgell, *Radical Squibs and Royal Ripostes* (Adams and Dart, 1971).

Steinbach, Susie, *Women in England 1760-1914* (Weidenfeld and Nicolson, 2004).

Thompson, Edward Palmer, *The Making of the English Working Class* (Penguin, 1970).

Thorne R. G., *The House of Commons 1790-1820* (Secker and Warburg, 1986).

Trow, M. J., *Enemies of the State, The Cato Street Conspiracy 1820* (Pen and Sword 2010).

Uglow, Jenny, *In These Years* (Faber and Faber, 2015).

Waller, John, *The Real Oliver Twist* (Icon Books, 2006).

White, Reginald, *Waterloo to Peterloo* (Penguin, 1968).

Index